WINGS OF KNOWLEDGE

AIRLINE OPERATIONS IN THE 21ST CENTURY

DR SUMEET SUSEELAN

ISBN

Paperback 979-8-89632-440-9
Hardcase 979-8-89673-375-1

WORLD BOOK
OF RECORDS
LONDON

CERTIFICATE

Dr. Sumeet Suseelan

Chairman, International Institute of Aviation

Bengaluru, Karnataka, India

Has been included for
being Youngest Aviation Author at the
age of 34 years on 4 July 2022.

INDIA EDITION

C.No.-WBR/RC/986/2022

Date : 17th August, 2022

Santosh shukla

Santosh Shukla
Barrister
President & CEO

WORLD BOOK OF RECORDS
UNITED KINGDOM ■ INDIA ■ SWITZERLAND

www.worldbookofrecords.uk

iudex.

DIGITAL CERTIFICATE

Contents

The chapter introduces the student to various aspects of commercial aviation, covering the different operations involved, such as air taxi services, private handling operations, and charters in the air. It explores different functions and services that have been put in place to support these operations and their importance to the industry.

This aspect of the chapter that deals with baggage handling and management gives information on reconciliation and trolley management. It gives details on procedures and technologies in making sure efficient and secure baggage handling within airports.

The chapter considers ramp operations, procedures regarding handling process, procedures of flight dispatch, SLPC, loading and unloading procedures, and lastly, emergency handling. Coordination between ramp and other departments is discussed, while directing basic safety and efficiency in airside operations.

The chapter details the passenger arrival and baggage handling processes, including baggage breakup areas, conveyor management, and lost baggage procedures. It also covers priority handling and settlement procedures related to passenger problems.

This chapter covers some of the measures taken to ensure safety and security in air transport. These are: aviation security orders, access control, explosive device recognition, patrolling, screening procedures, emergency protocols, roles of various agencies, and regulations that ensure the security of this particular mode of transportation.

Covering the logistics of air cargo, this chapter discusses cargo types, documentation, customs processes, warehousing, and the role of logistics in supply chain management. It provides insights into cargo handling, loading and unloading procedures, and the impact of load restrictions on cargo operations.

This chapter deals with the business and marketing strategies of the airlines. The issues discussed are market segmentation, marketing principles, fleet scheduling, collaboration with travel agencies, brand building and revenue-sharing between GSA and airlines. Customers' relations and promotional strategies are also dealt with.

This chapter describes the benefits and services offered to frequent flier program members. The issues considered in this book concern membership benefits, lounge access, the mileage points, and how upgrading is done. What is more, customer loyalty and added value for frequent flier programs are emphasized in the chapter.

CHAPTER-9: AIRLINE OPERATION & SCHEDULING   230

This chapter on the intricacies of the operation of airlines discusses schedule planning tools, time-space networks, and commodity flow models. Efficient scheduling and resource allocation are identified as key factors in the optimization of the operation of an airline.

CHAPTER-10: FLEET ASSESSMENT PROBLEMS   260

This chapter handles problems associated with fleet valuation or management. It treats approaches to fleet management, itinerary-based models, and solving techniques for standard problems in fleet evaluation, which provide insights into fleet performance and efficiency optimization.

CHAPTER-11: AIRLINE CATERING – OUTLINE IN FOUR SECTIONS   291

This chapter deals with in-flight services and handles all aspects of airline catering, such as galley equipment, food and nutrition checks, handling techniques, and techniques on how the catering service is delivered onboard. It deals with menu planning, special meal codes, and hygiene in food service.

CHAPTER-12: DANGEROUS GOOD REGULATIONS   315

It also covers regulations and procedures in the handling of dangerous goods really connected with aviation. Such issues to be tackled are safety adviser roles, classification of dangerous goods, packaging and labeling, handling and stowage, transport equipment, security provisions, and so on. It states there that any undertaking which has something to do with hazardous materials must be under the umbrella of safety and compliance.

CHAPTER-13: LOAD & TRIM 329

It includes the principles of weight and balance as applied to aviation, the need for weight control, basic flight theory, balance terminology, and weight records. It also describes how to determine the center of gravity, aircraft loading and trim, and weight measuring equipment.

Preface

Aviation has since become a symbol of the trend of man for innovation and achievement. It has always pushed the boundaries to the impossible and brought the entire world closer together. Be it the infancy of flight, or the air travel industry now in its ultimate development, aviation has managed greatly to change connectivity across the globe, trade, and the way we see our world.

This book attempts to meet the demands of the Indian aviation industry in its entirety, with every one of its diverse aspects working in concert to make it a real well-oiled machine. It is not just meant for professionals in the industry but also for people who are passionate about aviation, students, and individuals interested in knowing how this sector, so humongous yet well-synchronized, works. Every chapter covers diverse aspects of aviation and breaks down complicated processes into easy-to-understand information.

Whether one is interested in commercial aviation and air cargo operations or safety protocols and airline marketing, this book covers the essentials of what makes the aviation industry tick. It aims to educate, inform, and inspire readers by providing a clear understanding of the systems, strategies, and standards that drive this dynamic field.

This book, if useful to the readers, will provide insight into the world of aviation as a profession or hobby. Human endeavor in the right processes and technologies keeps the skies safe and efficient. Thank you for choosing to read this book and take this journey through the world of aviation.

About the Book

This book provides an in-depth perspective on the various dimensions that constitute aviation. It serves as an authority reference for students, professionals, and enthusiasts to acquaint them with core elements in the industry and the players involved.

This book consists of thirteen chapters which are all focused on a single subject for that chapter, such as commercial aviation, air cargo operation, ramp management, the regulations on safety aspects, and airline marketing, among others. Its starting point is a basic introduction to commercial aviation, then gradually raises the discussion to very detailed aspects, like load and trim management and dangerous goods, and passenger services. This progressive sequence is very useful in allowing knowledge to increment step-by-step.

The book is full of plain language that breaks down complex aviation concepts into much easier writing and can be quite easily explained to understand by everyone. It uses real case studies, best practices, and regulatory guidelines to help understand how the aviation industry works and evolves in practice.

Whether one is interested in an aviation career, wants more training for an existing career, or is just curious about what happens behind the scenes at airports and airlines, this book is a great starting point. It is not simply a technical guide but a celebration of the marvel that is aviation, for it shows how countless professionals and systems work together to ensure safe, secure, and efficient air travel around the globe.

Chapter-1

Commercial Aviation

Introduction to Commercial Aviation

Commercial aviation is a marvel of modern engineering and a pillar of global connectedness. This chapter explores the complex operations that drive commercial flight. plane taxi services, private operations, and plane charters all contribute to air travel and transport's smooth operation.

Continuous innovation and expansion have shaped commercial aviation. Commercial aviation has transformed travel and business from the Wright brothers' maiden flight to today's sophisticated planes and complicated networks. It has promoted international trade, cultural interaction, and global connectivity, making the world more accessible than ever.

Commercial aviation relies on regulatory frameworks and safety standards to maximize safety and efficiency. These standards are set and enforced by regulatory authorities like the FAA, EASA, and ICAO. Their requirements include aircraft design, maintenance, pilot training, and operations, providing a strong safety net for the industry.

Commercial aviation includes scheduled passenger flights, freight transport, medical evacuations, and humanitarian missions. Flexible and reliable, these services fulfill passenger and freight operator needs. They support the global economy, tourism, and emergency response infrastructure, making these services crucial.

Air taxis provide on-demand, point-to-point travel and are growing in commercial aviation. These services cater to corporate travelers and people who want private air travel without owning an aircraft. Air taxis are a good alternative to airlines for short-haul flights due to their flexibility and efficiency.

Private operations, including aircraft management, are also important in commercial aviation. These operations maintain, service, and operate private aircraft to the highest standards. Ground handling, maintenance, and airport and air traffic control cooperation are essential for private aviation clients' smooth experiences.

Air charters offer flexible travel choices for passengers and cargo. Charter services meet corporate travel, sports team, and time-sensitive cargo delivery needs with flexible scheduling and destinations. Air charters are useful for many clients due to their efficiency and personalization.

Students will learn about commercial aviation's complicated functions and services in this chapter. Readers will comprehend the many operations that make commercial aviation essential to modern life by studying air taxi, private handling, and flight charters.

Overview and Regulatory Frameworks

Commercial Aviation

Globally, commercial aviation forms the backbone of transportation since it offers necessary connections and helps economic development. Commercial aviation, defined as the operating of aircraft for the transportation of passengers or goods for hire, offers a broad spectrum of services from scheduled airline flights to air taxi operations and cargo charters.

Commercial aviation's historical growth is evidence of human creativity and technical advancement. The Wright brothers' first powered flight in 1903 signaled the beginning of controlled, continuous flying. Larger and more sophisticated aircraft were made possible by this discovery, which also helped the first commercial airlines to grow out of early 20th-century development Important turning points are the arrival of the jet engine in the 1950s, which transformed air travel by drastically lowering journey times and raising aircraft efficiency, and the arrival of wide-body jets in the 1970s, so enabling mass air transportation.

It is impossible to overestimate how commercial aviation influences world commerce and connectivity. By allowing things to be quickly transported across continents, so supporting tourism by making far-off locations accessible, and so promoting cultural interaction by linking people from all around the world. The industry is also very important for humanitarian projects since it provides necessary transportation for persons and medical supplies in crises.

Safety Standards and Regulatory Frameworks

The running of commercial aviation depends on regulatory systems and safety criteria, which guarantee that all facets of flight operations follow the best degrees of safety and efficiency. National and international aviation authorities—among them the Federal Aviation Administration (FAA) in the United States, the European Union Aviation Safety Agency (EASA), and the International Civil Aviation Organization (ICAO)—establish and enforce these rules.

Established in 1958, the FAA oversees all facets of United States civil aviation. Its responsibilities consist of certifying pilots and aircraft, supervising air traffic control, and enforcing safety rules. Beginning operations in 2003, the EASA harmonizes safety requirements among member states and improves the general safety of European aviation, therefore serving a comparable function inside the European Union. Developing worldwide standards and recommended practices, ICAO—a specialized agency of the United Nations—ensures the orderly and safe growth of world civil aviation. Originally founded in 1944, ICAO's goals are to establish universal aviation safety standards, enable worldwide air navigation, and advance international air travel development.

In commercial aviation, safety criteria include a broad spectrum covering aircraft design and manufacture, maintenance practices, pilot training, and operating procedures. To guarantee they satisfy high safety criteria, aircraft have to go through thorough testing and certification procedures. Equally strict maintenance techniques call for routine inspections and servicing to guarantee aircraft remain in best shape. From regular flights to emergency conditions, pilot training courses are meant to provide pilots the tools and information required to manage a variety of circumstances. Establishing operational protocols involving flight planning and air traffic control measures helps to guarantee the safe and effective movement of aircraft inside the airspace.

One cannot stress the value of these safety rules and legislative systems. Forming the backbone of the commercial aviation sector, they offer a consistent and regulated safety solution accepted and followed internationally. This guarantees correct and quick transportation of goods and passengers, hence building confidence in air travel.

Commercial Aviation Service Categories

Diverse and meeting a broad spectrum of needs and requirements, commercial aviation offers These services fall mostly into three main categories: passenger transportation, freight transportation, and specialty activities.

The foundation of commercial aviation is passenger transportation; scheduled carriers run frequent flights between locations. With several tiers of service—economy, business, and first class—these services are meant to satisfy the needs of business and leisure visitors. Aiming to differentiate themselves in a very competitive industry, airlines try to improve the passenger experience by means of improvements in in-flight entertainment, comfort, and customer service.

Another essential part of commercial aviation is cargo transportation, which helps items to be quickly moved all around. Industries that depend on quick and consistent delivery—including pharmaceuticals, electronics, and perishable goods—need air freight. To move goods, cargo airlines run specialized freighter aircraft and also make use of passenger aircraft's cargo compartment. To guarantee timely delivery, air freight logistics include complicated coordination involving customs clearance, warehouse, and ground transportation.

in commercial aviation, specialized operations consist of services such aerial surveying, medical evacuations, and humanitarian missions. Usually referred to as medevac, medical evacuation services offer vital transportation for individuals needing immediate medical assistance. To guarantee the safe and effective movement of patients, these operations are manned by qualified medical professionals and equipped with specialist equipment. Commercial aviation is used by humanitarian missions to provide supplies and help to disaster-torn regions, therefore offering vital support during a crisis. Environmental monitoring, land mapping, and resource exploration are just a few of the several uses for aerial surveying services, which employ aircraft to gather data.

All things considered, commercial aviation is a complex sector that is absolutely essential for world connectivity and economic growth. By means of its varied spectrum of offerings, it promotes global trade, travel, and humanitarian endeavors, fostering connectivity and accessibility of the world. The greatest degrees of safety and efficiency guaranteed by the regulatory systems and safety criteria set by aviation authorities help to build confidence in air travel by guaranteeing trust. The industry is still evidence of human creativity and the unrelenting quest of improvement even as it develops.

Air Taxi Operations

Air Taxi Services

One exciting and fast expanding part of the commercial aviation sector are air taxi services. Air taxis offer on-demand, point-to--point transport options catered to the particular needs of consumers unlike conventional scheduled airline services. These services mostly serve business travelers, high-net-worth people, and those looking for the ease and flexibility of private aviation travel free from the long-term commitment of owning a jet.

Usually seating four to eight passengers, air taxis run small aircraft. Designed for short-haul flights, these aircraft provide speedy and effective travel between smaller airports and other sites not serviced by larger carriers. The main benefit of air taxi services is its capacity to offer direct flights to locations may be inaccessible by conventional commercial planes, therefore drastically lowering journey time and improving client convenience.

Operational Guidelines and Needs

Running an air taxi business means following a sophisticated set of operating guidelines and legal regulations. Basic elements of guaranteeing the dependability and safety of air taxi operations are licensing and certification. Air taxi companies operating in the United States have to get a Part 135 certificate from the Federal Aviation Agency (FAA). The operator's aircraft, maintenance practices, pilot qualifications, and general operating policies are closely examined throughout this certification process. Other areas have similar laws under control by corresponding aviation authorities like the European Union Aviation Safety Agency (EASA), in Europe.

Flight planning, aircraft maintenance, and pilot training are primary operational processes used in air taxi companies. Flight planning is painstaking preparation meant to guarantee every flight's efficiency and safety. This covers choosing best paths, figuring gasoline needs, and working with air traffic control. Another essential component is aircraft maintenance, which depends on consistent inspections and servicing to keep airworthiness. Because air taxi aircraft fly more frequently and optimum dependability and safety must be ensured, maintenance procedures for them usually are more strict.

Comprehensive pilot training for air taxi businesses emphasizes customer service as well as technical ability. From regular flights to emergency events, pilots have to be skilled at managing a variety of circumstances. They also have to be very good communicators so they may engage passengers properly and guarantee a flawless and comfortable journey. Maintaining great levels of safety and service depends on ongoing education and evaluation.

Compliance and Regulatory Difficulties

The running of air taxi services naturally presents regulatory problems. Ensuring compliance with the several, sometimes strict rules set by different aviation authorities presents one of the main difficulties. This calls for a complete awareness of both domestic and international aviation rules as well as the capacity to modify operations to fit these criteria.

In the aviation sector, especially air taxi companies, environmental rules are becoming ever more important. Operators have to take care of issues about carbon emissions and noise pollution. Many areas have set emissions rules and noise abatement policies that air taxi companies have to follow. This has resulted in the acceptance of more modern, ecologically friendly aircraft and technologies meant to lower the effects of air taxi operations on the surroundings.

Maintaining the security of air taxi operations presents still another regulatory obstacle. This covers putting in place strong security measures to protect aircraft and passengers from possible hazards. Following security rules entails careful passenger and luggage screening as well as operational base security implementation during flights.

Case Studies and Models

Analyzing outstanding air taxi companies offers insightful analysis of the efficient running and management of these services. One prominent instance is Surf Air, a U.S.-based company that invented the subscription-based air taxi concept. For a monthly cost, Surf Air gives members unlimited flights between a few chosen destinations, therefore offering a great degree of convenience and flexibility. Successful implementation of this approach has drawn a devoted clientele of business travelers looking for dependable and quick air travel options.

Another such is the European company GlobeAir, running a fleet of Citation Mustang aircraft. Offering on-demand charter services to a large spectrum of locations, GlobeAir has become a top air taxi operator in Europe. Strong industry reputation for the organization comes from its focus on customer service, operational effectiveness, and safety.

Furthermore, significantly influencing the development of air taxi services are technological innovations. The business is about to be transformed by the creation of electric vertical takeoff and landing (eVTOL) aircraft. Leading innovators in this field include companies like Joby Aviation and Lilium, creating eVTOL aircraft meant to provide environmentally friendlier, quieter, more efficient air taxi services. Designed for metropolitan settings, these aircraft offer a solution for the mounting need for urban air mobility.

Future Developments and Novelties

With various trends and technologies ready to change the sector, air taxi services seem to have a bright future. Digital technologies including artificial intelligence (AI) and blockchain are projected to improve operational efficiency and customer experience by means of their growing integration. Blockchain technology can offer safe and open transactions; artificial intelligence can be utilized to maximize flight paths, forecast maintenance needs, and enhance customer service.

Still another noteworthy trend is the emergence of urban air mobility (UAM). UAM sees a system of air taxis running inside cities, offering speedy and effective mobility to help to ease traffic congestion. This idea is becoming popular as various cities all across the world investigate if it would be possible to include air taxis into their systems of mobility.

Another major priority is sustainability; the aviation sector is under more and more pressure to lower its environmental effect. A major first step towards reaching this is the evolution of electric and hybrid-electric aircraft. These aircraft provide to lower noise pollution and carbon emissions, so air taxi services become more socially acceptable and environmentally benign.

Finally, a dynamic and changing part of the commercial aviation sector are air taxi services. Air taxis present a convincing substitute for conventional airline travel given their emphasis on adaptability, ease of use, and economy. Running these services, though, calls on negotiating a challenging terrain of legal obligations. Examining successful operators and adopting technology changes can help the air taxi sector to keep growing and innovative, thereby changing our perspective on air travel.

Private Operations - Handling

Private Aviation

Serving people and businesses looking for customized and flexible air travel solutions, private aviation is a unique and exclusive part of the aviation business. Private aircraft provides customized services catered to the particular requirements of its customers, unlike commercial aviation, which runs on set itineraries and fixed schedules. This section covers a spectrum of activities, including repair, handling, and operation of private aircraft as well as their management.

Emphasizing privacy, convenience, and luxury, private aviation defines itself. Often high-net-worth people, celebrities, and business executives, clients prefer the opportunity to travel on their own schedules, visit far-off locations, and bypass the packed and sometimes difficult procedures linked with commercial airports. From little turboprops to big corporate jets, the aircraft utilized in private aviation varies greatly in comfort, range, and performance.

Handling and Management

Ensuring a flawless and joyful experience for clients depends on the way private aviation operations are handled and managed. Maintaining the high standards required by private aviation consumers depends much on ground handling services, which cover aircraft refueling, cleaning, catering, and passenger amenities.

Ground Handling Procedures

Private aviation ground handling policies are painstakingly designed and carried out to guarantee effectiveness and safety. Starting with airplane preparation—which includes extensive cleaning and maintenance checks—these operations start with Strict safety procedures guide refueling to avoid mishaps and guarantee aircraft readiness for its next flight. Customized meals and beverages offered by catering companies satisfy the tastes of the guests, therefore improving their in-flight experience.

Often known as Fixed Base Operators (FBOs), passenger services at private aircraft facilities are meant to be highly comfortable and convenient. Private lounges, conference rooms, and concierge services—which FBOs offer let guests unwind and conduct business as they wait for their plane. Usually quickening the check-in and security procedures at FBOs helps to lower waiting times and improve the whole travel experience.

Maintenance and Servicing

Essential elements of private aviation, maintenance and service guarantee aircraft's dependability and safety. Frequent maintenance inspections help to find and fix any possible problems before they might compromise the operation of the aircraft. This covers standard airframe, engine, avionics, and other vital system inspections. Highly skilled experts following stringent industry norms and guidelines do maintenance chores.

Apart from routine maintenance, private aircraft receive enhancements and changes to improve their comfort and performance. This can cover engine enhancements, interior renovations, and sophisticated avionics systems' installation. These improvements guarantee that the aircraft stays competitive in the market as well as increase its capabilities.

Coordination with Airports and Air Traffic Control

The seamless running of private aviation flights depends on efficient cooperation between airports and air traffic control (ATC). Private flights can demand flexible routing and scheduling unlike commercial aircraft, which follow set paths and schedules. This means tight cooperation with ATC to get the required clearances and guarantee that aircraft may go without delays.

Working closely with airports, private aviation operators arrange handling and parking for their aircraft. This covers scheduling ground handling services, negotiating landing and takeoff times, and making sure all required permits and paperwork are in order. In congested airspace, where private flights must be closely controlled to prevent problems with commercial traffic, good coordination with ATC is especially crucial.

Customer Experience and Service Excellence

Providing outstanding customer service determines the success of private aviation activities. Customers in this category want a degree of service that transcends what commercial aviation usually provides. This covers tailored attention, flawless logistics, and a dedication to both meeting and surpassing their expectations.

Personalized Services for Private Aviation Clients

Private aviation is fundamentally based on tailored services. This starts with the first booking procedure, in which customers can indicate their choices for aircraft type, inside layout, cuisine, and in-flight entertainment. To guarantee that every element of the client's vacation is customized to their requirements, private aviation firms frequently designate committed account managers to supervise all facets of the travel.

Another area where private aviation shines are in-flight services. Passengers can access fast internet, eat exquisite meals created by top chefs, and have a large array of entertainment choices. Trained to deliver discreet and attentive service, the cabin staff guarantees a comfortable and fun journey for the guests.

Enhancing Passenger Comfort and Convenience

In private aviation, improving passenger comfort and convenience is the first goal. This covers offering modern conveniences, roomy and beautiful cabin furnishings, and a quiet and pleasant ride. Larger windows, sophisticated climate control systems, and ergonomic seating are just a few of the innovations aircraft builders constantly bring to the interior designs.

On the ground, improving the passenger experience depends much on FBOs. These establishments provide private lounges with pleasant seating, beverages, and entertainment choices. Concierge services, which can organize ground transportation, lodging, and other travel-related needs, let passengers also benefit.

Case Studies of Exceptional Private Handling Services

Several private aviation firms have set standards for first-rate handling capabilities. One of the biggest private jet operators in the world, NetJets, for instance, offers a fractional ownership program giving customers access to an aircraft fleet. With a strong focus on safety, dependability, and tailored service, NetJets is known for its exacting attention to detail and dedication to customer satisfaction.

One such noteworthy example is VistaJet, a worldwide corporate aviation company running Bombardier aircraft. VistaJet stands out from other airlines by using a subscription-based approach, which lets customers access its fleet free from the ownership complications. The company's dedication to provide a consistent and first-rate experience over its worldwide network has attracted a devoted customer base.

Unmatched ease, comfort, and flexibility make private aircraft the height of individualized air travel. Ground handling, maintenance, and coordination with airports and ATC all together need careful planning and execution in the administration of private operations. The focus on individualized care and passenger comfort guarantees that customers get a travel experience that either meets or surpasses their expectations.

The business is ready to develop and change, including fresh technologies and service advancements as the market for private aviation keeps expanding. Businesses who excel in upholding high operating standards and providing outstanding customer service will keep growing in this unique and exciting part of the aviation sector.

Air Charters

Air Charter Services

Composing a flexible and active part of the commercial aviation sector, air charter services offer custom travel solutions for freight as well as passengers. Unlike planned airline services, air charters allow flexibility to run flights on demand, therefore meeting particular demands and preferences of customers. For many different industries, including corporate travel, sports teams, entertainment groups, and time-sensitive cargo deliveries, this adaptability makes air charters appealing.

Passenger charters and cargo charters help to generally classify air charter services. Often for business, leisure, or special occasions, passenger charters satisfy groups or individuals needing tailored travel plans. Conversely, cargo charters concentrate on delivering commodities that require quick or specialist handling—that instance, perishable things, high-value goods, or large cargo.

Operational Procedures and Best Practices

Running an air charter service calls for careful preparation and adherence to highest standards to guarantee customer happiness, safety, and efficiency. Route choice, acquiring required permits, organizing ground handling services, and liaising with air traffic control (ATC) constitute a few of the several important stages in charter flight planning.

Flight Planning and Execution

Air charter flight planning is a thorough procedure beginning with customer needs. This covers passenger count, kind and volume of cargo, preferred departure and arrival times, and any specific demands. This data helps operators choose the suitable aircraft and path taking into account flight length, fuel consumption, and weather.

Operators have to get required licenses and certifications from aviation authorities after the flight plan is developed. This entails working with ATC to guarantee airspace and airport slots, therefore enabling the flight to run free from delays. Ground handling operations including passenger services, catering, and fuelling are set to guarantee a flawless client experience.

Safety and Regulatory Compliance

Air charter operations put great emphasis on safety, hence operators have to follow strict rules established by aviation authorities. This covers keeping aircraft to the best of standards, doing frequent safety checks, and making sure crew members and pilots are correctly certified and qualified.

Particularly for passenger charters, regulatory compliance often covers security policies. To protect against any hazards, operators have to apply strong security procedures including passenger screening and baggage checks. Additional security steps can be needed for cargo charters carrying sensitive or valuable items.

Effective Coordination of Charter Activities

Effective management of charter operations include best use of resources and simplification of procedures to improve operational performance. This covers keeping a fleet of dependable and modern aircraft, guaranteeing timely maintenance and repairs, and efficiently running crew schedules.

Operating efficiency is considerably enhanced by technology. Advanced flight management systems can maximize paths, track aircraft performance in real-time, and forecast maintenance requirements, so lowering downtime and improving dependability. Systems for customer relationship management (CRM) enable operators to control client contacts and offer individualized service, hence enhancing client happiness and loyalty.

Business and Financial Aspects

From pricing strategies to revenue management to market dynamics to competition, air charter services' business and financial sides are complex.

Revenue Management and Pricing Policies

Many elements affect air charter service pricing: aircraft type, flight length, fuel prices, and extra services asked for by customers. Usually, operators choose a mix of fixed and variable pricing strategies to decide the charter flight cost. While variable costs include gasoline, landing fees, and catering, fixed costs cover expenses such as aircraft procurement, maintenance, and crew compensation.

In the air charter sector, revenue management is the process of besting profitability by means of pricing methods. This covers examining market trends, price changes depending on demand, and dynamic pricing choices. To draw frequent customers and create consistent income sources, operators can also offer bulk buy discounts or membership programs.

Competitive Landscape and Principal Actors

There are many operators fighting for customers in the very competitive air charter industry. Important actors in the sector are established charter corporations, aircraft management organizations, and boutique operators focused in niche markets. Offering first-rate service, contemporary, well-maintaining aircraft, and creative pricing policies helps successful operators set themselves apart.

Air charter firms have to keep competitive by always improving their fleet, changing their service offers, and using new technologies. Long-term performance also depends critically on developing close links with suppliers, customers, and aviation authorities.

Opportunities and Challenges

Running an air charter business comes with a lot of difficulties including changing gasoline costs, legal compliance, and financial uncertainty. Dealing with these difficulties calls for strategic planning, careful use of resources, and a dedication to upholding high safety and service standards.

Notwithstanding these difficulties, the air charter business presents tremendous growth potential. The sector is growing in response to growing demand for customized travel options, developments in aviation technology, and urban air mobility (UAM). Those who can use new technologies and adjust to shifting market conditions are positioned to grab these possibilities.

Case Studies with Real-World Illustrations

Analyzing successful air charter companies offers insightful information about sound business policies and procedures. Two particularly noteworthy examples are Air Partner and VistaJet.

Vista jet

Operating Bombardier aircraft, VistaJet is a global business aviation firm providing on-demand charter services to customers all around. With its subscription-based approach, the company gives flexibility and convenience by letting customers access its fleet free from the complications of ownership. VistaJet is well-known in the sector for excellence since it emphasizes providing consistent, high-quality service over its worldwide fleet.

Air Partner

Leading air charter firm Air Partner offers customized travel solutions for goods as well as passengers. The company provides private jet charters, group charters, and goods charters among its several services. Corporate travel, sports, and logistics are just a few of the industries that Air Partner has established as trusting partners based on its dedication to safety, dependability, and customer satisfaction.

Modern Ideas and Future Directions

Innovations in aircraft technologies, digital platforms, and sustainable aviation practices are driving future expansion in the always changing air charter sector. Electric and hybrid-electric aircraft research promises to lower running costs and environmental effect, therefore increasing the availability and sustainability of air charter operations.

By giving customers rapid access to charter alternatives, pricing information, and real-time updates, digital platforms and smartphone apps are transforming the booking process. These systems improve openness and convenience, facilitating client flight booking and management.

As operators look for ways to lower carbon emissions and lessen their environmental impact, sustainable aviation methods are gathering popularity. Investing in fuel-efficient aircraft, using carbon offset programs, and putting environmentally friendly operational policies into effect are part of this.

All things considered, air charter services provide a flexible and dynamic travel alternative that meets a broad spectrum of passenger and cargo requirements. Success in this cutthroat industry depends mostly on good management, respect of safety and legal requirements, and customer happiness. Embracing sustainable practices and technology advancements can help air charter operators keep expanding and flourishing in the changing aviation scene.

Chapter-2

BMA

Introduction to Baggage Reconciliation

Overview of Baggage Reconciliation

An essential operation in the aviation sector, baggage reconciliation guarantees that every piece of checked luggage is precisely matched with its corresponding passenger and flight. The seamless running of airports and airlines depends on this process, which also helps to ensure operational effectiveness and passenger happiness. Fundamentally, baggage reconciliation is tracking and confirming the movement of bags from check-in to loading aboard the aircraft, then to passenger pickup at their destination. This procedure reduces the possibility of missing or misdirected bags, which may cause major delays, higher running expenses, and unhappy consumers.

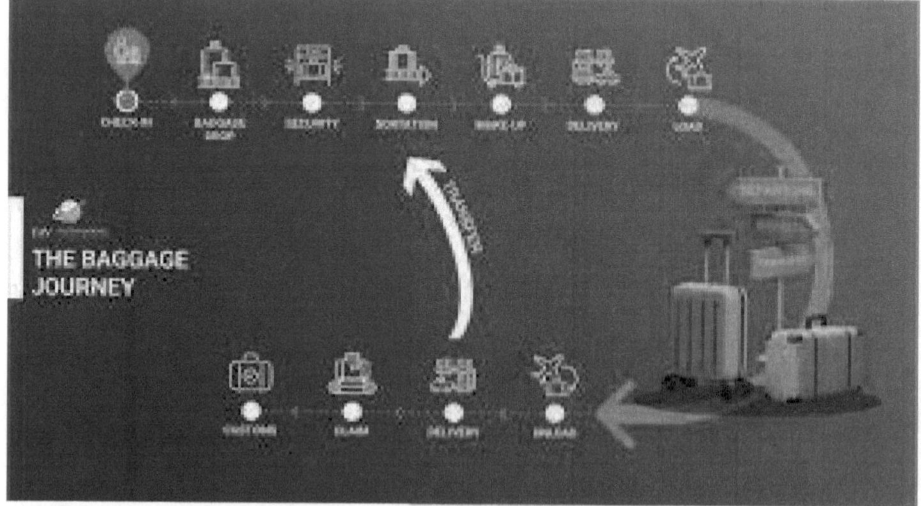

In several countries, baggage reconciliation is a legal obligation rather than only a logistical need. Guidelines and standards developed by several international aviation agencies, including the International Civil Aviation Organization (ICAO) and the International Air Transport Association (IATA), guarantee the efficiency and security of baggage handling operations. By preventing illegal baggage from being loaded aboard airplanes, these criteria are meant to increase the general safety of air travel by lowering the danger of security breaches and so raising passenger confidence in air travel.

Objectives of Baggage Reconciliation

Making sure every checked item is properly linked to the matching passenger and flight is the main goal of baggage reconciliation. This is accomplished by means of several checks and verifications conducted at several phases of the baggage handling operations. Important goals comprise:

Ensuring Security: By confirming that all checked baggage belongs to a verified passenger who is also on board, baggage reconciliation helps prevent unauthorized items from being transported. Maintaining passenger and staff safety and reducing security risk depend on this security precaution.

Enhancing Operational Efficiency: Efficient baggage reconciliation minimizes the risk of delays caused by baggage-related issues. Maintaining on-time performance, lowering turnaround times, and best utilization of airport resources depend on this.

Improving Customer Satisfaction: Passengers expect their luggage to arrive at their destination promptly and intact. Good baggage reconciliation lowers the possibility of lost or delayed luggage, improving the whole travel experience and raising passenger satisfaction.

Compliance with Regulations: Airlines and airports have to follow different laws for handling baggage. Good reconciliation systems guarantee adherence to these rules, therefore preventing any penalties and legal problems.

Challenges in Baggage Reconciliation

Baggage reconciliation is still a difficult and demanding chore even with the technological developments and strong system implementation. Several elements support these difficulties:

Large volume of baggage: Every day major airports handle thousands of bags. Managing such a high volume calls for both sophisticated systems and processes as well as speedy resolution of any problems that develop.

Diverse Operating Environments: Airports vary significantly in terms of size, layout, and infrastructure. This variety can make it difficult to apply uniform reconciliation procedures and calls for specific solutions fit for every airport's situation.

Human Error: Despite automation, human involvement is still necessary in many aspects of baggage handling. Manual tagging, scanning, and loading procedures can all cause mistakes that result in misrouted or lost bags.

Interlining and Transfer Baggage: Particularly those involving different airlines, baggage that needs to be moved between several flights adds still another level of difficulty. Ensuring flawless baggage transfer and juggling several carriers might be difficult.

Security Threats: The constant threat of security breaches necessitates stringent checks and verifications, which can slow down the reconciliation process. It is a difficult and continuous task to strike security against efficiency.

The Process of Baggage Reconciliation

Baggage reconciliation consists in numerous important phases, each of which is absolutely important for guaranteeing the correct and effective handling of bags. These phases consist:

Check-In and Tagging: At the check-in counter, each piece of luggage is tagged with a unique identifier, typically in the form of a barcode or RFID tag. The passenger's ticket and flight details link this identification.

Sorting and Screening: Tagged baggage is sorted and directed to the appropriate screening area. Bags are checked for illegal goods at this level to guarantee they are free.

Tracking and Loading: Once screened, baggage is tracked as it moves through the airport's baggage handling system. At several checkpoints, automated systems scan the tags to make sure every suitcase is headed toward its intended plane.

Loading Verification: Before loading onto the aircraft, baggage is cross-referenced with passenger lists to ensure that only bags belonging to checked-in passengers are loaded. This phase resolves any discrepancies.

Unloading and Delivery: Upon arrival, baggage is unloaded and directed to the appropriate carousel for passenger retrieval. The tracking mechanism guarantees that bags go to the right place.

Technologies in Baggage Reconciliation

The accuracy and effectiveness of baggage reconciliation systems have been considerably enhanced by technological developments. Some important technologies are:

Barcode Systems: Traditional barcode systems have been the backbone of baggage reconciliation for decades. Every bag has a barcode scanned at several points that offers real-time tracking data.

RFID Technology: Radio Frequency Identification (RFID) technology offers several advantages over traditional barcode systems. More accurate and effective tracking is made possible by RFID tags' ability to be read remotely and their absence of line-of-sight requirement. RFID technologies can help to drastically lower the frequency of misplaced or misdirected goods.

Automated Baggage Handling Systems (BHS): Modern airports are equipped with sophisticated BHS that automate the sorting, screening, and tracking of baggage. To expedite baggage processing, these systems combine several technologies including robotics, scanners, and conveyor belts.

Software Solutions: Advanced software platforms provide end-to-end visibility and control over the baggage handling process. These systems provide preventive management of any problems by integrating with databases of airports and airlines, therefore offering real-time updates.

Essential for guaranteeing security, efficiency, and satisfaction of air travel, baggage reconciliation is a part of airport operations. Technological developments have greatly improved the capacity of baggage reconciliation systems despite the difficulties related to high numbers, different operation settings, and human mistake possibility. Using barcode systems, RFID technology, automated handling systems, and sophisticated software solutions will help airports and airlines increase baggage handling process accuracy and efficiency. Not only guarantees regulatory compliance but also improves operational performance and passenger pleasure by effective baggage reconciliation, thereby helping the airline sector to be generally successful.

Baggage Reconciliation Procedure

Definition and Purpose of Baggage Reconciliation

Modern airport operations depend critically on baggage reconciliation, which guarantees that every piece of checked luggage is precisely matched with the person who has flown on the aircraft. By reducing events of lost or misdirected baggage, baggage reconciliation mostly serves to improve security, simplify processes, and guarantee passenger happiness. The efficiency and dependability of air travel are maintained in great part by this procedure, which directly influences the whole passenger experience.

The increased complexity of air travel and the rising demand for strict security policies help to explain the beginnings of baggage reconciliation. Losing and monitoring bags grew more difficult when bigger planes and more passengers came along. This resulted in the creation of systems and protocols meant to guarantee that, both on departure and arrival, every piece of luggage is tallied for.

Steps Involved in the Reconciliation Process

From the moment luggage is checked in until it reaches its final destination, the baggage reconciliation process consists of various crucial stages meant to guarantee correct tracking and treatment of bags. Every stage in this procedure is painstakingly designed and carried out to avoid any security or efficiency breaches.

Baggage check-in:

Passengers show their bags at the check-in desk, which is then RFID-tagged or barcoded. Important information on this tag includes the passenger's flight information, destination, and distinctive ID.

Once the bags are weighed, any required security inspections are carried out. The tag is read, and the baggage handling system (BHS) of the airport gets the data entered.

Following check-in, the bags are moved to a security screening section where different searches for banned goods take place. Usually this calls for X-ray machines, explosive detection systems (EDS), and occasionally hand inspections.

Should the bags pass security inspections, they go to the sorting section. If not, security staff notes it for more investigation.

The baggage is guided to the suitable conveyor belts depending on its destination in the sorting section. Using the data from the baggage tags, automated sorting systems guarantee that every piece of luggage finds its proper place.

Luggage handlers load bags onto carts or containers, which are then carried to the airplane. The tags are scanned once again to ensure that every piece of luggage matches the right flight before it is loaded onboard the airplane.

Baggage handlers follow particular protocols during loading to guarantee that the bags are put in the correct compartments of the aircraft. For weight distribution as much as security depends on this.

Once the bags are placed into the aircraft, the baggage tags are once more scanned once more to provide a last check that every piece is tallied for.

A reconciliation check is conducted to guarantee that all checked items match passengers who have flown the aircraft before it leaves. Should a passenger not board, their bags are discovered and taken off the airplane in order to minimize possible security concerns.

To guarantee accuracy and efficiency, this stage calls for strong cooperation among gate agents, luggage handlers, and the flight crew.

Arrival and emptying:

The bags are unloaded from the aircraft and moved to the baggage claim area when one reaches the destination. The baggage tags are checked to guarantee that every piece is counted for during unloading.

The bags are next arranged and run on conveyor belts so people may access them.

Passengers pick their bags in the baggage claim area using the special tags supplied during check-in. Every unclaimed item is underlined for more inquiry to find the owner and fix any problems.

Staff members at airports are ready to help consumers with any issues including delayed or missing luggage.

Lost and Found Procedures:

In cases where baggage is lost or misdirected, the information from the baggage tags and the BHS is used to trace the luggage and reunite it with its owner. This could need cooperation across several airports and airlines.

Passengers can make claims for missing bags; the customer support crew of the airline tries to quickly address the matter.

Baggage Tracking Technologies and Systems:

The baggage reconciliation process's accuracy and efficiency have been much raised by technological developments. Several important technologies and techniques are used to monitor and handle bags all through the trip.

Barcode Systems:

Traditional barcode systems involve attaching a tag with a printed barcode to each piece of luggage. To follow its whereabouts, these barcodes are read at several points during the luggage handling process.

Though efficient, barcode systems have many drawbacks like susceptibility to breakage and line-of-sight scanning requirements.

Radio Frequency Identification (RFID):

RFID technology uses tags embedded with microchips that transmit unique identifiers via radio waves. Because RFID tags do not depend on line-of-sight scanning, precise and quick tracking is made possible.

RFID technology is becoming more and more used by airports and airlines to improve baggage reconciliation. To increase baggage handling accuracy, the IATA (International Air Transport Association) has supported the worldwide acceptance of RFID.

Baggage Handling Systems (BHS):

The BHS is an integrated network of conveyor belts, scanners, and sorting machines that automate the movement and tracking of baggage within an airport. The BHS guides bags to the suitable locations using information from baggage tags.

Advanced BHS reduces the possibility of mistakes and delays by handling big amounts of baggage with great accuracy and speed.

Real-Time Tracking Systems:

Real-time tracking systems provide continuous updates on the location and status of baggage. These systems provide real-time information to airport personnel and passengers using a mix of RFID, GPS, and mobile technology.

Online systems and mobile apps let travelers monitor their bags all along their trip, therefore improving customer happiness and openness.

Automated Sortation Systems:

Automated sortation systems use advanced algorithms and machinery to sort baggage based on flight and destination information. These systems require little human involvement to handle thousands of bags every hour.

Using robotics and artificial intelligence in sorting systems is a new trend with even more accuracy and efficiency promised.

Baggage Management Software:

Baggage management software integrates various technologies and data sources to provide a comprehensive view of the baggage handling process. This program enables airport personnel to instantly spot and fix problems, monitor and control bags in real-time, so maximize operational effectiveness.

Baggage management systems are progressively including predictive analytics and machine learning features to foresee and minimize possible issues before they start.

Challenges and Solutions in Baggage Reconciliation

The baggage reconciliation procedure has various difficulties despite technology developments that call for constant innovation and improvement.

Handling High Volumes of Baggage:

During peak travel seasons and at busy airports, the sheer volume of baggage can overwhelm handling systems, leading to delays and errors. In order to effectively handle rising loads, airports make investments in highly capacity BHS and automated sortation systems.

Ensuring Security:

Luggage reconciliation gives security first concern. The difficulty is juggling operational effectiveness with strict security policies. Strict adherence to security rules, real-time tracking, and sophisticated screening technology help to lower hazards.

Minimizing Human Error:

Human error can occur at various stages of the baggage handling process, from tagging to loading. Training courses, automation, and artificial intelligence monitoring and assistance for human operators help to greatly lower the possibility of errors.

Dealing with Irregular Operations:

Weather disruptions, technical issues, and other irregular operations can complicate baggage handling. Effective management of such events depends on contingency preparations, real-time communication networks, and adaptable operational procedures.

Inter-Airport Coordination:

For baggage that involves multiple airports and connecting flights, coordination between different airports and airlines is crucial. Standardized procedures, data exchange, and joint platforms improve inter-airport coordination and baggage handling streamlining.

Passenger Expectations:

Passengers expect their baggage to arrive on time and in good condition. Dealing with these expectations calls for ongoing technological, procedural, and customer service development. Real-time tracking and proactive communication help to raise passenger confidence and satisfaction.

Future Trends and Innovations in Baggage Reconciliation

Several developing trends and ideas meant to improve efficiency, security, and passenger experience will help baggage reconciliation going forward.

Biometric Verification: Integrating biometric verification with baggage handling systems can improve security and reduce the need for manual checks. Passengers can easily attach biometric data—such as face recognition—that links them to their bags.

Blockchain Technology: Blockchain offers a decentralized and secure way to track and manage baggage information. It can improve openness, stop data manipulation, and simplify cooperation amongst many parties.

Artificial Intelligence and Machine Learning: AI and machine learning can optimize various aspects of baggage handling, from predicting baggage volumes to identifying potential issues before they occur. Additionally able to improve automated tracking and sorting systems are these technologies.

Sustainable Practices: Aviation is giving sustainability top priority more and more. Using energy-efficient technologies, cutting waste, and besting resource use will help baggage handling systems contribute.

Passenger Self-Service: Self-service technologies, such as automated bag drop kiosks and mobile check-in, empower passengers to manage their baggage handling process, reducing waiting times and improving efficiency.

Smart Luggage: Smart luggage equipped with GPS, RFID, and IoT capabilities allows passengers to track their bags in real-time and receive alerts if their luggage is opened or lost. These changes improve passenger comfort of mind and security.

Trolley Management Overview

Importance of Trolley Management in Airport Operations

One of the most important but sometimes disregarded components of airport operations is trolley management. Good trolley management guarantees seamless luggage handling, therefore enhancing the general operational effectiveness and passenger pleasure. Between check-in desks, security screening sections, baggage sorting zones, and airplane loading facilities, trolleys—also known as baggage carts—are indispensable for moving bags between several sites around the airport.

Good trolley management improves the customer experience generally, reduces congestion in important operational areas, and helps prevent delays in luggage handling. Airlines can keep a flawless flow of operations by making sure trolleys are easily available where and when they are needed, therefore lowering waiting times and raising the quality of services.

Different Types of Trolleys Used for Baggage Handling

Each of the many trolleys utilized in baggage handling is meant to fulfill particular requirements within the airport surroundings. Effective trolley control depends on knowledge of the several kinds of trolleys and their uses.

Typical baggage trolleys:

Passenger luggage is usually carried on these most often used kinds of trolleys. Usually found in public places such as parking lots, check-in desks, and baggage claim areas, Standard baggage trolleys are made to be easily usable and fit for several luggage sizes.

Motorized trolleys:

Long distances within the airport are covered by motorized carts carrying significant baggage quantities. Large airports where manual transportation would be ineffective find them especially helpful.

Advanced technologies including GPS tracking and automatic routing can also be included into motorized trolleys.

Container trolleys:

Between the aircraft and the baggage handling system, bags, containers or ULDs are carried using container trolleys. These trolleys are made to guarantee the safe transfer of containers without damaging the contents of the bags by handling big weights.

Specialized Trolleys:

Designed for certain purposes, such as moving delicate or large objects, specialized trolleys are To fit different types of baggage, these trolleys could include extra features including padding, harnesses, or special forms, therefore guaranteeing their safe and effective handling.

Catering and Service Trolleys:

Although they are mostly used for moving food and other in-flight service products, catering trolleys can help with general airport trolley management. Proper management of these carts helps to keep punctuality and simplify service operations.

Challenges in Trolley Management and Their Impact on Operations

Good trolley management has certain difficulties. Many problems could develop that affect the effectiveness of trolley use and, hence, the whole baggage handling operation.

Distribution and availability:

Making sure trolleys are on hand where they are most required presents one of the main difficulties. In baggage handling facilities, poor distribution can cause congestion that delays and irritates travelers.

Dealing with this difficulty depends on effective trolley allocation and redistribution.

Care and Durability:

Trolleys are constantly used, hence they experience a lot of damage. Maintaining their optimal functioning depends on regular maintenance. Broken or malfunctioning trolleys could cause safety hazards and slow down business. It is really vital to use fast repair procedures and a strong maintenance routine.

Organization and Communication:

Good trolley management calls for flawless cooperation among several airport departments—including ground services, luggage handling, and repair crews. Effective trolley use and allocation resulting from communication breakdowns affects general operating efficiency.

Issues of security:

Unattended or badly controlled trolleys might provide security concerns. Maintaining airport security and safety requirements depends on trolleys not blocking important areas and being accurately tallied for.

Passenger Interaction:

Many times, passengers leave trolleys in odd places or abuse them, which results in clutter and ineffective utilization. This problem can be reduced by teaching passengers correct trolley use and including facilities for trolley returns.

Approaches for Effective Trolley Management

Using sensible trolley management techniques will help to greatly improve operational effectiveness and passenger pleasure. These are some ideal practices:

Systems of real-time tracking:

Tracking trolleys in real-time by means of GPS and RFID technologies helps control their availability and distribution. Real-time tracking minimizes delays by allowing rapid identification and trolley movement to highly demand regions.

Systems for Automated Retrieval:

Trolleys can be constantly available where needed and their collecting and redistribution automated systems help to lower the demand for manual handling. These systems move trolleys back to specific locations using robotics and conveyor belts.

Predictive analytics:

Using real-time flight schedules and past data, predictive analytics may project trolley demand. This lets airport personnel proactively distribute trolleys to busy locations, therefore increasing efficiency and lowering wait times.

Regular Maintenance Plans:

Maintaining proper operational condition of trolleys depends on a regular maintenance program. Early repairs and proactive replacements help to stop operational interruptions brought on by malfunctioning trolleys.

Passenger Encouragement and Instruction:

Trolley management can be improved by teaching travelers on correct trolley use and offering incentives for returning them to specified locations. Appropriate use is encouraged by clear signs and handy trolley return stations.

Cooperative Coordination:

Clearly defined channels of communication and cooperative procedures among several airport departments guarantees that trolley management is included into the whole operational plan. Frequent meetings and updates allow one to quickly handle any problems.

Technology in Baggage Management

Advanced Technologies Enhancing Baggage Handling Efficiency

Thanks to the incorporation of modern technologies, airport baggage handling has changed dramatically over the years. From check-in to ultimate destination, these technologies are absolutely essential for guaranteeing the safe and effective transfer of bags, therefore reducing mistakes and raising passenger comfort. Some of the main technologies applied in contemporary baggage handling systems are listed here.

Automated Conveyor Systems

The backbone of contemporary luggage handling is automated conveyor systems. From check-in counters to the airplane and subsequently the baggage claim area, these systems comprise a network of conveyor belts and sorting equipment moving bags. Automated conveyor systems primarily help with:

Speed and Efficiency:

Thousands of bags can be handled using automated conveyors, therefore drastically lowering the baggage processing time needed. Particularly during busy travel times, this helps to control excessive passenger counts.

Accuracy:

These systems minimize the possibility of misrouted or lost goods by precisely sorting and guiding bags to the right locations using barcode and RFID scanning.

Reduced Manual Handling:

Automation lessens the requirement for human labor, therefore accelerating the process and lowering the possibility of human mistake and workplace injury.

Bag tracking and reconciliation have been transformed by RFID technology. RFID tags have various benefits over conventional barcode systems in that they may be scanned from a wider distance and from without direct line of sight.

Real-Time Tracking:

Real-time baggage tracking made possible by RFID tagging helps throughout processing. Throughout the trip, passengers and airport personnel can track the whereabouts and state of bags at any one moment.

Greater accuracy:

By means of accurate and consistent tracking data, RFID devices lower the possibility of lost or misplaced goods. This raises general passenger happiness and efficiency.

Gathering Information:

By means of comprehensive data on luggage handling performance, RFID technology enables the analysis of which can help to pinpoint and solve system inefficiencies.

BHS (baggage handling system) software

Combining several parts of the baggage handling process, Baggage Handling System (BHS) software offers a complete management tool. The advantages and characteristics of BHS software include in:

Centralized Control:

By centralizing baggage handling operations' control and monitoring, BHS software lets airport personnel handle the whole process from one interface.

Operational Insights:

The program offers real-time analysis of baggage flow, system performance, and possible bottlenecks, therefore facilitating proactive management and fast resolution of problems.

Compatibility with Other Systems:

To guarantee flawless cooperation and information exchange, BHS software can interact with other airport systems including flight information displays and passenger check-in systems.

Security Measures in Baggage Handling

Importance of Security in Baggage Handling

Ensuring the safety and integrity of air travel depends mostly on security in baggage handling. Every piece of luggage must be devoid of forbidden goods and possible hazards since millions of people pass daily. Security lapses can have serious effects on passenger safety, legal penalties, and airline reputation harm as well as on other aspects. Maintaining confidence in air travel and protecting passengers, crew, and aircraft depends so on strict security policies. The sad events of September 11, 2001, brought attention to the weaknesses in aviation security and resulted in a major reform of security protocols all around. Since then, the aviation sector's attempts to stop such events depend critically on the combination of strict standards and cutting-edge technologies. A key component of this all-encompassing security system is baggage handling security, which guarantees that no harmful object finds its way on aircraft.

Screening Procedures for Checked Baggage

The first line of protection in making sure no harmful goods are flown commercially is screening processes. Several layers of security inspections are part of these operations. X-ray machines, which offer comprehensive images of the contents, run all checked bags. Trained to spot forbidden objects including bombs, guns, and other dangerous materials are security staff. Using dual-view technology, advanced X-ray systems offer two distinct angles of view of the contents of the bag, hence improving detecting powers.

Using sophisticated technology, explosive detection systems (EDS) automatically identify possible hazards and analyze the chemical composition of the baggage contents to detect explosive materials. Under ETD systems, luggage is swabbed for trace levels of explosive materials, which are then examined to find even minute concentrations of explosive residues. ETD is very helpful for spotting explosives that would not be readily apparent using standard X-ray or EDS technologies. Should X-ray or EDS systems indicate a bag, security staff may manually check it, physically opening and looking at the contents to make sure they do not include forbidden objects. Manual inspections guarantee that any questionable objects found by automatic methods are addressed and are comprehensive.

More finely detailed than conventional X-ray devices, CT scanners give a three-dimensional picture of the contents of a bag. Their accuracy and dependability in threat detection have made these even more valuable. Different kinds of materials can be distinguished using CT technology, enabling exact detection of any hazards. Security staff also receive training on how to spot any indicators of questionable conduct among guests. Although it has nothing to do with baggage, this method helps find people who could need more examination including their bags.

Regulatory Compliance and International Standards

Strong rules and international guidelines direct the security precautions taken in baggage handling. Setting worldwide standards and recommended methods for aviation security, including luggage screening and handling, the International Civil Aviation Organization (ICAO) Member nations must follow these guidelines if they are to guarantee consistency in security policies. Annex 17 of ICAO lists the security procedures member nations have to abide by, therefore guaranteeing a uniform aviation security strategy.

The TSA in the United States is in charge of baggage handling security policy execution. TSA rules provide particular screening techniques and equipment needs to guarantee the security of examined baggage. For instance, the TSA's 3-1-1 regulation controls the liquids, gels, and aerosols passengers could include in their checked bags. For EU members, EASA establishes aviation safety and security criteria to guarantee that EU airports and airlines follow strict security procedures. The rules of EASA guarantee strong security standards all throughout Europe by including thorough criteria for the screening and handling of checked luggage.

Every nation has an aviation authority in charge of nationally enforcing security rules. These authorities guarantee adherence to world norms and might enforce extra security policies as necessary. For baggage handling security in British airports, the Civil Aviation Authority (CAA) in the UK, for instance, lays particular rules. Harmonizing security policies among several countries depends on international cooperation. Working toward global development and promotion of similar security methods, organizations such as the ICAO and IATA (International Air Transport Association) guarantee that security policies are consistent independent of the airport or airline.

Roles of Various Agencies in Baggage Security

Many agencies work together to guarantee baggage handling procedures' security. Implementation and supervising of screening processes falls to airport security teams. When needed, they do hand inspections; they run X-ray equipment, EDS, ETD, and CT scanners. These staff members are taught to manage several security situations and guarantee that every item of baggage is properly examined.

Airlines have committed security staff members who work with airport security to make sure baggage handling procedures follow legal criteria. They might also go extra security for particular flights or locations. Development and use of security protocols catered to their operations involves also airline security professionals. Particularly for international flights, customs authorities may check bags to make sure no illegal items are carried across borders and that all commodities follow customs rules. Working closely with airport security, customs officials help to find and handle possible hazards in checked goods.

To handle baggage screening procedures, several airports and airlines use private security companies. These contractors have to follow all legal guidelines and operate under the direction of teams representing airports and airlines. Often bringing specific knowledge and technology to improve baggage security are private contractors. Reacting to security concerns found during baggage screening falls mostly on law enforcement departments. In case of possible hazards, they offer quick intervention to guarantee the security of travelers and staff of airports.

Enhancing Security through Technology

Advanced technologies greatly improve the security of luggage handling operations. Analyzing X-ray and CT pictures, artificial intelligence and machine learning algorithms find possible hazards more precisely than human operators by themselves. These systems can highlight dubious objects for more examination. Additionally able to learn from prior data, artificial intelligence systems can gradually raise their threat detecting capacity. Passenger IDs can be verified and matched with checked baggage using biometric technology including fingerprint scanning and facial recognition, therefore adding still another degree of protection to guarantee that no illegal person can carry bags. While improving security, biometric validation helps to simplify the check-in procedure.

Blockchain can guarantee that every stage of the luggage handling process is traceable and tamper-proof, therefore improving openness and responsibility by means of a safe and unchangeable record of baggage handling procedures. Blockchain can also let multiple stakeholders—including airports, security agencies, and airlines—share safe data. IoT devices can be fitted to bags to track their whereabouts and state in real time. These gadgets improve the capacity to track and control baggage over its travel by constantly updating on baggage movement and alerting security staff to any illegal access or manipulation.

For many different kinds of hazards, advanced screening technologies such backscatter X-ray systems and millimeter-wave scanners offer improved detection capacity. Liquids, non-metallic items, and other things that conventional X-ray systems could overlook can all be found by these sophisticated screening instruments.

Training and Awareness

In luggage handling, effective security depends also on well-trained staff and increased awareness. To operate complex screening tools and respond effectively to possible hazards, security staff members must receive thorough training. Regular refresher courses and drills guarantee staff members' current knowledge of the most recent security technologies and practices. Another absolutely vital element is passenger awareness. Reducing security hazards requires teaching passengers about security procedures including the kinds of things forbidden in checked baggage and the need of declaring hazardous chemicals. At airports, clear signs and communication help travelers navigate and stop unintended security lapses.

Challenges and Future Directions

Ensuring the best degrees of security in luggage handling still presents difficulties even with the technological developments and strict legislative rules. Security concerns are always changing as new techniques of hiding illegal objects surface often. Maintaining ahead of these challenges calls for both constant innovation and adaptation. One of the toughest tasks is juggling operational effectiveness with security. Sometimes rigorous security policies cause delays and congestion in luggage handling sections. It is imperative to find means of process simplification without sacrificing security.

Particularly for smaller airports with tighter budgets, ensuring that there are enough resources—including staff and technology—to uphold strong security requirements can be difficult. Consistent security methods worldwide depend on more harmony and cooperation. Although there are global norms, the application of security policies can differ throughout nations. Making sure travelers follow security rules can prove challenging. Maintaining security depends on ongoing efforts to teach travelers and ensure compliance.

The integrity and safety of air travel depend on security steps taken in baggage handling. Airports and airlines may properly control the security of checked goods by putting strict screening policies into operation, following regulatory guidelines, using modern technologies, and guaranteeing complete training and awareness. Maintaining high security standards and shielding passengers, crew, and aircraft from possible hazards depends on ongoing improvement and adaptation to new hazards.

Operational Procedures for Trolley Management

Workflow and Best Practices for Efficient Trolley Usage

Smooth operation of airport baggage handling systems depends on efficient trolley management. From their first deployment to maintenance and redistribution, the trolley management process consists of numerous important phases. Using best practices in every one of these phases helps to maximize the availability and state of trolleys, hence improving general effectiveness. Trolleys are positioned deliberately in heavy traffic areas including parking lots, baggage claim facilities, and check-in desks. Flight itineraries and passenger traffic statistics form the foundation of the deployment strategy to guarantee trolley availability where most required.

Trolleys' whereabouts and condition are tracked using real-time monitoring technologies like GPS and RFID. These technologies can determine when and where trolleys should be moved as well as offer ongoing information on trolley availability. From places where they are less required, trolleys are routinely gathered and sent to high-demand areas. Using conveyor belts and robotics to move trolleys back to specified collecting places, automated retrieval systems and dedicated trolley management personnel simplify this operation.

Maintaining trolleys in good running order depends on regular maintenance. Periodic inspections help trollers find and fix any problems. To guarantee quick repairs and replacements, airports set maintenance plans and procedures, therefore preventing operating interruptions. Particularly for those with bulky or heavy bags, airport personnel are ready to help guests with trolleys. This service not only raises passenger happiness but also guarantees correct usage of trolleys and return to assigned locations. There are obviously marked trolley return points all around the airport. Announcements and signage help passengers to return trolleys to designated places, therefore minimizing clutter and increasing availability for other users.

Passenger comments and tracking system data are examined to maximize trolley operations. Demand forecasts made by predictive analytics allow deployment plans to be changed. These realizations guide the implementation of constant improvement projects.

Maintenance and Management of Trolley Fleets

Maintaining a fleet of trolleys calls for frequent inspections, repairs, and replacements to guarantee they stay in best shape. Routine checks for indicators of wear and tear—broken wheels, damaged handles, structural problems—are part of effective maintenance and management policies. Trained maintenance personnel who follow set checklists handle inspections to guarantee comprehensive assessments.

Schedules of preventive maintenance are set to handle possible problems before they cause breakdowns. This covers changing out worn components, tightening bolts, and lubricating moving parts. Preventive maintenance lowers the possibility of unexpected breakdowns and helps trolleys last for more years. When trolleys are discovered to be defective, they are promptly taken off line and sent for repairs to maintenance facilities. Safety and functionality come first in repair procedures, hence trolleys are rebuilt to running order before being used.

Trolleys that are beyond repair or have reached the end of their useful life are replaced with new units. Spare trolleys kept at airports help to enable quick replacements and reduce disturbance of business operations. Good inventory control guarantees always enough trolleys to satisfy demand. Inventory management systems let airports monitor trolley counts in storage, in-service, and in-repair. This guides future replacement and purchase planning.

Coordination Between Ground Staff and Baggage Handling Teams

Good trolley management calls for strong cooperation between luggage handling teams and ground staff. Good communication and teamwork guarantee that trolleys are used effectively and available when and where they are required. Establishing clear communication channels helps several teams to exchange information. Frequent meetings and updates enable coordination of activities and quick resolution of any problems that develop.

Teams of ground crew and baggage handlers coordinate to track trolley availability and usage. Tracking systems' real-time data is distributed around teams to guarantee everyone receives current information. This synchronization guarantees a seamless operating flow and helps to avoid traffic jams. To guarantee that every staff member engaged in trolley management knows their roles and responsibilities, training courses are run. Frequent training courses help staff members remain current on new technology and best practices, therefore improving general effectiveness.

Trolley Management Future Trends and Innovations

Many developing trends and ideas will help trolley management in airports to flourish. Integration of cutting-edge technology including the Internet of Things (IoT) and artificial intelligence (AI) is supposed to transform trolley administration. While IoT devices can offer real-time data on trolley state and position, artificial intelligence can be utilized to forecast demand trends and maximize trolley deployment. These technologies will increase operational effectiveness and lower the necessity of human involvement.

Another important trend influencing trolley control going forward is sustainability. embracing electric trolleys and running recycling programs for former trolleys are just two of the ecologically friendly policies airports are embracing more and more. These projects match more general sustainability objectives and help to lessen the environmental effects of airport activities.

Furthermore, trolley control is increasingly being done using smartphone apps. These tools improve the passenger experience by letting users find trolleys, ask help, and offer comments, therefore simplifying processes. By allowing airport employees to better monitor and control trolleys, mobile apps also help to guarantee that they are always available where necessary.

To run airport baggage handling systems effectively, effective trolley management is therefore absolutely essential. Airports can guarantee that trolleys are constantly available and in good condition by applying best practices, using cutting-edge technologies, and encouraging strong cooperation between ground crew and luggage handling teams. Adopting future trends and technologies will help trolley management to be even more sustainable and efficient, therefore enhancing the whole passenger experience.

Chapter-3

Ramp Operations (Airside Operations)

Handling Procedures

Overview of Ramp Operations

Often called airside operations, ramp operations form the foundation of airport operations. These activities cover all that takes place on the airport ramp—where aircraft are parked, loaded, unloaded, refueled, and maintained. The seamless running of the whole airport depends on the efficiency and safety of ramp operations, therefore affecting everything including flight plans and customer happiness. Among the many duties ramp staff members handle are escorting airplanes to their parking locations, making sure all ground handling tools are correctly positioned, and preserving a safe workplace. It is impossible to overestimate the need of thorough training and following safety procedures given the high-risk character of operating near aircraft and large gear.

Standard Operating Techniques (SOPs)

Carefully crafted rules, Standard Operating Procedures (SOPs), must be followed by ramp staff to guarantee the effective and safe handling of aircraft on the ramp. These processes address all facets of ramp operations and offer thorough guidelines on how to safely and correctly complete each chore. Maintaining consistency and reducing risk of mistakes or mishaps depend on SOPs. Marshaling is guiding aircraft using standard hand signals to reach their assigned parking areas. To properly interact with pilots, ramp staff members must be well knowledgeable in these signs. Correct marshaling guarantees aircraft are positioned as needed, therefore facilitating later loading, unloading, and service operations. Placing wedges—chocks—against an aircraft's wheels to stop it from moving when parked is known as choking. On the ramp, this operation is absolutely vital for the protection of people and equipment. Chocks have to be set in place right away upon the aircraft's complete halt and stay until it is ready to take off. Attaching ground power units, laying safety cones around the aircraft, and linking passenger boarding bridges or stairs are only a few of the various actions required in securing the aircraft. These steps assist to guarantee that the airplane stays steady and safe for ground handling procedures. Effective ramp operations depend on ground handling equipment—including baggage carts, fuel trucks, and catering vehicles—being properly positioned. Equipment needs to be positioned far enough to prevent interfering with other operations or creating a safety risk but still close enough to carry out their purposes.

Safety Protocols

Because staff members operate in a high-risk area, safety is first priority in ramp operations. Moving aircraft, heavy machinery, and different ground handling operations call for strict safety procedures to guard workers and tools. Appropriate Personal Protective Equipment (PPE) must be worn by ramp workers including gloves, safety shoes, high-visibility vests, and hearing protection. Protecting workers from the several hazards on the ramp—including loud noises, moving cars, and heavy equipment—PPE is absolutely vital. Training courses stress hazard awareness, teaching staff to identify possible hazards and implement preventative action. This covers knowing jet blast zones, avoiding walking beneath planes, and keeping a safe distance from moving vehicles. Clearly indicated safety zones on the ramp feature regions set aside for particular uses such fueling, loading, and maintenance. Following these zones guarantees that activities do not coincide and that staff members are aware of their surroundings, helping to prevent mishaps. Maintaining ramp safety calls for effective communication. To coordinate actions and notify one another to possible hazards, ramp staff members utilize radios, hand signals, and other communication devices. Effective, succinct communication guarantees that every team member is aware of continuous operations and helps to avoid misinterpretation. Improving safety procedures depends on timely incident reporting including near-misses. Ramp staff members are urged to promptly report any dangerous situations or events, therefore enabling speedy resolution and the application of preventative action.

Equipment and Vehicle Operations

A major element of ramp operations is the safe running of ground handling machinery and vehicles. Among the several jobs done using equipment and trucks are airplane towing, baggage transportation, and refueling. Strict adherence to standards and frequent maintenance help to guarantee that these activities are carried out effectively and safely. Comprehensive training on the correct operation and use of ground handling equipment is required of ramp staff. This covers understanding of safety elements, equipment controls, and emergency protocols. Frequent training updates help to keep staff members current about new tools and techniques. Tugs, gasoline trucks, baggage carts—vehicles utilized on the ramp—have to be driven very carefully.

Drivers are obliged to defer to aircraft and other vehicles, respect speed restrictions, and follow designated driving paths. Preventing mishaps and guaranteeing flawless ramp operations depend on proper vehicle performance. The safe running of equipment and vehicles depends on regular maintenance and inspections of them. Manufacturer advice and operational requirements guide the creation of maintenance schedules. Before every usage, inspections look for any wear or damage that can threaten safety.

Emergency Procedures

Ramp operations are highly risky, so fully defined emergency protocols are absolutely crucial. These protocols guarantee that ramp staff members can react fast and forcefully to several kinds of crises including medical events, fuel leaks, and fires. Regular inspections of fire extinguishers, appropriate handling and storage of combustible items, and instruction on the use of firefighting equipment include fire safety practices. Ramp staff members have to be ready to react fast to stop fires from spreading and doing major damage. Because of their combustible nature and possibility for environmental contamination, fuel leaks create a major hazard on the ramp. Fuel spills call for quick containment, notifying relevant authorities, and safe cleanup techniques among other emergency plans. Training ramp staff members in medical emergencies—including first aid and CPR—is essential. While waiting for competent medical aid, emergency medical operations guarantee that wounded workers get fast and suitable treatment. Should a severe incident—such as an aircraft accident or security threat—occur, ramp staff members have to be conversant with evacuation protocols. This covers knowing where emergency exits, assembly areas, and the all-person accounting method are located.

Coordination and Collaboration

Good ramp operations call for perfect cooperation across several departments and teams. This guarantees that every activity is timed and that any possible conflicts or delays are reduced. To organize chores and distribute information, ramp staff members must closely interact with one another. Frequent debriefings and briefings help to guarantee that every team member understands their roles and duties. Smooth operations depend on ramp operations working with other airport departments like flight operations, maintenance, and security. This entails constant communication and coordination to handle any problems that develop and guarantee that every activity complements each other. Real-time tracking systems and automated communication tools among other advanced technologies help to coordinate and increase efficiency. These systems serve to simplify procedures and give ramp staff current information.

Continuous Improvement

A basic idea of ramp operations is constant improvement. Regular review of operations and performance helps airports to find areas needing development and carry out adjustments to increase efficiency and safety. Frequent observation of ramp operations performance helps spot patterns and areas for development. Tracking key performance indicators (KPIs) including incident rates and on-time performance helps one evaluate progress. Ramp staff comments are quite helpful in pointing up problems and suggesting fixes. Regular seminars and training courses guarantee that staff members are current on new techniques and best practices. Constant process optimization is the evaluation and improvement of methods meant to remove inefficiencies and improve safety. This includes changing SOPs, using best practices from other airports, and embracing new technologies.

A key component of ramp operations, handling processes guarantee the safe and effective handling of aircraft on the ramp. Following SOPs, giving safety top priority, keeping equipment, and encouraging coordination and ongoing development can help airports guarantee seamless and efficient ramp operations.

Flight Dispatch

Role of Flight Dispatch

Flight dispatchers play a crucial role in the aviation industry, ensuring that flights are planned, coordinated, and operated efficiently and safely. To handle any problems that develop during a flight, they behind-the-scenes construct flight plans, track flights in real-time, and contact pilots and other ground staff. Flight dispatchers have duties in weather analysis, fuel computation, flight route planning, and aviation rule compliance assurance. Flight dispatchers assist to guarantee that flights run on time and that any possible dangers are reduced by controlling these important chores.

Pre-Flight Preparations

Operations in flight dispatch depend critically on pre-flight preparations. These get ready entail a thorough evaluation of all elements influencing the flight. Analyzing the weather both at the destination and along the intended path is one of the main chores. Sophisticated weather forecasting technologies help dispatchers find any possible flight-affecting dangers such as thunderstorms, turbulence, or icing conditions. This study might lead them to propose different strategies to escape unfavorable conditions.

Determining the fuel needs for the flight is another crucial component of getting ready for takeoff. Including allowances for alternative airports, possible delays, and unanticipated events, dispatchers have to make sure the airplane has enough gasoline to get to the destination. This calls for weighing elements including the weight of the aircraft, the distance to be flown, the state of the weather, and any anticipated air traffic control limitations.

Pre-flight preparations also heavily rely on flight route planning. Using flight planning software, dispatchers find the most effective path considering elements including air traffic control regulations, airspace limits, and fuel economy. The chosen path has to be consistent with all pertinent aviation rules and offer the most effective and safest way to get to the destination.

Communication and Coordination

The good running of flight dispatch depends on effective cooperation and communication. To guarantee that everyone is aware of the flight plan and any possible changes, dispatchers have to keep continual contact with pilots, air traffic controllers, and other ground staff. This correspondence guarantees flawless operation of flights and rapid resolution of any problems.

Dispatchers help to communicate using a range of methods and technologies. These cover digital messaging systems, satellite communication systems, and radio transmission. By means of real-time communication, dispatchers enable pilots with revised weather information, route adjustments, and other vital information during the flight. This guarantees pilots' most recent knowledge to guide their decisions.

Additionally vital is cooperation between flight dispatchers and other airport divisions. Working together with ground handling teams, maintenance crews, and security guards, dispatchers make sure the flight runs well in all facets. This covers making sure the aircraft is correctly loaded, maintained, and fueled as well as that all security inspections are finished before takeoff.

Monitoring and Adjustments

The dispatcher's job starts once the airplane is airborne since they real-time monitor it. This entails making sure the aircraft follows the intended path and tracking its development with flight tracking equipment. Dispatchers check air traffic, weather, and other elements that can affect the trip constantly. Should any problems—such as unanticipated weather or air traffic congestion—occur, dispatchers are in charge of modifying the flight plan to guarantee flying efficiency and safety.

Real-time monitoring tools give dispatchers vital information on the state of the aircraft including position, altitude, speed, and fuel levels. This data lets dispatchers spot any flight plan deviations and act with corrections. Should the aircraft experience unanticipated turbulence, for instance, the dispatcher can coordinate with air traffic control to find a more straight flying path.

Apart from tracking the flight, dispatchers also handle organizing any required adjustments with the flight crew. This could call for changing the altitude to maximize fuel economy, rerouting the aircraft to evade bad weather, or working with other flights to prevent air traffic congestion. To guarantee that any changes are carried out seamlessly and that the flight keeps running safely and effectively, good coordination and communication are absolutely vital.

Emergency Response

Managing events that arise during a flight depends critically on flight dispatchers. During an emergency, dispatchers are in charge of giving the flight crew the tools and knowledge they require to manage the circumstances. To guarantee a quick and efficient reaction, this can entail liaising with air traffic control, emergency services, and other pertinent authorities.

Medical emergencies, technical breakdowns, and security concerns are among the several emergency situations taught to dispatchers. In every instance, the dispatcher has to evaluate the circumstances, compile pertinent data, and let the flight crew know what direction and support they need. This could call for determining the closest appropriate airport for an emergency landing, arranging medical aid for a sick passenger, or offering technical support for an in-flight failure.

Good emergency response calls for coordinated communication with all pertinent stakeholders. To guarantee that everyone is aware of the situation and can react correctly, dispatchers have to keep continuous contact with the aircraft crew, air traffic control, and emergency services. Timeliness and accuracy in information delivery by dispatchers help to guarantee flight and passenger safety.

Training and Certification

A flight dispatcher's employment calls for a lot of training and certification to guarantee they are qualified to manage their duties. Rigid training courses spanning a broad spectrum of subjects—including meteorology, navigation, flight planning, aviation rules, and emergency procedures—must be completed by dispatchers. This instruction gives dispatchers the knowledge and abilities required to carry out their responsibilities.

Apart from first instruction, dispatchers have to keep their accreditation by means of continuous learning and training. This could entail going to refresher classes, helping in simulations and exercises, and keeping current with the most recent advancements in aviation technology and laws. Constant training guarantees dispatchers are ready to meet the changing demands of the aviation sector and uphold the best standards of safety and effectiveness.

Tools and Technologies

Effective performance of flight dispatchers depends on a range of tools and technology. These instruments give dispatchers the knowledge and resources they need to schedule, track, and real-time flight adjustments. Key instruments and technology applied in flight dispatch include:

Flight Planning Software:

By means of flight planning software, dispatchers can build comprehensive flight plans considering elements such weather conditions, airspace constraints, and fuel economy. These instruments let dispatchers maximize flight paths and guarantee aviation rule compliance.

Tools for weather forecasts:

Planning and monitoring flights depend on accurate meteorological data. Advanced weather forecasting tools are used by dispatchers to examine both at the destination and along the intended path weather conditions. These instruments give dispatchers real-time weather pattern updates, therefore guiding their judgments.

System of Flight Tracking:

Real-time flight tracking systems give dispatchers comprehensive knowledge on the position, altitude, speed, and fuel levels of the aircraft. These tools let dispatchers track the development of the flight and make necessary corrections to guarantee effectiveness and safety.

Communication Networks:

Flight dispersion requires effective communication. To keep regular contact with the flight crew, air traffic control, and other pertinent parties, dispatchers use a range of communication methods including radios, satellite communication, and digital messaging platforms.

Emergency Reaction Mechanisms:

Emergency response systems help dispatchers deliver the flight crew the information and support they need during an emergency. To guarantee a quick and efficient response, these systems comprise tools for liaising with air traffic control, emergency services, and other authorities.

Challenges and Future Directions

The job of flight dispatchers is always changing, and they have numerous difficulties guaranteeing the effective and safe running of flights. Managing the rising complexity of air traffic—more flights running in crowded areas—is one of the main difficulties. Dispatchers have to negotiate these complexities to maximize flying paths and reduce delays.

Keeping current with quickly developing technology and evolving aviation rules is still another difficulty. To properly use new tools and follow revised rules, dispatchers have to be constantly improving their knowledge and abilities. Dealing with these issues calls for constant education and training.

Looking ahead, technological developments should help flight dispatchers to become even more capable. Artificial intelligence and machine learning combined into flight planning and monitoring systems could help to increase the accuracy and efficiency of dispatch operations. To find ideal flight paths, forecast weather, and offer real-time decision support, these systems can examine enormous volumes of data.

Furthermore, the growing application of automation in air traffic control would probably affect the function of flight dispatchers. Routine chores can be automated to free dispatchers to concentrate on more difficult and strategic decisions. To guarantee dependability and safety, however, it is imperative to strike a balance between automation and human supervision.

To sum up, the effective and safe running of flights depends much on flight dispatchers. Their duties cover pre-flight preparations, real-time monitoring, correspondence, and emergency reaction. Using cutting-edge tools and technologies will help dispatchers maximize flight operations and handle any difficulties that develop. Maintaining high standards of safety and efficiency in flight deployment depends on ongoing training and adaptation to changing technology and laws.

SLPC (Scheduled Load Plan Control)

Introduction to SLPC

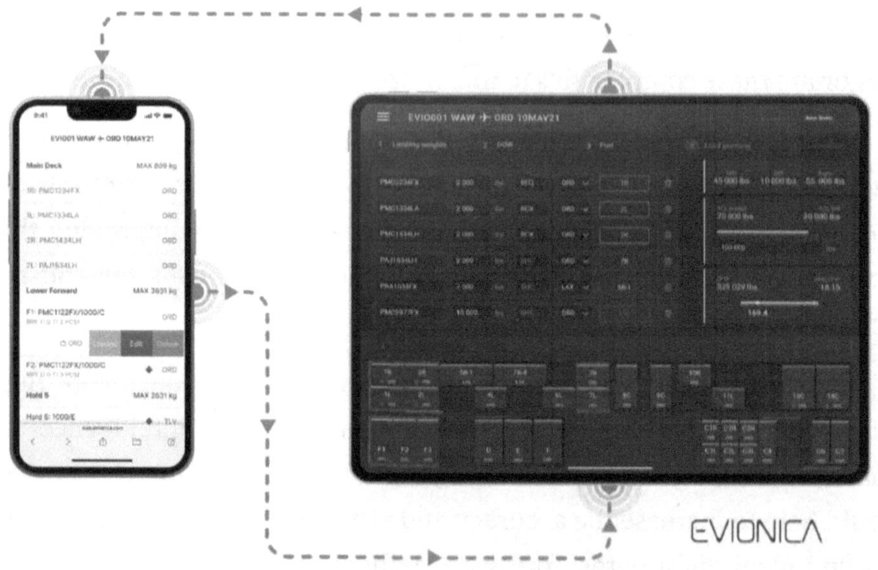

Crucially important for aviation operations, scheduled load plan control (SLPC) guarantees safe and effective loading of aircraft. To guarantee best weight distribution and balance, SLPC entails the meticulous planning and management of an aircraft's load—including passengers, cargo, and fuel. Not only does appropriate load planning ensure flight safety but also helps to maximize fuel economy and follow regulations. To develop a complete load plan that improves operational efficiency and safety, SLPC combines many elements including aircraft type, flight length, weather circumstances, and cargo details.

Importance of Load Planning

A basic feature of flight operations, load planning directly affects the performance, fuel consumption, and general safety of the aircraft. An correct load schedule guarantees that the center of gravity of the aircraft stays within reasonable limits all during the flight. Stability and control of the aircraft depend on this. In severe circumstances, improper weight distribution can endanger flight safety; in other cases, it can cause problems including higher fuel consumption and aircraft control trouble.

Furthermore, helping to save costs is effective load planning. One of the most important running expenses, fuel consumption can be lowered by airlines maximizing the load. Furthermore, correct load planning reduces the possibility of overloading, which may result in fines and higher maintenance expenses because of too much aircraft wear and tear. Hence, in both safety in aircraft operations and economic efficiency, SLPC is absolutely essential.

Creating Load Plans

Making a load plan calls for multiple phases and the application of advanced tools to guarantee accuracy and aviation rule compliance. The process starts with compiling comprehensive flight data including aircraft type, path, weather, passenger count, and cargo characteristics. Development of a load plan that satisfies all safety and efficiency criteria depends on this knowledge.

Calculating the aircraft's overall weight—including its basic operating weight, payload, and fuel—next comes Passenger, luggage, and cargo make up the payload. Determining the proper fuel load—which must be enough for the trip length, including reserves for alternate routes and unanticipated events—requires accurate weight estimates. Advanced flight planning tools guarantee accuracy and regulatory conformity by helping in these computations.

Distribution of the weight in the aircraft comes next once the overall weight has been ascertained. This entails arranging goods and baggage in particular sections to keep the aircraft's center of gravity within reasonable bounds. The thorough weight distribution advice given by the SLPC program helps to guarantee that the aircraft stays balanced and steady all through the flight. Before being sent to the ground handling and flight crew, qualified individuals—load masters and flight dispatchers—review and approve the final load plan.

Monitoring and Adjustments

Two key elements of SLPC are closely observing and modifying the load schedule. It is imperative to guarantee that the actual loading corresponds with the intended distribution during the loading process. Ground workers and load masters must thus constantly oversee the loading processes. Any differences between the expected and real load have to be fixed right away to prevent problems with performance and safety.

Sometimes last-minute changes—such as extra cargo, passenger no-shows, or changing weather—cause modifications to the load plan to be required. Real-time updates and load plan modifications made possible by the SLPC system help to guarantee that the aircraft may still run safely and effectively. To keep the proper center of gravity and weight restrictions, ground crew and load masters employ revised load plans to make required adjustments like cargo distribution or fuel load changes.

During this phase, good communication among the aircraft crew, flight dispatchers, and ground handling personnel is absolutely vital. Any modifications to the load schedule have to be immediately shared so that everyone engaged knows of them and their consequences. Even in case of unanticipated changes, this coordination helps to preserve the flight's safety and efficiency.

Compliance and Regulatory Challenges

Compliance with aviation rules is absolutely essential for SLPC. Strict rules for load planning and weight distribution are defined by regulatory authorities including the European Union Aviation Safety Agency (EASA) and the Federal Aviation Administration (FAA), therefore guaranteeing the safety of flying operations. These rules address many facets, including weight distribution restrictions, fuel needs, and maximum takeoff and landing weights.

Airlines have to make sure their load schedules follow these rules in order to stay free from fines and guarantee the integrity of their activities. Maintaining accurate records of all load plans, utilizing approved software for load planning, and performing frequent audits to confirm compliance—this entails Any deviations from legal criteria have to be taken care of right away and with corrective action meant to stop recurrence.

Following international guidelines for cargo management also counts as regulatory compliance, particularly with regard to hazardous commodities. Established by groups like the International Air Transport Association (IATA), these criteria offer direction for the secure movement of hazardous products. These criteria have to be included into SLPC systems to guarantee that every cargo is handled and loaded securely, so reducing the danger of mishaps.

Technologies in SLPC

Technological developments have greatly improved SLPC system capabilities by offering load planning and management more safety, efficiency, and accuracy. From weight calculations to weight distribution and compliance tests, modern SLPC systems automate many facets of load planning using complex algorithms and software.

Advanced flight planning software is one of SLPC's main technologies applied here. To provide comprehensive and accurate load plans, this program combines many data sources—including flight schedules, weather predictions, and aircraft specs. Real-time monitoring and modifications are also included in the program, which lets load masters and ground crew rapidly and effectively make required changes.

Tracking goods and baggage using barcode systems and RFID (Radio Frequency Identification) is another vital technology. By giving real-time data on the weight and location of every item, these systems help to guarantee correct weight computation and application. Additionally improving loading process efficiency are RFID and barcode technologies, therefore lowering the chance of mistakes and delays.

Additionally being included into SLPC systems are artificial intelligence (AI) and machine learning to enhance predictive powers and load planning optimization. By means of historical data and present situations, artificial intelligence algorithms can forecast possible problems and provide ideal load schedules. By learning from prior events, machine learning models may always raise their accuracy, improving the general efficiency and safety of SLPC.

Case Studies and Best Practices

SLPC technologies have been effectively used by several airlines to improve load planning and management procedures. To maximize its freight and passenger load planning, for instance, a big international airline applied sophisticated SLPC software. The airline cut fuel use by 5% by combining predictive analytics with real-time data, therefore saving major costs and benefiting the environment.

Another instance is a smaller airline tracking goods and baggage using RFID and barcode technology. By enabling nearly flawless weight estimates and distribution, this technology helped the airline lower danger of overloading and enhance on-time performance. Improved loading process efficiency helped the airline additionally by lowering turnaround times and raising general operational effectiveness.

Regular training and certification for loadmasters and ground crew are best practices for SLPC since they guarantee that they are competent in using the newest technology and following legal criteria. Maintaining accuracy and compliance also depends on load plan constant monitoring and audit of correctness. Modern SLPC systems and technologies should also be investments for airlines to improve their capacity and remain competitive in the market.

Future Trends in SLPC

Rising regulatory standards and continuous technological development should help to define SPLC's future. Integration of artificial intelligence and machine learning into SLPC systems is one of the main trends since it offers better predictive capacities and optimization. Analyzing enormous volumes of data, AI-powered SLPC systems can find ideal load plans, project possible problems, and instantly suggest changes.

Load planning and management is seeing more and more use of robotics and automation as well. With little human involvement, automated systems can manage several chores including tracking objects, loading and unloading goods, and changing load plans. This increases safety and lowers the danger of mistakes while nevertheless improving productivity.

With airlines trying to lessen their environmental effect, sustainability is also starting to take front stage in SLPC. Through more accurate load plans and weight distribution, advanced SLPC systems can assist maximize fuel economy and reduce pollutants. Furthermore projected to be more common are the application of sustainable materials and techniques in loading and freight handling.

To sum up, SLPC is an indispensable part of aviation activities since it guarantees the effective and safe loading of aircraft. Airlines can improve their load planning and management systems by including cutting-edge technologies, following rules, and using best practices in conjunction. Maintaining high criteria of safety, efficiency, and sustainability in SLPC operations depends on constant improvement and adaptation to new trends.

LIR / Loading & Offloading Procedure

Loading Procedures

An aircraft's loading process is a carefully thought out process meant to guarantee compliance with legal criteria, safety, and efficiency. Good loading is the deliberate arrangement of cargo, baggage, and other objects to preserve the aircraft's balance and center of gravity. This procedure starts long before the airplane reaches the airport and runs until it's ready for takeoff.

Building a thorough load plan comes first in the loading process. This proposal comprises details on the type of aircraft, cargo and baggage weight and volume, and item allocation inside the aircraft. The load plan guarantees that the airplane stays balanced and that its center of gravity stays within reasonable limits all during the flight. Maintaining the flight stability and control depends on this.

Ground handling staff load the aircraft using specialist tools once the load plan is set. Cargo loaders, conveyor belts, and container transporters—which help to safely and quickly move goods into the cargo holds of the aircraft—are among these equipment. Every cargo and luggage item is checked and weighed to make sure it corresponds with the load plan's specifics. To guarantee equal distribution of weight, items are subsequently positioned in designated areas within the cargo holds per plan.

Ground handling employees have to follow rigorous safety procedures throughout the loading process to stop mishaps and injuries. This covers donning gloves, safety shoes, and high-visibility vests—personal protection gear (PPE). Procedures for handling hazardous goods must also be followed by staff members to guarantee correct packaging and labeling as well as appropriate storage of these things in specified aircraft sections.

Offloading Procedures

Equally vital and entails the secure and quick removal of goods and baggage from the aircraft upon arrival at its destination is the unloading process. Like loading, unloading needs meticulous planning and coordination to guarantee that every item is handled properly and that the aircraft stays balanced during the operation.

Arriving, the airplane is directed to its allocated parking spot and ground handling crew starts the offloading operation. Using specialist tools like belt loaders and container carriers, this entails clearing goods and luggage from the cargo compartments of the airplane. Every item is scanned and noted to make sure it corresponds with the flight manifest and points to the suitable airport location.

Following correct weight distribution techniques is crucial during offloading to help to reduce aircraft instability. The heaviest objects should be taken out first since ground handling personnel have to carefully remove objects in a manner that preserves the balance of the aircraft. This guarantees the persons involved safety and helps the aircraft not to tip.

Handling Special Cargo

Special cargo including dangerous products, perishable goods, and large things calls for extra care and handling. Unique handling and storage needs of special cargo sometimes call for meeting in order to guarantee its safe transportation.

For example, hazardous materials have to be labeled and packed strictly following rules. Usually loaded and offloaded in specified places of the aircraft, these objects help to reduce the possibility of contamination or mishaps. To guarantee their safe management of hazardous materials, ground handling personnel need specific training in their handling.

Food and medical supplies, among perishable items, call for temperature-regulated handling and storage. Often carried in refrigerated containers, these goods need to be loaded and offloaded fast to stop deterioration. Ground handling employees have to work closely with the receiving party to guarantee that perishable items arrive in good shape and right away.

Oversized objects, such machinery or big equipment, could call for specific loading and unloading tools. These objects have to be tightly fastened inside the airplane to stop movement during flight. To guarantee the safe transportation of big goods, ground handling personnel have to follow particular guidelines for securing and handling them.

Compliance and Safety

In loading and unloading processes, following aviation rules and safety criteria is absolutely vital. To guarantee the safety of flight operations, regulatory authorities including the European Union Aviation Safety Agency (EASA) and the Federal Aviation Administration (FAA) impose rigorous rules for the handling of goods and baggage. These rules address weight restrictions, packaging needs, and handling of hazardous goods among other areas.

Ground handling firms and airlines have to make sure their processes follow these rules to prevent fines and guarantee the integrity of their operations by guaranteeing their safety. For ground handling employees, this entails frequent training and certification; the use of certified tools; and strict safety procedures.

All loading and unloading activities first concern safety. Following safety procedures helps ground handling employees avoid mishaps and injuries. This covers knowing possible hazards, using tools properly, and applying right lifting methods. Frequent safety audits and inspections guarantee accurate application of processes and quick resolution of any problems.

Finally, the loading and unloading processes are essential parts of airside operations since they guarantee the effective and safe handling of goods and baggage. Airlines and ground handling firms can guarantee the seamless running of their flights and the safety of their staff by means of thorough load plans, adherence to safety procedures, and regulatory compliance.

Offloading the Pax - Due to Emergency

Importance of Emergency Offloading Procedures

Passenger and crew safety depends critically on emergency offloading processes during unanticipated situations. These operations are meant to rapidly and effectively remove passengers from an aircraft in circumstances that compromise their safety, including fires, technical problems, security concerns, or medical issues. Minimizing risk and guaranteeing that every passenger and crew member is securely taken off the airplane as quickly as feasible is the main objective. Effective implementation of emergency offloading techniques can save lives and avoid injuries, therefore stressing the need for thorough training and preparedness for all the concerned workers.

Types of Emergencies Requiring Offloading

Different emergencies could call for the quick passenger offloading. Whether they start on board systems or outside sources, fires represent a major hazard and call for quick evacuation to stop damage or death. Technical problems include engine problems, loss of cabin pressure, or malfunction of landing gear may also call for emergency offloading to guarantee passenger safety. Threats to security—including bomb threats, attempts at hijacking, or suspicious behavior—demand quick response to protect crew members and passengers. Medical emergencies—such as major health events involving crew members or passengers—may also call for speedy offloading to offer immediate medical care.

Steps in Emergency Offloading Procedures

Several important elements are part of emergency offloading processes to guarantee the effectiveness and safety of the evacuation process. The flight crew's quick situational assessment comes first since they decide on the type and degree of the emergency. This judgment drives the flight crew to start the established protocols-based emergency unloading processes. Clearly and succinctly guiding the evacuation procedure, the captain or assigned crew member tells both passengers and staff of the necessity of evacuation.

Directed to the closest exits—which could comprise doors, emergency exits, and over-wing exits—passengers are Opening these exits and, should needed, distributing evacuation slides to the personnel. Managing the evacuation depends much on flight attendants, who also guarantee that passengers stay calm and follow instructions. To guarantee their safe evacuation, they also help travelers with specific needs such those of impairments, elderly passengers, children, and others.

Ground crew and emergency responders take control once passengers have left the airplane and lead them to safe regions distant from the aircraft. Medical staff members are ready to offer anyone who requires instantaneous help. After a last search of the aircraft to make sure nobody is left behind, the flight crew leaves themselves.

Training and Preparedness

Good emergency offloading systems call for thorough training and readiness for every staff member engaged. Regular training courses for flight crews feature simulated versions of many emergency situations. These simulations guarantee that crew members may react quickly and successfully by helping them to practice their duties and responsibilities during an emergency evacuation. To guarantee flawless coordination during a real disaster, ground personnel and emergency responders also take part in these training courses.

Training courses stress the need for concise communication, fast judgment, and good crowd control. Trained to assist passengers with special needs and use evacuation tools including slides and life vests, crew members Refresher courses and regular drills guarantee that every staff member stays competent in emergency offloading techniques.

Communication and Coordination

During an emergency offloading, good coordination and open communication are absolutely vital. Using a calm and forceful voice to preserve order and stop panic, the flight crew has to give passengers precise, succinct directions. Passengers are guided to the exits using standardized emergency commands and signs, therefore guaranteeing a flawless evacuation.

Crucially important is cooperation among the flight crew, ground crew, and emergency personnel. The flight crew tells ground staff members about the type of emergency and the need of evacuation; they then get ready to help passengers get off the plane. Alerted and ready to offer quick aid are emergency responders including medical professionals and firefighters.

Real-time information exchange among all the participants is made possible by efficient communication instruments including radios and intercom systems. This cooperation guarantees that the evacuation is carried out effectively and that once passengers get off the plane they get the required help and support.

Challenges and Solutions

Adopting emergency offloading policies calls for numerous issues that need to be resolved if their efficacy is guaranteed. Managing passenger panic and guaranteeing everyone stays calm during the evacuation is one of the biggest difficulties. Maintaining order and avoiding anarchy depend on effective communication and strong flight crew authoritative directions.

Helping passengers with unique needs—that of impairments, elderly customers, youngsters, and so on—present another difficulty. Ground workers and flight attendants have to be taught to give the required help and support so these passengers may safely depart. Additionally vital is coordination with emergency personnel since they might be required to offer further help.

Time limits provide still another major obstacle since situations may call for quick response to stop damage or death. Training courses stress the need for rapid decision-making and effective operation of operations to guarantee that the evacuation is finished within the required critical period.

Continuous Improvement

Emergency offloading processes must be constantly improved if they are to remain efficient and flexible enough to meet fresh problems.

Based on comments from drills and actual events, regular assessments and updates of procedures assist pinpoint areas needing work and carry out required modifications. Furthermore helping to drive ongoing development are advanced training courses and simulations including the newest technologies and best practices.

Airlines work with industry groups and regulatory authorities to keep current on fresh trends in emergency evacuation. Exchange of industry best practices and experiences helps improve general responsiveness and preparation. Airlines may guarantee that their emergency offloading protocols stay efficient and compliant with the highest safety criteria by encouraging a culture of ongoing development.

Ultimately, flight operations depend critically on emergency offloading processes to guarantee passenger and crew safety in unanticipated circumstances. Airlines may improve their capacity for readiness and reaction by putting well defined policies into effect, offering thorough training, and encouraging good coordination and communication. Constant improvement initiatives help to guarantee that these processes stay efficient and compliant with industry best standards, therefore preserving the life of people on board.

WCHR/WCHS/WCHC

Recognizing Special Assistance Codes

International Air Transport Association (IATA) designations WCHR, WCHS, and WCHC help to pinpoint the particular support needs of passengers with limited mobility. These rules guarantee that travelers with disabilities have a safe and enjoyable travel experience and help airlines and airport employees offer suitable assistance. Planning and coordination depend on each code matching a varying degree of help needed.

Wheelchair Ramp, or WCHR for short, marks those who can walk short distances and climb stairs but need a wheelchair for longer distances. Wheelchair Steps, or WCHS, are for those who can walk limited distances but cannot climb stairs. Wheelchair Cabin Seat, or WCHC, is the term used to describe travelers who always need a wheelchair but require help to and from their seat. Providing the proper degree of care and guaranteeing seamless operations from check-in to boarding and disembarkation depend on an awareness of these codes.

Coordination for Pre-flight

For those requiring particular support, pre-flight coordination starts at the time of booking. Passengers or their representatives let the airline know what kind of help is needed, therefore allowing the carrier to make essential plans. This data is absolutely essential to guarantee that enough personnel and tools are ready to satisfy the needs of the travelers.

Airlines prepare for the required equipment, including wheelchairs and ambulifts, working with airport authorities. They also make sure qualified staff members are on hand to help these travelers. Verifying that the aircraft can carry people with limited mobility—that is, by means of accessible seats and appropriately arranged lavatories—is part of pre-flight coordination.

The airline's system notes special help requests, and notifies all pertinent departments—including ground handling, cabin crew, and security agents. This guarantees that everyone engaged in the travel of the passenger is conscious of their needs and ready to offer the necessary help.

Check-In and Boarding

The passenger check-in process is meant to be as seamless and stress-free as feasible for those needing particular help. Often used to speed the procedure are dedicated check-in desks or priority lanes. Ground crew guarantees that guests get the required assistance by helping with check-in processes, baggage handling, and security inspections.

Reduced mobility travelers typically receive first priority when boarding so they have enough time to reach their seats without feeling hurried. From the check-in desk to the boarding gate and from there to their seats, ground crew help these guests. Specialized equipment such as ambulifts or aisle wheelchairs is used to aid passengers who cannot walk at all (WCHC) or who require assistance climbing stairs (WCHS) board.

Trained to help passengers with limited movement, flight attendants guarantee their comfort and security in their seats. This covers assisting with seat belts, stow-on carry-on bags, and emergency procedure instructions.

In-Flight Assistance

For travelers with limited mobility, in-flight support emphasizes on their comfort and safety all during the voyage. Regular check-ins by flight attendants help to access the lavatory, guarantee that passengers have what they need for a comfortable trip, and The crew is trained to assist passengers who need continuous help (WCHC) with moving inside the cabin and to handle any particular requirements that might develop.

The cabin crew also makes sure all passengers are familiar with the safety protocols and that emergency tools including aisle wheelchairs are easily accessible. Meal and beverage assistance in-flight helps to accommodate dietary restrictions, guarantee that passengers can clearly express their wants, and so meets needs.

Disembarkation and Post-Flight Assistance

Passenger reduced mobility disembarkation processes are meticulously designed to guarantee a safe and quick airplane exit. Often the last to go, these passengers let the personnel offer targeted help free from the strain of other passengers straying across the aisles.

Using ambulifts or aisle wheelchairs if necessary, ground crew meets the aircraft to help with disembarkation. Whether it's a connecting flight, baggage claim, or ground transportation, they assist travelers retrieve their carry-on bags and guide them across the airport to their next point of contact.

Ground crew works to guarantee flawless transitions between flights for passengers with connecting flights. This covers giving current boarding cards, helping with security checks, and making sure travelers are cozily settled at the next boarding gate.

Continuous Improvement and Feedback

Airports and airlines work constantly to provide travelers with limited mobility better services. Finding areas of development and making sure the help given satisfies their needs depend on passenger comments. Ground crew and flight attendants must receive regular training if they are to remain current on best practices and new tools meant to help passengers.

To improve the travel experience for consumers with special needs, airlines also make investments in improved technology and equipment. To guarantee clear and efficient interactions with consumers, this covers more pleasant and accessible seating choices, better boarding and disembarkation aids, and advanced communication tools.

Challenges and Solutions

Helping travelers with limited mobility comes with various difficulties, including guaranteeing timely and effective service, coordinating across several airport departments, and managing unanticipated events as delays or equipment failures. Airlines and airports invest in new technologies, run strong training programs, and help workers to develop a culture of empathy and responsiveness in order to meet these difficulties.

Overcoming these obstacles mostly requires good collaboration and communication. Any problems that develop can be quickly resolved by keeping open lines of contact between passengers, airline staff, and airport authorities thereby guaranteeing a seamless and stress-free travel experience for all.

To give travelers with limited mobility customized help, WCHR, WCHS, and WCHC codes are therefore absolutely essential. Airlines and airports can guarantee that every customer gets the support they need for a safe and comfortable travel by means of deliberate pre-flight planning, focused check-in and boarding procedures, attentive in-flight assistance, and effective disembarkation techniques. Efforts at constant improvement and efficient handling of problems improve the travel experience even more for passengers needing particular help.

Chapter-4

Arrival Management

Recognizing Special Assistance Codes

Introduction to IATA Codes

For those with limited mobility especially, air travel can be a difficult and demanding experience. The International Air Transport Association (IATA) has created a uniform system of special assistance codes to guarantee these travelers get the required support and services. Among these, WCHR, WCHS, and WCHC are crucial in determining the particular needs of consumers needing varying degrees of help. These rules guarantee that travelers with disabilities have a safe and comfortable travel experience in addition to helping to guarantee efficient planning and coordination.

For several purposes, the IATA codes are quite essential. They enable staff members of airports and airlines to rapidly determine the kind of help a passenger needs, therefore guaranteeing the allocation of the suitable tools and personnel. For those with specific requirements, our method guarantees a flawless travel experience by helping to eliminate uncertainty and delays. Staff members of airlines and airports can greatly raise the level of service given to passengers with limited mobility by knowing and applying these rules effectively.

Details of Each Code

Providing the appropriate degree of attention and assistance depends on an awareness of the details of every IATA code. Every code relates to a particular degree of help needed; so, planning and implementing a flawless travel experience depends on understanding these differences.

WCHR: Wheelchair Ramp

For those who can walk short distances and climb stairs but need a wheelchair for longer distances within the airport, WCHR—Wheelchair Ramp—is used. Usually, these people can control the airplane without any extra help. These passengers mostly need these things while they are traveling through the airport, as the distances between check-in desks, security checkpoints, boarding gates, and baggage claim areas can be somewhat large.

Airport personnel must make sure wheelchairs are available at key locations all throughout the airport for WCHR authorized guests. This guarantees that these people can move between several regions comfortably and effectively. Staff members have to be taught to be helpful without compromising the passenger's sense of independence; they should assist when needed and back off when the passenger can handle on their own.

WCHS: Wheelchair Steps

Wheelchair Steps, or WCHS, are patrons who can walk limited distances but cannot climb stairs. These travelers need help getting on and off the plane as well as a wheelchair to get about the airport. Should the airport lack jet bridges or ramps, they could also require assistance for climbing and descending airplane stairs.

Staff members at airports and airlines must work together to give WCHS passengers flawless assistance. This covers the availability of stair lifts or ambulifts to help with boarding and disembarking. Staff members should also be ready to assist these travelers with their carry-on bags and guarantee their comfortable and safe seating.

WCHC: Wheelchair Cabin Seat

Passengers who always need a wheelchair and require help to and from their seat are designated WCHC, or Wheelchair Cabin Seat. These travelers require thorough assistance all during their trip, including at boarding, disembarking, and in-flight; they cannot move on their own.

Airlines have to make sure aisle wheelchairs are accessible for WCHC passengers to move about the cabin. Training in helping these passengers with boarding and seat-belts and stowing carry-on bags is very important for flight attendants. These passengers could need help getting to the restroom and with other needs in-flight. Thus, to guarantee their comfort and safety, one must be highly attentive and caring.

The Role of Special Assistance Codes in Planning and Coordination

Effective assistance of travelers with limited mobility depends on good collaboration and planning. This process depends critically on the usage of special assistance codes such as WCHR, WCHS, and WCHC, which let airports and airlines be ready and guarantee that the required tools and staff are in place.

Booking and Pre-Flight Arrangements

Special support starts the process right when one books. Passengers or their representatives have to let the airline know their particular needs so that the booking system may record the relevant IATA code. This early warning is absolutely vital since it sets off a set of pre-flight procedures meant to satisfy the passenger's needs.

Airlines have to work with airport officials to plan for required tools including wheelchairs and ambulifts. They must also make sure that qualified employees are on hand to help these travelers all during their trip. This covers looking at the aircraft's accessibility elements, including the availability of suitable lavatories and accessible seats.

The system of the airline logs requests for special help and alerts all pertinent departments, including security, cabin crew, and ground handling. This all-encompassing alert system guarantees that every person engaged in the passenger's trip knows their needs and is ready to provide the necessary assistance.

Check-In and Security

Passenger requests for special help have their check-in process tailored to be as smooth and stress-free as feasible. Often set to speed the procedure are dedicated check-in desks or priority lanes. Assisting with check-in processes, baggage handling, and passenger seamless clearance of security checks falls to ground crew.

Wheelchairs have to be easily available at the check-in desk for WCHR travelers. Training staff members to help these guests through the check-in and security process will help to avoid needless delays or pain. Extra help including specialist tools and qualified staff is needed for WCHS and WCHC passengers to enable their passage across security and to the boarding gate.

Boarding and In-Flight Assistance

One important phase where the degree of help needed depends much on the IATA code is boarding. Reduced mobility passengers usually get first boarding so they have enough time to reach their seats without feeling hurried. From the check-in desk to the boarding gate and then to their airplane seats, ground staff help WCHR passengers. While aisle wheelchairs are given to WCHC passengers to enable them reach their seats, ambulifts or stair lifts are employed to assist WCHS guests with boarding.

The duties change in-flight to fall to the cabin staff, who have to make sure travelers with limited movement are safe and comfortable. This covers helping with seat belts, stowing carry-on bags, and offering information about emergency protocols. Flight attendants have to be ready to offer WCHC passengers continuous support including assistance with restroom access and other needs all during the flight.

Ensuring a Positive Travel Experience

Giving travelers with limited mobility a good travel experience transcends their physical demands. It also entails making sure they have support, respect, and value all along their path. From every staff member engaged, this calls for a mix of empathy, training, and clear communication.

Training and Empathy

Ensuring staff members are ready to help travelers with limited mobility depends on their receiving training. Technical instruction on how to use wheelchairs and ambulifts as well as sensitivity training to grasp the difficulties these clients experience and how to assist them with dignity and respect are part of this also.

In this regard, empathy is quite important. Staff members ought to be able to understand the tension and anxiety travel might bring for the passenger. Staff members can greatly improve the travel experience of a passenger by displaying compassion and offering attentive, customized service.

Effective Communication

Ensuring that passengers with limited mobility get the support they require depends mostly on clear and effective communication. From check-in to boarding and disembarkation, this covers giving clear directions and information at every phase of the journey. Employees should also be attentive listeners ready to answer any inquiries or worries the passengers could have.

Clear language, avoidance of jargon, and patience help to guarantee efficient communication. Particularly for guests with hearing or cognitive problems, visual aids and written directions might also be helpful.

Continuous Improvement and Feedback

Maintaining great standards of service for travelers with limited mobility depends on ongoing development. Airlines and airports have to routinely go over their policies, get comments from customers, and make required changes to raise the caliber of the given service.

Gathering and Analyzing Feedback

Passenger comments are a great source of information for pointing up areas needing work. Airlines and airports should inspire travelers to share their stories and offer ideas for improvement of the services. Surveys, comment cards, and direct staff interactions help one compile this input.

By means of analysis of this input, common problems and trends can be found, enabling airports and airlines to solve these methodically. For instance, if several passengers say they find trouble with a certain element of the boarding procedure, this suggests focused enhancements are needed.

Implementing Improvements

The comments received should guide airlines and airports in implementing enhancements to their policies and offerings. To better satisfy the demands of passengers with limited mobility, this can entail changing policies, updating training programs, or purchasing new equipment.

Additionally crucial to guarantee staff members remain educated about best practices and new technology are regular training updates and refreshers courses. Airlines and airports may guarantee that they regularly deliver all customers high-quality service by encouraging a culture of ongoing development.

Ultimately, supplying passengers with limited mobility with efficient support depends on knowing and appreciating particular assistance codes such as WCHR, WCHS, and WCHC. These guidelines guarantee that suitable tools and staff are in place to satisfy the demands of the passengers, therefore facilitating planning and coordination. Airlines and airports can guarantee a safe, comfortable, and happy travel experience for every passenger with disabilities by means of thorough training, empathy, good communication, and a dedication to ongoing improvement.

Coordination for Pre-Flight

Importance of Pre-Flight Coordination

Giving passengers with limited mobility efficient help depends mostly on pre-flight cooperation. Beginning well before the passenger reaches the airport, this procedure entails careful planning and communication to guarantee that all required preparations are in place. From the time a passenger books their ticket until they reach their final destination, the aim is to provide a flawless travel experience for those with special needs, therefore guaranteeing their safety, comfort, and convenience. Good pre-flight coordination calls for several stakeholders—the airline, airport authorities, ground handling personnel, flight crew—all of which cooperate to satisfy passenger needs with limited mobility.

Booking and Initial Notification

Pre-flight coordination begins the moment a ticket is booked. Passengers or their representatives have to let the airline know about their particular needs for help, therefore enabling the carrier to make required plans. This first alert is absolutely important since it guarantees that the passenger's needs are recorded and forwarded to the pertinent departments and prepares the ground for all later activities.

Usually prompted to submit thorough information about their condition and the kind of support they need, passengers with limited mobility are purchasing flights. This covers defining the IATA code (WCHR, WCHS, or WCHC) that fits their requirements as well as any other pertinent information, including if they will be using a personal wheelchair or need help with particular medical equipment.

Once this data is entered into the airline's reservation system, it is This system is intended to highlight special assistance requests and create alerts to all pertinent departments, therefore guaranteeing that everyone engaged in the passenger's journey is aware of their needs and ready to offer the required support.

Coordination with Airport Authorities

Following the first booking and alert, the airline works with airport authorities to schedule the required tools and staff. This entails making sure that various specialized equipment including ambulifts, wheelchairs, and other tools are accessible and in excellent operating order. It also ensures that there are enough qualified employees to help travelers with limited mobility at several places around the airport, including security checks, check-in desks, and boarding gates.

Ensuring that the physical infrastructure of the airport is accessible to travelers with limited mobility mostly depends on the authorities of airports. This includes making sure paths are clear and free of hazards as well as furnishing easily available check-in counters, restrooms, and waiting areas. Any possible accessibility problems and guarantee that all required accommodations are in place depend on cooperation between the airline and airport authorities.

Verification of Aircraft Accessibility

Verifying that the airplane can carry passengers with limited mobility is another crucial component of pre-flight coordination. This entails making sure the airplane offers any other required accommodations, reasonably sized bathrooms, and accessible seating choices. The airline has to make sure that the assigned seats for passengers with limited mobility are accessible and satisfy all comfort and safety standards.

Sometimes the airline might have to make extra plans to guarantee the passenger could travel comfortably. To meet the needs of the passenger, this can entail changing seating arrangements, making sure aisle wheelchairs are accessible, or otherwise making additional changes. These configurations have to be precisely coordinated to guarantee that they do not compromise the general flight operation or safety.

Notification to pertinent departments

Good pre-flight coordination calls for thorough notification to all pertinent departments in the airline and airport. Ground handling staff, cabin crew, security guards, and any other staff member engaged in the passenger's journey counts here. Every department has to know the particular needs of the traveler and is ready to offer the necessary help.

For check-in, luggage handling, and security checks, ground handling employees, for instance, must be ready to help. The cabin staff has to be ready to help the customer to and from their seat, guaranteeing their comfort and safety during the trip. In-flight support is another thing they provide. Any particular plans needed for passenger and equipment screening should be known to security staff.

This communication is much facilitated by the reservation system of the airline. Entering a special assistance request into the system creates notifications directed to all pertinent departments. These alerts provide comprehensive information on the passenger's needs as well as any particular instructions or plans developed. This guarantees that every person engaged in the trip of the passenger is totally educated and ready to offer the required assistance.

Equipment Preparation

A major component of pre-flight coordination is making sure the right tools are accessible and in good operating condition. This covers wheelchairs, ambulifts, aisle chairs, and any other specific tool needed to help guests with limited mobility. To guarantee that all required tools are ready and easily available, airlines have to cooperate closely with ground handling businesses and airport officials.

Good working condition of the equipment depends on regular maintenance and inspections. Any problems or breakdowns have to be fixed quickly to prevent delays or inconveniences on the day of travel. Backup tools should also be ready for unanticipated issues or extra help requirements.

Staff Training and Allocation

Giving passengers with limited mobility efficient help depends on proper staff distribution and training. This entails making sure every employee who will be dealing with these customers have sufficient knowledge in the pertinent best practices and procedures. Among the several subjects this training should address are emergency protocols, communication styles, and proper equipment use.

Empathy and understanding are also very important when dealing with customers with special needs, hence staff training should also stress this. This covers being courgent, patient, and sensitive to the demands and worries of the traveler. Airlines can make sure passengers with limited mobility feel appreciated and assisted all through their travel by encouraging a culture of empathy and responsiveness.

Additionally crucial is staffing enough to help travelers with limited mobility. This covers making sure that, at important spots around the airport—check-in desks, security checkpoints, boarding gates—there are sufficient personnel on hand. Working with the cabin crew also helps to guarantee their readiness to offer in-flight help.

Contingency Planning

Pre-flight coordination depends much on contingency planning, which guarantees that airlines are ready to manage any unanticipated problems or obstacles. This covers contingency preparations for personnel and coordination as well as backup tools.

For instance, there should be a backup ready should a wheelchair or ambulift break down to prevent delays or disturbances. Likewise, should a staff member be absent for illness or another cause, there should be a strategy in place to guarantee that another qualified staff member may cover for the required support.

Contingency planning also entails working with other pertinent stakeholders and airport authorities to handle any possible accessibility problems or other difficulties that would develop. Airlines may guarantee that they are ready to manage any unanticipated events and give passengers with limited mobility flawless support by including a well-considered backup plan.

Continuous Improvement and Feedback

Maintaining the effectiveness and responsiveness to the needs of passengers with limited mobility depends on constant improvement and feedback. Pre-flight coordination systems must thus stay strong. Airlines should routinely assess their policies by means of passenger and worker comments, therefore pointing up areas needing development.

Direct passenger and staff encounters as well as surveys and comment cards help one compile this input. Analyzing these comments helps airlines to spot trends and common problems, which will help them to make focused changes to their operations and offerings.

Additionally crucial to guarantee staff members remain informed about best practices and new technology are regular training updates and refreshers courses. Airlines may guarantee that they regularly offer passengers with limited mobility premium service by encouraging a culture of ongoing development.

Check-In and Boarding

Streamlined Check-In Process

Passenger reduced mobility (PRMs) have a check-in process intended to be as simple and stress-free as feasible. Airlines and airports set special check-in desks or priority lanes to guarantee these travelers get the required help fast and effectively. These designated lanes serve to speed up the check-in process, therefore lowering wait times and perhaps stressing PRMs less.

Arriving at the airport, PRMs are led to these specific check-in areas where qualified personnel are ready to help with security checks, baggage handling, and check-in processes. From generating boarding tickets to tagging and baggage transportation, ground crew members at these counters are well equipped to meet a spectrum of needs. They give the boarding procedure and any other services the passenger could need succinct and unambiguous information.

The airline's reservation system already notes the needs of guests who have pre- ordered particular assistance. This lets check-in employees get ready ahead of time so that any required tools, including wheelchairs or ambulifts, are ready and accessible. This pre-planning guarantees that the passenger's trip throughout the airport is as seamless as feasible and helps to minimize any possible delays.

By confirming their travel documentation, checking in their bags, and walking PRMs through the security process, the check-in personnel helps them. A wheelchair is supplied at the check-in area to get WCHR passengers—who can walk short distances and climb stairs—through the airport—that they require for longer distances. Security personnel make sure suitable actions are made to assist WCHS passengers—who can walk limited distances but cannot climb stairs—in their screening, which can include using accessible screening lanes or assigning extra personnel to help with the procedure. Staff assist WCHC passengers— who always need a wheelchair—with the transfer from their personal wheelchair to an airport-provided wheelchair should be needed, and guarantee that all mobility aids and medical devices are vetted correctly.

During security searches, good communication is absolutely vital. Clear, patient explanations of every procedure step by security staff will help to guarantee that PRMs know what is happening and what they need to do. This helps to lower anxiety and guarantees courteous and effective completion of the screening procedure.

Priority Boarding Process

One important phase where the degree of help needed depends much on the IATA code allocated to PRMs. is boarding. For these people, the boarding process depends critically on priority boarding. By allowing PRMs to board the plane ahead of other passengers, this practice gives them more time and space to relax into their seats without feeling hurried.

Usually initially called to the gate, PRMs are the ones starting the boarding procedure. From the check-in desk to the boarding gate and then to their seats on the airplane, ground staff helps these guests. For WCHR travelers, this may mean wheelchairs guiding them across the airport. Particularly if the aircraft is parked at a remote stand and boarding via stairs is necessary, specific equipment including ambulifts or stair lifts is employed to help WCHS passengers board.

Aisles wheelchairs are supplied to WCHC passengers, who require support to and from their seat, therefore enabling them to negotiate the small aircraft aisles. Working together, ground personnel and cabin crew makes sure these guests are comfortably and safely moved to their seats. This covers assisting with seat belts, stowing carry-on bags, and offering any other needed assistance.

Once PRMs are onboard, the comfort and safety of them depend much on the cabin crew. They are taught to provide individualized help catered to these passengers' particular needs. Aiding PRMs to settle into their seats starts this process; this could include moving them from an aisle wheelchair to their seat, aiding with seat belts, and stowing carry-on bags. Flight attendants check that WCHC customers are comfortably seated and that all required goods are within reach.

voyage attendants often check to see whether PRMs require any more help over the voyage. Helping with restroom access, seat adjustments, item retrieval from carry-on bags, or meal and drink provision could all be part of this. To guarantee that the passenger feels supported and cared for, flight attendants should be sensitive to their needs and ready to help with any requests.

Smooth support of PRMs depends on efficient cooperation between ground workers and cabin crew. The pre-flight briefing marks the start of this cooperation since it tells the cabin staff about any guests needing particular help and their particular requirements. After that, the cabin is ready using this knowledge and guarantees that all required tools are in place.

Ground staff closely interacts with the cabin crew during boarding to enable the seamless movement of PRMs from the gate to their seats. This entails offering physical help if necessary and employing specialized tools including ambulifts and aisle wheelchairs. Ground staff and cabin crew keep in constant communication throughout the flight to handle any problems and guarantee that the needs of the passenger are satisfied.

Ultimately, the check-in and boarding procedures for those with limited mobility call for careful planning, cooperation, and understanding. Airlines and airports may guarantee that these customers get the help they require for safe and comfortable travel by setting aside specific check-in counters, priority boarding, and thorough in-flight support. Efforts at constant improvement and good handling of unforeseen events increase the travel experience for PRMs even more, therefore promoting a more inclusive and easily available air transport sector.

In-Flight Assistance

Ensuring Comfort and Safety Onboard

Once passengers with limited mobility (PRMs) board, the emphasis moves to making sure they remain comfortable and safe all during the journey. A good and stress-free travel experience is created in great part by flight attendants' provision of the required aid and support to these passengers. This covers making sure all safety procedures are followed, offering individualized help as needed, and preserving clear, efficient communication.

Personalized Assistance

Training teaches flight attendants to provide individualized support catered to the particular needs of PRMs. Helping passengers settle into their seats starts this process; this could include moving them from an aisle wheelchair to their seat, helping with seat belts, and stowing carry-on baggage. Flight attendants make sure that all required goods are within reach and that WCHC passengers—who need ongoing help—are comfortably seated.

Voyage attendants often check to see whether PRMs require any more help over the voyage. Helping with restroom access, seat adjustments, item retrieval from carry-on bags, or meal and drink provision could all be part of this. Flight attendants should be sensitive to the needs of the passenger and ready to help with any requests so that the passenger feels supported and cared for.

Accessing In-Flight Services

Meal, beverage, entertainment, lavatory facilities—all of which PRMs should have access to in-flight—as other passengers do. Maintaining the comfort and happiness of PRMs throughout the flight depends on these services being simply available and accessible.

Meals and Beverages

Flight attendants assist PRMs with meal and beverage service, taking into account any dietary restrictions or special requirements. Helping customers open packaging, cutting food, and arranging products in simple reach could all be part of this. Flight attendants discreetly and respectfully assist guests who require help with feeding so they may comfortably enjoy their meal.

In-Flight Entertainment

Access to in-flight entertainment systems is an important aspect of the travel experience. Flight attendants assist PRMs with running personal entertainment devices, changing screen orientations, and choosing material. Flight attendants should be conversant with the accessibility tools of the entertainment system, including audio descriptions and closed captions, and help passengers in using them for those with visual or hearing problems.

Lavatory Access

Ensuring that PRMs can access lavatory facilities safely and comfortably is a key responsibility of the cabin crew. Flight attendants use aisle wheelchairs to assist WCHC passengers—who need help with mobility—in getting around the cabin and to reach the restroom. Training flight attendants to offer this unobtrusive and polite help guarantees the passenger's dignity and privacy is preserved.

Emergency Policies and Safety Measures

Safety is the first concern for every passenger, particularly those of PRMs. Flight attendants have to make sure PRMs are conversant with the equipment and safety policies of the aircraft. This covers the placement and functioning of emergency exits, the usage of oxygen masks and life vests, and the processes to follow in case of an emergency. Personalized safety briefings covering this also encompass

Personalized Safety Briefings

For PRMs, a standard safety demonstration may not be sufficient. Customized briefings considering the particular requirements and capabilities of the passenger should be given by flight attendants. One-on-one safety equipment demonstrations, emergency exit usage explained, and passenger understanding of what to do in certain emergency situations could all be part of this.

Emergency Equipment

Flight attendants should ensure that any specialized equipment needed by PRMs, such as aisle wheelchairs and medical devices, is readily accessible and in good working condition. Flight attendants are taught to help PRMs safely evacuate the aircraft in an emergency. This covers guiding them to the closest exit, deploying evacuation slides if needed, and, if at all possible, making sure their mobility aids are packed.

Communication and Support

Giving in-flight help to PRMs depends on good communication. Attractive listeners, flight attendants should make sure they grasp the demands and worries of the passenger. Effective communication guarantees that PRMs feel free to ask for help when necessary and helps to build confidence.

Flight attendants should get good at active listening—that is, giving the customer their whole attention, noting their needs, and answering suitably. This guarantees correct and timely meeting of the passenger's needs.

Instead of waiting for PRMs to beg for assistance, flight attendants should aggressively offer it to them. The travel experience of the traveler can be much improved by regular check-ins, courteous conversations, and a readiness to help with any needs. By means of proactive support, the cabin crew and the guest develop a good rapport, therefore promoting inclusion and care.

Challenges and Solutions

Giving PRMs in-flight help can be difficult in several ways: resolving medical emergencies, managing unanticipated demands, and making sure every passenger gets the attention they need. Airlines have to make investments in thorough training for flight attendants, create an empathetic and responsive culture, and apply efficient policies for handling in-flight support if they are to meet these demands.

Medical Emergencies: Flight attendants must be prepared to handle medical emergencies that may arise during the flight. This covers learning how to use medical equipment on board, first aid and CPR training, and ground-level medical professional coordination. Clear protocols for handling medical situations guarantees flight attendants' quick and efficient response ability.

Unexpected Needs: During the journey, PRMs can find themselves uncomfortable or require extra medical supplies. Flight attendants should be adaptable and imaginative, devising original ideas to meet these needs. This could entail working with the ground crew of the airline to schedule extra supplies or changing the seating configurations for the customer.

Balancing Attention: Flight attendants must balance their attention between PRMs and other passengers, ensuring that everyone receives the assistance they need. This calls for good time management, open communication, and a team-based support system. Working together, flight attendants can make sure every customer enjoys and finds comfort in their voyage.

Continuous Improvement and Feedback

Maintaining good standards of in-flight assistance for PRMs depends on ongoing development. Airlines should routinely go over their policies, get comments from flight attendants and customers, and apply required adjustments to improve the caliber of the given services.

Getting comments from PRMs is quite helpful in pointing up areas needing development. Airlines should inspire travelers to share their stories and offer ideas for improvement of the services. Surveys, comment cards, and direct conversations with flight attendants help one compile this input.

Using the comments collected, airlines should make focused changes to their in-flight assistance protocols. To better serve PRMs, this could entail changing policies, funding new equipment, or updating training courses. Frequent training updates and refresher courses guarantee flight attendants' continuing awareness of best practices and new advancements.

To guarantee passengers' pleasure and safety during the journey, efficient in-flight help for those with limited mobility is therefore absolutely vital. Flight attendants may make a good and encouraging environment for PRMs by providing individualized help, keeping clear communication, and being ready for crises. Efforts at constant improvement and a proactive approach to solve problems help to increase the quality of in-flight assistance, therefore promoting a more inclusive and easily available air travel experience for every passenger.

Disembarkation and Post-Flight Assistance

In the travel experience of passengers with limited mobility (PRMs), disembarkation is a crucial element. Appropriately timed disembarkation guarantees that these passengers comfortably and safely leave the airplane. Ground crew and cabin crew must carefully organize and execute this process to prevent delays and guarantee a flawless transfer from the airplane to the airport buildings. Good disembarkation practices enable PRMs to have a happy end to their voyage, therefore preserving their dignity and respect.

Disembarkation processes for PRMs are meant to minimize any possible discomfort or difficulty while also offering the required assistance. Usually the last to leave, PRMs let the cabin crew provide concentrated help free from the strain of other passengers straying across the aisles. Usually ready at the gate to receive the aircraft and help with disembarkation, ground workers are For WCHR passengers—who can walk short distances—assistance could include wheelchair provision at the aircraft door and airport navigation help. Particularly if the aircraft is parked at a remote stand, WCHS passengers employ specialist equipment as ambulifts or stair lifts to assist them in getting off the aircraft.

A wheelchair is utilized to assist WCHC passengers—who always need one—in navigating the airplane aisles toward the exit. To make sure these people are safe and comfortable throughout the move from their seat to the aisle wheelchair, cabin crew help. Additionally helping PRMs with their personal items and carry-on baggage is the cabin crew. This guarantees that the disembarkation process is more seamless and efficient since the traveler does not have to fight with getting goods from under-seat storage or overhead bins.

The duty for their care passes from the cabin crew to the ground workers once PRMs leave the aircraft. This handover has to be flawless and well-coordinated to guarantee that the given help is without any gaps. Ground crew guides and supports PRMs as they negotiate the airport from the airplane door. Whether it's a connecting flight, baggage claim, or ground transportation, this covers helping them find their next point of contact, leading them through customs and immigration, and assisting with recovering checked bags.

Many times, airports provide specific spaces designated for special assistance where PRMs may relax and get further help as needed. To give PRMs a pleasant and encouraging surroundings as they wait for their next actions, these facilities have information desks, toilets, and chairs.

More coordination is needed for PRMs with connected flights to guarantee a flawless change between planes. Ground crew members are very important in enabling this process since they support and guide PRMs so they may reach their connecting gates on schedule. Ground crew members help PRMs get revised boarding permits for their connecting flights, therefore guaranteeing that all required information is presented clearly. This includes verifying gate numbers, boarding schedules, and any unique plans perhaps created.

Should further security inspections be needed for connecting flights, ground crew members aid PRMs in navigating these procedures seamlessly. This includes making sure any mobility devices or medical equipment are checked suitably and returned to the passenger right away. Ground staff arrange shuttle buses or motorized carts for occasions when PRMs must move between terminals. This guarantees that PRMs can minimize any stress or pain by moving comfortably and fast between several areas of the airport.

Delays and unanticipated events can arise during disembarkation and post-flight assistance notwithstanding meticulous planning. Effective and quick resolution of these problems depends on contingency plans being in place. Managing delays and surprising events depends on good communication. Ground crew and cabin crew have to keep PRMs updated about any delays or modifications by means of consistent updates and unambiguous directions on future action. This helps to lower anxiety and guarantee that PRMs have knowledgeable support.

Where delays are notable, further help would be needed. This could call for food and drink, planning rest spots, or, if necessary, working with the medical team. Ground crew should be ready to provide these services and make sure PRMs are comfortable and well-cared for throughout waiting. Coordination with airport medical services is crucial for PRMs with medical requirements. Ground crew members should be taught to realize when medical help is needed and how to rapidly access the relevant resources. This guarantees that any medical problems are taken care of quickly and satisfactorily, therefore preserving the passenger's safety and welfare.

Maintaining high criteria of disembarkation and post-flight assistance for PRMs depends on constant improvement. Airlines and airports should routinely go over their policies, get comments from employees and customers, and apply required improvements to improve the caliber of the given services. Finding areas of development depends much on the comments of PR managers. Airlines and airports should inspire travelers to share their stories and offer ideas for improvement of the services. Surveys, remark cards, and direct interactions with ground workers and cabin crew help one compile this input.

Airlines and airports should apply focused improvements to their disembarkation and post-flight assistance systems based on received comments. To better serve PRMs, this could entail changing policies, funding new equipment, or updating training courses. Frequent training updates and refresher sessions guarantee staff members remain informed about best practices and new advancements.

To sum up, for PRMs the travel experience consists mostly in disembarkation and post-flight assistance. Airlines and airports may guarantee that PRMs get the help they require for safe and comfortable travel by means of coordinated support, guaranteed seamless transitions, and unexpected situation readiness. Efforts at constant improvement and efficient handling of obstacles help PRMs to have even better travel experiences, therefore promoting a more inclusive and accessible air transport sector.

Chapter-5

Air Transport Safety & Security

Annex 17 and Aviation Security Orders/Circulars

Overview of Annex 17

A pillar of aviation security is the International Civil Aviation Organization's (ICAO) Annex 17. Formally titled "Security: Safeguarding International Civil Aviation Against Acts of Unlawful Interference," it lays out the guidelines and suggested actions (SARPs) required to preserve international aviation from illegal interference. Annex 17's main objective is to establish a basis of security policies to be followed by every ICAO member state, therefore guaranteeing a consistent aviation security approach all around.

Originally approved in March 1974, Annex 17 has been changed many times to include fresh technologies and approaches to handle changing security concerns. The paper describes how several stakeholders—including state authorities, airport operators, and airlines—have established and kept strong security measures. To guarantee a flawless and efficient security system, it underlines the need for cooperation and coordination across several agencies.

Key Provisions of Annex 17

Annex 17's obligation for member states to create a national civil aviation security program is among its most important clauses. This program has to specify the duties and obligations of every engaged entity as well as the policies for stopping and handling actions of illegal intervention.

Furthermore required in Annex 17 are frequent security audits and inspections meant to guarantee adherence to the set security policies.

Annex 17 further emphasizes the requirement of thorough training courses for every employee engaged in aviation security. These courses have to address several facets of security, including threat detection, emergency reaction, and equipment use. Moreover, the Annex calls on states to create backup strategies for handling security events, therefore guaranteeing that there are unambiguous guidelines for handling crises.

Aviation Security Orders

Directives issued by national regulating agencies to carry out and execute Annex 17's regulations are aviation security instructions. These directives offer thorough instructions on the particular security policies that airlines, airports, and other players of influence have to follow. Regular updates reflect changes in the threat environment and they are customized to meet the particular security issues of every state.

Topics covered by aviation security rules span widely from cargo security to passenger and baggage screening to access control. They also spell out how security events—such as bomb threats or hijackings—are handled. These directives guarantee that all entities engaged in aviation security know their obligations and have the required tools and skills to carry them out by offering clear, practical rules.

Security Circulars

Another crucial means of spreading knowledge and direction on aviation security is security circles. Security circulars are advisory notes offering best practices and ideas for improving security procedures, unlike legally mandated aviation security regulations. Both national and international regulatory authorities issue them, and they are a great tool for keeping current on the most recent advancements in aviation security.

Often covering developing hazards, security circles offer direction on how to reduce them. A circular might, for instance, offer ideas on how to counteract the threat unmanned aerial vehicles (UAVs) present or on improving cybersecurity defenses against cyber-attacks. Maintaining the general security of the aviation industry depends much on security circulars informing stakeholders about emerging hazards and offering workable solutions for their addressing.

Implementation and Compliance

Effective implementation of Annex 17 and the related aviation security regulations and circulars calls for coordinated effort among all relevant stakeholders. State authorities have to guarantee that the required legal and regulatory systems are in place and that enough supervision exists to track compliance. Airlines and airport operators have to follow the recommended security protocols and make sure their employees are suitably qualified to perform their responsibilities.

Regular audits and inspections carried out by both national and international regulatory authorities track adherence to the security policies described in Annex 17. These audits point up areas for development and evaluate the success of the security initiatives. States that disobey the recommended security policies could suffer fines or other consequences, thereby underlining the need of keeping a strong and efficient security system.

Challenges and Future Directions

Although Annex 17 offers a whole framework for aviation security, its use is not without difficulties. The difficulty lies mostly in juggling security with the ease of air travel. Effective security measures should be able to stop acts of illegal interference, but they shouldn't unnecessarily stop passenger or freight flow either. Reaching this harmony calls for constant innovation as well as the acceptance of fresh technology and approaches.

The changing character of security issues presents still another difficulty. Annex 17's clauses and the related security directives and circulars have to be routinely revised to handle newly arising hazards. This calls for constant study and cooperation among security specialists, industry players, and regulatory authorities.

Looking ahead, the application of cutting-edge technology such as artificial intelligence and biometrics to improve aviation security is increasingly underlined. More efficient and effective these technologies are since they might enhance threat detection and simplify security procedures. Adoption of them, however, also brings fresh difficulties including the necessity to guarantee the compatibility of several systems and solve privacy issues.

Roles of Various Agencies

Governmental Agencies

Establishing and preserving aviation security depends critically on governmental institutions. Formulating and implementing aviation security rules falls to national agencies like the Transportation Security Administration (TSA) in the United States or the Directorate General of Civil Aviation (DGCA) in India. These organizations create thorough security plans compliant with global norms, such those described in Annex 17 of ICAO. They supervise the application of security policies at airports, guarantee adherence to legal criteria, and carry out routine audits and inspections.

Globally, companies like the European Union Aviation Safety Agency (EASA) and the International Civil Aviation Organization (ICAO) establish standards and enable member state collaboration. By means of its Aviation Security Program, ICAO offers countries direction, technical support, and training to enable them to improve their security systems. To guarantee conformance to world standards, it also does security audits and evaluations. Working together with national authorities, these agencies synchronize security measures and handle developing concerns, therefore guaranteeing a coordinated and efficient worldwide aviation security system.

Frontline of aviation security, airport security officers are in charge of implementing and preserving security procedures on airport grounds. Their responsibilities cover a broad spectrum from entrance control to passenger and luggage screening to patrolling to handling security events. These staff members are educated to identify illegal objects and possible hazards using cutting-edge screening technologies including body scanners and X-ray machines.

Apart from regular screening duties, airport security personnel also oversee and regulate access to limited areas. This entails verifying credentials and identification, running haphazard searches, and making sure just authorized staff members access private areas. In an emergency, they also are quite important since they coordinate with law enforcement and other agencies to control security events, evacuate areas, and handle other issues.

Staff members in airport security depend critically on training and ongoing professional development. To carry out their responsibilities, they have to be current on the newest security technologies, threat analyses, and best practices. Frequent drills and simulations help them to be ready for many situations, therefore guaranteeing a high degree of competency.

Airline Security Teams

Airline security professionals protect aircraft, passengers, and crew in concert with airport authorities. Among their duties include monitoring access to aircraft, passenger and baggage screening, and security implementation on board flights. Airlines have to follow national and international security rules; regulatory bodies regularly monitor and check their security initiatives.

Pre-flight screenings and checks are one of the main purposes of airline security staff. This includes confirming passenger names, looking over checked and carry-on bags, and making sure no forbidden goods are packed aboard. Working closely with airport security, airline security staff are educated to identify suspicious activity and possible hazards.

A flawless security operation depends on cooperation among airport officials and airline security. This entails distributing knowledge on possible hazards, organizing security protocols during boarding and disembarkation, and working on emergency response strategies. The general security and safety of air travel depend on efficient communication and coordination among several agencies.

Coordination with Law Enforcement

Working with airport and airline security teams to prevent and respond to security concerns, law enforcement authorities are absolutely crucial in aviation security. Their involvement spans regular patrols and surveillance to managing significant security events including terrorist attacks or hijackings. Trained to handle a variety of circumstances, law enforcement personnel guarantee the safety and security of travelers and airport employees.

Joint operations, information exchange, and integrated response plans help to coordinate law enforcement agencies' activities with aviation security. Law enforcement personnel may be positioned at strategic locations, including boarding gates and checkpoints, at airports to enhance even more security. To discourage and identify illegal activity, they also routinely police airport grounds including parking lots and perimeter areas.

Should a security incident arise, law enforcement departments lead in handling the reaction. This calls for investigating, mitigating hazards, and evacuating impacted areas. Working closely with airport and airline security professionals, they guarantee a coordinated and effective reaction, therefore reducing the effect on passengers and airport operations.

Good cooperation between law enforcement and aviation security depends on effective communication and teamwork. Regular meetings, combined training programs, and set procedures for information exchange help to accomplish this. Working together, these organizations may improve their combined capacity and offer a strong security system for the aviation industry.

The Role of Intelligence Agencies

Through quick and useful information about possible hazards, intelligence services also significantly contribute to aviation security. To find developing security concerns, these organizations compile and examine information from several sources—including cyber monitoring, informants, and surveillance activities. Their intelligence enables law enforcement and airline security staff to foresee and lessen risks before they become reality.

Maintaining a proactive security posture requires cooperation among intelligence agencies and aviation security organizations. Regular briefings, danger assessments, and intelligence exchange guarantee that every participant knows of present hazards and can modify their security protocols. This cooperative approach helps create a dynamic and responsive security environment ready to change with changing threats.

Access Control

People Access Control

A basic feature of aviation security is managing the access of people on airport grounds. This system combines technology and approaches meant to guarantee that only authorized users and passengers can access restricted areas. Using security checkpoints at several points of entrance is one of the main strategies followed. People at these checkpoints have to show legitimate flight permits and identity, which security staff checks. Modern technologies are being applied more and more to simplify this process and improve security: biometric scanners and automated gates. Effective in preventing illegal access, biometric systems—which comprise fingerprint, facial recognition, and iris scanning—have great degree of accuracy and are challenging to fabricate.

Apart from physical inspections, airports use technological access control mechanisms. Access cards or key fobs are used in these systems to let limited regions be accessed. Every card is set with certain access permissions, therefore guaranteeing that people may only enter spaces pertinent to their employment. Through centralized control rooms, security staff can follow individual movement within the airport and react quickly to any illegal efforts, effectively monitoring and regulating access in real-time.

Background screening of airport personnel and contractors is another absolutely important component of people's access control. People have to complete extensive background checks to make sure they do not create a security risk before being let into sensitive places. Checks on criminal records, work histories, and—in some cases—security clearance from federal agencies comprise this process. By spotting any changes in a person's situation that can affect their security clearance, constant monitoring and regular re-screening aid to preserve a safe surroundings.

Vehicle Access Control

Maintaining airport security depends also on vehicle access management. The systems and policies for controlling vehicle access to restricted regions are meant to stop illegal vehicles from accessing sensitive zones and to reduce the possibility of vehicle-borne diseases. Vehicle checks placed at key sites surrounding the airport are one of the main techniques applied. Security staff at these checkpoints examine cars, confirm driver credentials, and look for any illegal or suspicious objects.

Restricted area entry is often managed with automated vehicle barriers and bollards. Depending on the vehicle's authorization status, these physical barriers can be raised or lowered to let or obstruct vehicle entrance. Another technical fix used in many airports are license plate recognition (LPR) devices. To enable quick and safe entry control, LPR systems automatically scan and verify license plates of cars against a database of approved vehicles.

Apart from physical and technological restrictions, airports use surveillance systems to track vehicle traffic. To offer real-time surveillance, CCTV cameras are positioned deliberately inside limited regions and around vehicle entry points. Control room security staff can watch vehicle activity and react swiftly to any suspicious conduct or security lapses. Combining these surveillance technologies with access control strategies improves the whole security architecture.

Controlling service and delivery trucks is another important component of vehicle access control. These vehicles have to be closely watched and regulated since they sometimes need access to different areas of the airport for running operations. While the cars themselves may be subject to frequent inspections, drivers of service vehicles must go through background checks and get appropriate permission. Strict procedures for service and delivery trucks guarantees that only authorized people and vehicles may access sensitive areas and helps reduce the possibility of security breaches.

Landside Security

Landside security is concerned with safeguarding public areas including terminals, parking lots, and other airport facilities that are open to everyone. Since these locations are generally the initial point of contact for guests and passengers, their security is absolutely vital. One of the main tactics for landside security is the obvious presence of security guards. Patrolling public locations, uniformed security guards discourage possible threats and help guests and visitors.

Apart from actual security presence, airports use sophisticated surveillance technologies to keep an eye on ground level areas. High-definition and night-vision CCTV cameras are positioned deliberately all over terminals, parking lots, and other public areas. These cameras let security staff constantly monitor and let them rapidly spot and react to unusual behavior. Usually captured and kept, the video from these cameras offers priceless evidence should an incident occur.

Crowd control management is yet another crucial component of landside security. Different strategies are used by airports to control visitor and passenger traffic, therefore lowering the possibility of congestion and possible security concerns. This covers the use of extra security staff during busy travel times and barriers and signage to lead people through approved paths. Good crowd control helps passenger experience generally as well as security.

Landside areas are also covered via screening processes. This covers screening baggage and other objects carried into terminals using sniffer dogs and bomb detecting equipment. To find and deal with any possible hazards, random patrols and checks are carried out. These steps will help airports to lower the danger of security events and improve the security of landside areas.

Improving landside security depends critically on the integration of technology. Surveillance footage is analyzed and anomalies in real-time found using advanced analytics and artificial intelligence. These technologies let security staff react quickly by spotting odd activity or missed objects. Moreover, the usage of communication tools and mobile apps helps security personnel coordinate better, therefore guaranteeing a quick and efficient reaction to any security issues.

All things considered, aviation security depends critically on access control—that which relates to persons, vehicles, or landside locations as well as other elements. Advanced technologies, strict policies, and coordinated efforts among security staff members help airports to provide a safe environment for visitors, employees, and passengers. Preventing illegal access, reducing security risks, and preserving the general integrity of the aviation sector depend on strong access control mechanisms being maintained.

Recognition and Handling of Explosive Devices & Other Prohibited Articles

Explosive Device Recognition

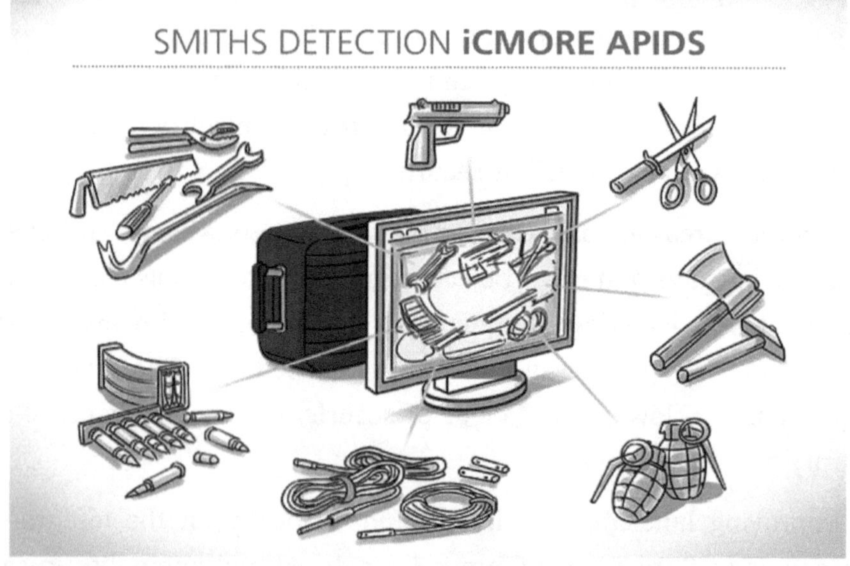

A key component of aviation security, recognition of explosive devices calls for both strict procedures and specific training. Law enforcement officials and airport security staff among other security agents have to participate in thorough training courses meant to provide them the tools and knowledge required to spot such hazards. These courses address several facets of explosive device recognition, including the kinds of explosives often employed, their appearance, and the techniques of concealment possible.

Usually, training consists of theoretical instruction mixed with hands-on tasks. Trainees study the chemical and physical characteristics of several explosives, how to build improvised explosive devices (IEDs), and the signs of a possible explosive threat. Simulated situations in which trainees must spot and react to suspicious objects or actions abound in practical exercises. These drills give participants hands-on experience in a controlled atmosphere, thereby simulating real-life events as practically practicable.

Apart from first training, continuous education and refresher courses are crucial to keep security staff current on the most recent hazards and detection methods. With new kinds of explosives and concealing techniques developing routinely, the scene of aviation security is always changing. Regular training guarantees that staff members stay alert and ready to spot even the most complex hazards.

Handling Prohibited Articles

Maintaining airport security mostly depends on the recognition and handling of forbidden objects. Not just explosives but also guns, dangerous materials, and other objects that can endanger aircraft or passenger safety are banned. To guarantee they do not affect aviation security, security staff members should be well knowledgeable in the methods for spotting and handling these objects.

At airports, screening processes are meant to find forbidden objects before they can be carried on an airplane. Advanced screening technologies—X-ray machines, metal detectors, and explosive trace detection (ETD) systems—are used here. Trained to run these devices and decipher the signals and images these machines generate is security staff. When needed, they are also instructed in hand searching personal items and bags.

When a forbidden object is discovered, security staff members have to act strictly to securely manage the matter. Usually, this entails separating the object, alerting the relevant authorities, and applying accepted methods for disposal. Bomb disposal units and other specialized teams may be called in to control the threat in circumstances where an object is thought to be an explosive device.

During such events, law enforcement, security staff, and other pertinent agencies must coordinate clearly and effectively. Ensuring that all those engaged know their roles and duties helps to control the matter properly and reduce disturbance of airport operations.

Building and Area Search Procedures

Finding hazards inside airport buildings and grounds calls for methodical search techniques. These processes are meant to guarantee that every possible hiding location for explosive devices and other forbidden objects is carefully investigated, therefore reducing the possibility of an unnoticed threat.

Usually starting with a risk assessment to find high-risk areas needing immediate attention, search operations These might be passenger waiting lounges, baggage claim sections, toilets, and storage spaces. Visual inspections, hand searches, and the use of detection gear including metal detectors and ETD systems are among the several methods and approaches security staff members employ to do these searches.

Building and area searches frequently call for canine units, taught to identify bombs and other contraband. These dogs can quickly cover great distances and are quite good in spotting hidden hazards. Their handlers are taught to interact with the dogs and decipher their signals, therefore guaranteeing quick resolution of any possible hazards.

Search techniques have to be systematic and exhaustive, covering all possible hiding spots inside the allocated area. This includes looking behind panels and walls, within and under furniture, in ventilation systems, and in other hidden areas. Security staff members also need to be taught to spot indicators of environmental unusual changes or tampering that would point to the existence of a concealed device.

Throughout search activities, effective coordination and communication are absolutely vital. Security teams have to cooperate perfectly, exchanging data and guaranteeing that every region is covered. Maintaining thorough records of the search procedure, including the regions searched and the results, can help to guarantee responsibility and enable follow-up activities should needed.

Patrolling and Guarding

Methodologies of Patrol

A pillar of airport security, effective patrolling guarantees that every part of the facility is routinely watched over and offers a clear deterrent to possible hazards. Although the particular needs and layout of the airport will affect the patrolling methods, normally foot patrols, vehicle patrols, and stationary posts are used.

Usually found in high traffic locations such baggage claim areas, check-in counters, and terminals, foot patrols are Walking over various locations, security staff keeps a clear presence and interacts with staff members and guests. This visibility lets security staff respond fast to any events and helps to discourage possible hazards.

Larger portions of the airport—including parking lots, surrounding walls, and access roads—are watched by vehicle patrols. Patrolling these locations, security staff search for indications of suspicious behavior or illegal access using marked and unmarked vehicles. Vehicle patrols let security guards swiftly cover more terrain and react to events in outlying parts of the airport.

Monitoring particular high-risk sites including security checkpoints, sensitive facilities, entrance and exit points, and stationery posts is done using CCTV cameras to support their monitoring activities, security guards at these posts maintain eye over their assigned areas. They also oversee access to these spaces, therefore guaranteeing that only authorized staff members may pass through.

Regular and random patrols make it challenging for possible hazards to forecast security patterns and help to keep security staff attentive. Whether by direct involvement or by informing the relevant authorities, security staff members have to be educated to identify suspicious activity and act accordingly.

Safety Measures

Maintaining security also depends critically on protecting private portions of the airport. Control towers, fuel storage facilities, maintenance hangars, and other sites that, should they be compromised, might seriously jeopardize airport operations and safety.

Best practices for security of these spaces combine access control policies, physical obstacles, and ongoing observation. Unauthorized access is discouraged in part by physical barriers such gates, fences, and security doors. Many times, these obstacles have electronic access control systems that need biometric verification or identification cards to access.

Apart from physical obstacles, security staff members are positioned at strategic points of access to validate credentials and execute security inspections. Their training teaches them to spot and handle possible hazards such as security breaches, dubious activity, and illegal access attempts. Constant surveillance via CCTV cameras and other monitoring tools adds still another level of protection, enabling security staff to instantly identify and handle events.

Maintaining the efficacy of guarding techniques depends on routine security audits and assessments. These audits assess the systems of access control, physical security, and monitoring in place to find any flaws or areas needing development. To remain current on the newest risks and best practices in protecting private areas, security staff members also have to be constantly learning.

Examining and Searching

Essential elements of airport security, screening and search processes are meant to find and stop forbidden objects from being carried onboard planes. Advanced technology including X-ray machines, metal detectors, and explosive trace detection systems are used in these operations together with hand searches carried out by qualified security staff.

Beginning at the security checkpoint, passengers must pass through metal detectors and have their carry-on bags X-ray machines inspected. Trained to decipher the images these devices create, security staff can spot any objects that might be dangerous. Should an anomaly be found, passengers might also be subjected to further screening including body scans or pat-down inspections.

Equally crucial is baggage screening, whereby both checked and carry-on bags are carefully examined. Usually, explosive detection devices and high-powered X-ray equipment screen checked bags. Any unusual objects found throughout the screening process are noted for more investigation. At security checkpoints, carry-on bags are checked; if needed, security staff do hand searches.

Procedures of screening and search ought to be exhaustive and consistent to guarantee that no forbidden objects go unnoticed. From explosive devices to dangerous chemicals, security staff members have to be educated to identify and manage a broad spectrum of hazards. Passenger and airport personnel safety depends on well defined methods for handling discovered risks including isolation and removal processes.

Methods of Protection and Inspection

Guarding Parked Vehicles

A key component of airport security is ensuring parked aircraft against illegal access. Targets for vulnerability are aircraft, hence illegal access could cause theft, damage, or other security breaches. Protection of parked aircraft calls for access control, surveillance, and physical security mixed together.

Using gates and fences to stop illegal people from reaching parked airplanes is one of the physical security precautions. Many times, aircraft are parked in approved secure zones under observation by security guards and cameras. To discourage illegal access, these facilities could additionally feature security lighting and alarms.

Parking aircraft's protection depends also on access control. These sections are only accessible to authorized staff members including maintenance teams and airline employees. Security staff members examine credentials and guarantee that only those having justifiable causes are allowed access. By limiting access to authorized people only, electronic access control systems including biometric scanners and key cards add still another level of protection.

Monitoring parked airplanes depends much on surveillance. CCTV cameras are positioned deliberately to cover aircraft parking lots continuously. Real-time monitoring of these cameras by security staff in control rooms searches for any evidence of illegal access or suspicious activities. Every incident is promptly notified to on-site security teams, who can react to handle the threat.

Frequent security audits and inspections help to guarantee that the steps used to guard parked aircraft are successful. By assessing the physical security, access control, and surveillance systems, these audits find any areas that might need development. Security staff members also need ongoing education to be informed of the newest risks and best techniques for safeguarding parked aircraft.

Manual Examination of Cargo

Ensuring airline security depends mostly on the physical screening of baggage. Although extremely successful advanced screening technologies including X-ray machines and explosive trace detection systems are available, occasionally a hand check is required. This can result from a random security check or from an anomaly found during the first screening phase.

Security staff members open and check suitcase contents during manual checks to find any forbidden objects or any hazards. Along with following rigorous procedures to guarantee the safety of the inspector and the passenger's possessions, this process calls for great attention to detail and thoroughness.

Security staff search for evidence of tampering, unexpected changes, or concealed compartments hiding illegal objects during a physical check. They are taught to identify a broad spectrum of hazards, including guns, explosives, and dangerous chemicals. Standard practice is the wearing of gloves and other protective gear to guarantee the inspector's safety.

Usually present during the physical check of their bags, passengers provide security staff chances to ask questions and address any issues. Passenger understanding of the process and the causes for the inspection depends on clear communication. This helps to uphold openness and faith in the security protocols.

When a forbidden object or possible threat is found, security staff members apply accepted procedures to manage the matter securely. This could call for separating the object, contacting the relevant authorities, and, should more inspections be needed, doing more investigations. The object is then taken out and disposed of in line with legal criteria so as to guarantee that it does not endanger aviation security.

Carrier of Arms and Ammunition by Air

Strict rules and procedures govern the air carrying of weapons and ammunition to guarantee the crew and passenger safety. These laws let for the transportation of weapons and ammunition under specified circumstances while deterring illegal access to them.

Those who must carry weapons and ammunition—law enforcement agents or hunters—have to follow particular rules. Guns have to be unloaded and tightly packed in a secured, hard-sided container. Usually in their original packaging or another container that offers protection against accidental discharge, ammunition must be packed apart from the gun.

At check-in, passengers carrying firearms and ammunition have to disclose these goods. Security staff make sure all legal criteria are followed and confirm the weapons are unloaded and correctly packaged. After that, apart from the passenger cabin, the weapons and ammunition are moved in the cargo hold of the airplane to stop illegal access during the flight.

Special procedures are in place for the transport of weapons by police enforcement personnel or other people who might have to carry one on their person. These people are subject to extra security checks and have to get approval from the airline and the pertinent agencies. Maintaining the safety of every passenger depends on cooperation among the airline, security staff, and law enforcement to guarantee adherence to these procedures.

Finally, fundamental elements of aviation security include awareness and handling of explosive devices and other forbidden articles, patrolling and guarding, and protection and inspection procedures. These steps guarantee that possible hazards are found and controlled thereby preserving passenger, staff, and airport operations' safety and security. Maintaining a strong and efficient aviation security system depends on ongoing education, cutting-edge technologies, and coordinated actions among law enforcement, security staff, and other pertinent agencies.

Emergencies and Contingencies

Emergency Response Plans

Ensuring passenger, personnel, and airport infrastructure safety and security during an emergency depends on the formulation and execution of emergency response plans. These all-encompassing plans are thorough tactics meant to handle a variety of possible events, from terrorist acts to natural disasters. An emergency response plan's main objective is to offer a clear, methodical way to handle emergencies, reducing their effects on property and human life, and so enabling fast restoration of normal operations.

Developing a good emergency response strategy calls for several important phases. First, a careful risk analysis looks for possible weaknesses and hazards. This evaluation takes into account things including the location of the airport, the kinds of aircraft it manages, and its general security posture. This assessment helps to create particular scenarios that highlight the several kinds of crises that might strike.

Establishing standards and procedures for handling any kind of emergency comes next once possible scenarios are recognized. This includes assigning duties and obligations to all pertinent staff members including management, emergency responders, and airport security officers. Command systems and open lines of communication are set up to guarantee that during an emergency information is passed fast and precisely.

An efficient emergency response strategy depends mostly on training and frequent simulations. Every employee ought to be conversant with the strategy and their particular responsibilities inside it. Regular drills and simulations provide staff members a chance to practice their reaction in a controlled setting and help to find any flaws or gaps in the strategy. Often working with local law enforcement, fire agencies, and medical services, these drills guarantee a coordinated and complete response.

Contingency Planning

Getting ready for unanticipated security events that can strike an airport depends on contingency planning in great part. Cont contingency plans offer a flexible framework for managing a broad spectrum of unanticipated events unlike emergency response plans, which are intended for particular situations. Contingency planning is to make sure the airport may keep running effectively and safely even in the presence of unanticipated events.

Good contingency planning starts with determining which important processes and functions have to be kept running through an emergency. This covers basics including baggage handling, passenger screening, and air traffic control. By giving these duties top priority, airport administration can guarantee that important operations are not disrupted and more wisely deploy resources.

Additionally included in contingency plans are techniques for preserving collaboration and communication during a crisis. Establishing backup channels of contact and methods for distributing data to employees, customers, and outside organizations is part of this. Redundant systems are set up to guarantee that important infrastructure stays running, including data backup facilities and alternate energy sources.

Contingency planning also depends critically on the development of recovery protocols. Once the crisis has been under control, these protocols show the actions needed to resume regular operations. Repairing damaged infrastructure, doing extensive security checks, and supporting impacted passengers and personnel might all be part of this. Recovery protocols are made to be adaptable, therefore enabling airport management to fit the particular situation of every occurrence.

Escorting People & Consignment

At airports, a key security precaution is escorting precious consignments and high-risk people. While expensive consignments can range from high-value goods to sensitive documents, high-risk individuals could be dignitaries, celebrities, or anyone under danger. Escorting these people and consignments has as its main goal guaranteeing their safety and security all while their trip inside the airport.

Usually combining physical security elements with coordinated efforts among security staff, protocols for escorting high-risk individuals Assigning a specific security detail to go with the person, guaranteeing safe transportation, and making sure all access points and paths are under observation and control could all help here. Training security staff members in crowd control and media presence management can help them to identify and handle possible hazards.

Likewise, important consignments call for strict security protocols to stop loss, theft, or manipulation. Usually carried in safe containers and escorted by security guards all during the handling procedure, these consignments Just authorized people are allowed to handle or move the carefully regulated consignments. Real-time monitoring of the consignments' position and status is frequently accomplished with tracking systems including GPS or RFID tags.

Escorting important consignments and high-risk patients depends on good coordination and communication. To guarantee a flawless and safe process, security staff members must cooperate closely with airport officials, airline employees, and other agencies. This covers pathways of pre-planning, time coordination, and contingency preparation for any unanticipated events.

Emerging Threats and Advanced Security Measures

Behavior Detection

A proactive security tool called behavior detection watches and examines people's actions to spot possible hazards. While conventional security systems concentrate on spotting forbidden objects, behavior detection seeks to spot suspicious activity suggesting hostile intent. This strategy is predicated on the idea that those preparing or executing security risks sometimes show specific behavioral traits.

Trained in behavior detection, security staff members learn to identify particular signals and patterns suggestive of suspicious activity. These indications could include anxiousness, evasiveness, or other odd behavior. Observing people in several airport environments—security checkpoints, boarding gates, public areas—behavior detection officers interact with those displaying suspicious conduct to further evaluate their intent.

Good behavior identification calls for situational awareness, expertise, and training all taken together. Security guards have to be able to tell natural stress or anxiety brought on by air travel from conduct suggesting a real threat. Real-world experience and ongoing education assist behavior detection agents hone their abilities to precisely identify possible hazards.

Insider Threat

Since they involve people with authorized access to safe places who could use their position for malevolent intent, insider threats seriously compromise aviation security. Employees of airports, contractors, or other staff members with legal access to private information and infrastructure can all pose these risks. Finding and reducing insider risks is a difficult task needing a multifarious strategy.

Strong background screening and vetting procedures for every employee are among the main tools for handling insider threats. This covers exhaustive investigations on a person's criminal record, work experience, and affiliations. Frequent re-screening and ongoing observation enable one to spot any changes in a person's situation that can endanger security.

Reducing insider risks also depends much on access control policies. This entails limiting access to private spaces depending on a person's position and obligations and applying biometric authentication to confirm identities. Security staff members also have to be educated to spot among their colleagues questionable behavior or activity and to quickly report any issues.

Apart from physical security policies, it is imperative to develop a culture of security consciousness and alertness. Frequent training and awareness campaigns equip staff members with knowledge of the possible hazards and inspire them to participate actively in spotting and documenting insider threats. The general security posture of the airport can be much improved by staff members developing responsibility and accountability.

Cyber Security

Cybersecurity has become a vital part of aviation security as digital technologies grow ever more important to aviation operations. From air traffic control systems to passenger data and infrastructure management, cyberthreats can target many facets of airport operations. Dealing with these challenges calls for a thorough strategy covering technological as well as psychological elements.

Using strong network security systems is one of the main steps toward improving cyber security. To guard against illegal access and cyber-attacks, this covers applying intrusion detection systems, encryption, and firewalls. Frequent security audits and vulnerability assessments assist to find and fix possible network infrastructure flaws.

Reducing cyber risks also depends much on employee knowledge and training. Many cyberattacks take use of human weaknesses including social engineering or phishing. Effective cyber-attacks can be greatly lowered by training courses teaching staff members safe internet activities, email recognition of suspicious messages, and reporting of possible cyber-threats.

Effective cyber security depends on cooperation and information exchange among aviation participants. Working together, airports, airlines, law enforcement authorities, and cyber security specialists may exchange threat intelligence, create best practices, and plan reactions to cyber events. By means of this cooperative method, a strong cyber security system capable of changing with changing threats is created.

Profiling

Profiling is a security method applied to improve aviation security by means of identification of people who might be more risk-bearing depending on particular characteristics. This method evaluates the possible danger connected with a passenger by means of an analysis of several elements, including travel habits, behavior, and personal data. Using profiling to augment conventional security protocols adds still another degree of protection.

In aviation security, risk-based profiling and behavioral profiling are two several forms of profiling applied. While risk-based profiling takes into account things like travel history, ticket buying methods, and relationships to recognized hazards, behavioral profiling concentrates on spotting suspicious activity. Combining these methods permits every passenger to have a thorough risk assessment.

Although profiling is a good security tool, it has to be done so in a way that honors people's rights and prevents prejudice. Ensuring that profiling methods are fair, open, and grounded on objective criteria depends on well defined policies and control. Continuous monitoring and training help to guarantee that profiling is applied suitably and powerfully.

Profiling methods are being improved with increased usage of advanced technology including artificial intelligence and machine learning. By use of extensive data analysis, these technologies can spot trends and abnormalities suggestive of a security problem. Integration of profiling with other security policies can help airports build a more strong and proactive security system.

In essence, aviation security depends critically on handling crises and contingency plans as well as on getting ready for new hazards and sophisticated security practices. Effective contingency planning, comprehensive emergency response plans, and procedures for escorting high-risk people and precious consignments serve to guarantee that airports can react properly to a wide spectrum of events. Behavior detection, insider threat reduction, cybersecurity, and profiling offer still another layer of defense against changing security risks. Constant adaptation and improvement of these policies will help airports to keep a safe surroundings for operations, personnel, and passengers.

Chapter-6

Air Cargo

Overview of Air Cargo

Globally, air cargo is essential for trade since it allows items to be quickly transported over continents and oceans. Time-sensitive and valuable goods choose air freight because, unlike other forms of transportation, it provides unmatched speed and dependability. Working together to guarantee the effective and safe movement of products, the air cargo sector includes airlines, goods forwarders, ground handling agencies, and customs officials among other stakeholders. Maintaining supply chain continuity, supporting e-commerce, and enabling worldwide trade all depend on air cargo in the linked world of today.

The importance of air cargo goes beyond simple product delivery to also promote economic development and growth. Fast and dependable delivery services from air cargo enable companies to satisfy consumer needs, lower inventory costs, and increase market share. Critical and life-saving commodities including medical equipment, drugs, and disaster relief supplies depend on air cargo as well. The capacity to swiftly relocate these goods emphasizes the need of a strong air cargo infrastructure since it may make a big difference in emergency conditions.

Types of Air Cargo

The type of the products being carried will help one to generally classify air freight into numerous groups. Each of these categories— general cargo, perishable items, hazardous chemicals, live animals— requires particular handling and transportation practices to guarantee compliance with laws and safety.

General Cargo: This section covers commonplace consumer goods including electronics, clothes, machines, and tools. Usually less sensitive to environmental conditions and without requiring particular handling, general cargo is the most often used kind of air freight.

Perishable Goods: Perishable goods, such as fresh produce, seafood, flowers, and pharmaceuticals, require temperature-controlled environments to maintain their quality and safety during transit. The conditions are watched and regulated throughout the trip using specialized containers and tools including refrigerated units and temperature loggers.

Hazardous Materials: Also known as dangerous goods, hazardous materials include items that pose a risk to health, safety, or the environment. Among examples are chemicals, batteries, and flammable substances. Airborne hazardous material transportation calls for rigorous adherence to rules established by entities as the International Civil Aviation Organization (ICAO) and the International Air Transport Association (IATA). The safe movement of these goods depends critically on accurate labeling, packaging, and documentation.

Live Animals: The transportation of live animals, including pets, livestock, and exotic species, requires special care and attention. Animals have to be kept in suitable containers that give enough comfort, ventilation, and room. To guarantee the wellbeing of the animals during travel, airlines have to follow particular rules and guidelines including those set in the IATA Live Animals Regulations (LAR).

Every kind of cargo has different difficulties and calls for different solutions to guarantee effective and secure movement. Using new technologies and best practices to improve operational efficiency and customer satisfaction, the air cargo sector constantly changes and innovates to address these challenges.

Air Cargo vs. Passenger Aircraft

Although passenger aircraft and air cargo both benefit the aviation sector, they are built and run with different priorities and standards. Appreciating the complexity of air freight operations requires one to understand the main variations between these two kinds of aircraft.

Design and Structure: Cargo aircraft are specifically designed to maximize cargo capacity and efficiency. To fit a variety of goods kinds and sizes, they have reinforced flooring, big cargo doors, and sophisticated loading mechanisms. Passenger airplanes, on the other hand, with seating configurations, in-flight entertainment systems, and other conveniences, are essentially built for the comfort and safety of the passengers. To provide more flexibility, certain passenger aircraft— known as "combi" aircraft—are built to carry both goods and people in different sections.

Functionality and Operations: Usually flying at night to minimize traffic and maximize asset use, cargo aircraft follow predetermined cargo routes. These paths could comprise several stops for loading and unloading and are designed for cargo demand. Usually based on cargo demand rather than set plans, cargo flights give more freedom to shippers. Conversely, passenger aircraft concentrate on getting people between big airports and hubs and run set routes and timetables.

Regulatory Requirements: Both cargo and passenger aircraft must comply with stringent aviation regulations to ensure safety and security. Still, the particular criteria can change based on the kind of cargo being moved. For instance, compared to passenger airplanes, hazardous items carried by cargo planes must be packaged and labeled differently. Cargo planes may also come under distinct customs clearance procedures and security screening policies.

Economic Considerations: Running cargo instead of passenger aircraft also has quite different economics. Goods demand, industry pricing, and logistical effectiveness influence cargo operations. Airlines have to weigh the income from goods services against the expenses of running focused cargo trips. Nonetheless, passenger airlines mostly make money from ticket sales; auxiliary income comes from things like baggage fees and in-flight sales.

In essence, although both air cargo and passenger aircraft are vital components of the aviation sector, their design, functioning, and operations are geared to satisfy the particular needs of product transportation over passengers. Appreciating the complexity and challenges of air cargo operations as well as their important importance in world trade and logistics depends on an awareness of these variations.

Documentation and Regulations

Documents Involved

A highly regulated sector, air cargo transportation depends on a multitude of paperwork to guarantee the legal, safe, and effective transfer of commodities. These records guarantee that shipments are tracked and controlled properly, help different stakeholders communicate, and supply required information for customs and regulatory compliance. Airway bills, commercial invoices, packing lists, and certificates of origin are a few of the key records required in air freight operations.

Airway Bill (AWB): The airway bill is one of the most critical documents in air cargo. Detailing the terms and conditions of the cargo, it acts as a contract of carriage between the shipper and the airline. The AWB contains information including description of the products, weight and measurements, shipper and consignee details, and routing facts. Additionally acting as a guide for handling and delivering the cargo and a receipt of goods for the shipper is The house airway bill (HAWB) issued by the goods forwarder and the master airway bill (MAWB) issued by the airline are the two varieties of airways bills.

Commercial Invoice: The commercial invoice is a document provided by the seller to the buyer, detailing the goods sold and their value. It covers basic details including the names and addresses of the buyer and seller, a goods description, quantity and unit price, shipment total value, terms of sale and payment. Customs clearance depends on this paper since it forms the foundation for evaluating taxes and obligations.

Packing List: The packing list is a detailed document that provides information about the contents of each package in a shipment. It covers the goods' descriptions, weight and dimensions of every box, and any specific handling directions. Customs officials and goods forwarders can check the contents of the cargo and guarantee that everything is accounted for using the packing list.

Certificate of Origin: The certificate of origin is a document that certifies the country in which the goods were manufactured. Customs authorities sometimes demand that one ascertain the relevance of trade agreements and taxes. Usually issued by a chamber of commerce or other approved entity, this paper contains information including the nation of origin, a commodities description, and exporter and importer details.

The foundation of the documentation process in air freight operations is these records as well as others like export licenses, import permits, and inspection certifications. < They guarantee that every person engaged possesses the required knowledge to manage the cargo properly and follow legal criteria.

FIATA Rules

Representing the interests of freight forwarders worldwide, the International Federation of Freight Forwarders Associations (FIATA) In order to enable global trade and increase the dependability and efficiency of goods forwarding services, FIATA creates and advocates consistent regulations and standards. The operational procedures and legal structure of air cargo transportation are much shaped by the FIATA guidelines.

Widely used in the sector, FIATA has created a set of consistent papers and forms. Among these is the FIATA Multimodal Transport Bill of Lading (FBL), a negotiable document of title and a contract of carriage for multimodal goods. By means of a consistent structure for recording the terms and circumstances of transportation, the FBL lowers the possibility of conflicts and misinterpretation between the parties.

FIATA's establishment of best practices and policies for goods forwarders is yet another important contribution. These policies address many facets of goods forwarding, including liability, regulatory compliance, and risk control. Following FIATA's guidelines can help goods forwarders build reputation and dependability, therefore strengthening their relationship with clients and partners.

FIATA is also very important in promoting global interests of the goods forwarding sector. It interacts with trade associations, government agencies, and other interested parties to support laws and rules that enable seamless international commerce of goods. FIATA helps to create a more integrated and effective worldwide supply chain by speaking for goods forwarders collectively.

TACT Rules

Published by the International Air Transport Association (IATA), the rules known as the Air Cargo Tariff (TACT) are a thorough collection of guidelines and tariffs for the air cargo market. TACT offers consistent information on prices, fees, and policies relevant to air-based commodities transportation. For airlines, goods forwarders, and shippers—who depend on it as a vital reference tool—it guarantees continuous and open air cargo operations.

TACT primarily serves to offer current data on air freight rates and costs. This covers specifics about security fees, fuel surcharges, and other auxiliary expenses a shipment could incur. TACT enables shippers and goods forwarders to properly estimate the cost of air transportation and make wise route and career choice decisions by providing a single source of price information.

Apart from pricing data, TACT comprises thorough rules and procedures for the movement of different kinds of goods in addition. This encompasses everything from normal cargo to specialist shipments including perishable items, dangerous chemicals, and live animals. TACT guarantees that shipments follow international standards and legal criteria by outlining the particular needs for documentation, labeling, and packing.

Furthermore, quite important for standardizing air cargo terminology and procedures is TACT. Clear definitions and rules serve to lower uncertainty and guarantee that all those engaged in the air cargo supply chain understand the words and processes. In a worldwide sector where shipments sometimes include several carriers, forwarders, and regulatory organizations, this standardization is especially crucial.

TACT also assists the air freight sector's electronic documentation and processing deployment. TACT facilitates the efficiency and accuracy of cargo handling and documentation by encouraging the use of electronic airway bills (e-AWB) and other digital technologies, therefore helping to simplify operations and lower paperwork.

All things considered, the safe, quick, and compliant movement of products by air depends critically on the policies and documents controlling air cargo operations. For tracking and managing shipments, basic records including airway bills, commercial invoices, packing lists, and certificates of origin offer the required data. FIATA rules set consistent procedures and criteria for cargo forwarders, therefore improving the dependability and reputation of their offerings. Promoting consistency and openness in air cargo operations, TACT guidelines provide thorough knowledge about prices, charges, and policies. These components taken together create the basis of a strong and well-run air freight sector, therefore promoting world trade and economic development.

Customs and EXIM Operations

Customs Check - Process Involved

A vital part of air cargo operations, customs clearance guarantees that items arriving or leaving a nation follow all applicable laws and regulations. The procedure consists in various stages meant to enable the effective and safe flow of goods and deter criminal activity including importation of forbidden products or smuggling.

Turning in the necessary paperwork marks the first stage in the customs clearance process. Usually this covers the airway bill, business invoice, packing list, and any other pertinent permits or certifications. These records give vital details on the shipment—including its value, source, and contents—which customs authorities use to evaluate taxes and charges.

Customs inspectors analyze the files first to make sure all the necessary information is accurate and supplied once they have been turned in This review looks for any differences or absent details and confirms the coherence of the material among several papers. Should any problems arise, the cargo can be kept until required remedies are done.

The physical examination of the goods comes next. Customs authorities may decide to check the whole cargo or a random sample depending on the risk assessment and the kind of goods being moved. Opening packages, looking for forbidden materials, and confirming that the contents line the stated information comprise this examination. This process is sometimes facilitated and its precision is improved by advanced technology such as X-ray equipment and scanners.

Customs personnel figure the taxes and fees due for the shipment after the examination. This computation is predicated on the products' declared value, their Harmonized System (HS) code categorization, and any relevant trade agreements or levies. Before the items may be delivered, the shipper or consignee must next pay these taxes and charges.

Once all checks are finished and all relevant fees paid, customs officials release an order permitting the items to reach their intended use. Presenting this release order is absolutely essential to get the goods from the cargo handling or airport facility. Clear communication and coordination among customs officials, cargo forwarders, and other stakeholders is crucial to guarantee seamless and effective clearance throughout the whole process.

EXIM Operations

At the core of worldwide trade, export and import (EXIM) activities help products to travel between nations. These activities call for careful planning and execution to properly negotiate a complex interaction of logistics, regulatory compliance, and market concerns.

Export Operations: The export process begins with the preparation of goods for shipment. This includes labeling, packaging, and making sure all required supporting material is exact and full. Important export documentation include certificates of origin, packing lists, commercial invasions, and export licenses—if necessary. Coordinating these activities and making sure the consignment conforms with the rules of exporting and importing nations depend much on freight forwarders.

The items are driven to the airport and turned over to the cargo handling agent once they are ready for shipment. Before the cargo is carried aboard the airplane, the agent does a basic check to confirm its condition and paperwork. Maintaining the integrity and security of the cargo is a priority throughout this process, particularly for delicate or valuable items.

Import Operations: Import operations involve several steps to ensure that goods entering a country comply with local laws and regulations. The process starts with the import documentation submission—commercial invoice, airway bill, packing list, and any necessary permissions or certificates. Reviewing these records, customs officials determine the taxes and obligations relevant to the cargo.

Arriving, the items are checked and cleared under customs policies. This entails physical inspections and the use of scanning technology to confirm the contents and guarantee adherence with import rules. The items are released to the consignee or their appointed agent once they cross customs; they then arrange for transportation to the end point.

Key Considerations and Challenges: Effective EXIM operations call for thorough awareness of the regulatory environment and market conditions in both the exporting and importing nations. Key factors include adherence to trade rules, tariffs and duties, currency exchange rates, logistical difficulties including transportation and warehouse space. Businesses also have to be ready to negotiate possible obstacles including changes in trade rules, customs delays, and demand swings.

Overcoming these obstacles depends on good coordination and communication among all the engaged parties. To guarantee seamless and effective processing of goods, this covers strong cooperation with customs officials, freight forwarders, logistics providers, and clients. Using technology and automation can also assist EXIM processes be more efficient generally and aid to lower risk of mistakes.

Role of Customs in Air Cargo

Maintaining security and compliance in air freight operations depends mostly on customs agencies. Their tasks go beyond just gathering taxes and taxes; they also include stopping illicit activity, safeguarding national security, and easing legal trade.

Customs mostly serves to make sure that everything entering or departing a nation follows relevant rules and regulations. This includes making sure shipments are correctly declared, determining the appropriate tariffs and taxes, and making sure forbidden or restricted commodities aren't shipped. To find any hazards and disparities, customs officials combine modern technologies such X-ray scanners and chemical detectors with hand inspections.

Maintaining the security of the air freight supply chain depends very heavily on customs authorities. This includes stopping smuggling, spotting fake goods, and intercepting illicit weapon or drug shipments. Customs help to guarantee public safety and preserve the integrity of international trade by means of extensive inspections and application of intelligence and risk assessment techniques.

Apart from their duties of enforcement, customs officers also have to help to enable legal trade. This entails simplifying clearance protocols, applying effective risk control techniques, and using technology to cut processing times. Through encouraging compliance and strengthening supply chain security, programs like the Authorized Economic Operator (AEO) initiative serve to improve cooperation between customs and the corporate sector.

In response to new issues and trends in air freight, customs officials also are rather important. This covers adjusting to trade policy changes, handling the growing amount of e-commerce shipments, and lessening the effects of world crises including natural disasters or pandemics. Customs can efficiently handle these difficulties and help international trade to flourish by always changing their procedures and using new technologies.

In essence, the effective and safe flow of products across borders depends on the customs clearing process, EXIM activities, and function of customs in air cargo. Customs authorities are very important in the worldwide air cargo sector since they guarantee compliance with rules, promote trade, and guard national security. Navigating the complexity of customs and EXIM processes depends on effective coordination, clear communication, and technology leverage; so, air cargo must keep supporting international trade and economic development.

Air Cargo Handling and Logistics

Air Freight Forwarders - Competition

Acting as middlemen between shippers and airlines, air goods forwarders are absolutely essential in the air cargo sector. They handle documents, arrange items' transportation, and offer several logistical services to guarantee that shipments are securely and effectively delivered. Driven by elements including service quality, pricing, worldwide network reach, and technical developments, the competitive scene for air goods forwarders is sharp.

Air freight forwarders have to constantly adjust to evolving customer expectations and market conditions if they are to remain competitive. To stand out from rivals, they provide value-added services such door-to---door delivery, customs brokerage, and warehouse space. Many forwarders also make technological investments to improve their operating effectiveness and offer real-time shipment tracking and view-through capability. As consumers want openness and frequent updates on their cargo status, this technology edge might be a major competitive advantage.

Air freight forwarders' rivalry also stimulates creativity in service offerings. Forwarders are always looking for means to maximize routing, cut transit times, and increase cost effectiveness. Common approaches to increase service capability and market reach are strategic alliances and cooperation among airlines, trucking firms, and other logistics providers. Forwarders that can provide dependable, reasonably priced, and flexible solutions are more suited to grab market share and create long-term customer relationships in this very competitive industry.

Cargo Charters

Essential for the air cargo sector, cargo charters offer tailored and flexible transportation options for big, urgent, or specialized items that cannot be fit on ordinary planned flights. Cargo charters are important because they allow different sectors—including automotive, aerospace, humanitarian relief, and military operations—specific solutions for different logistical problems.

Cargo charters have operational elements including thorough coordination and preparation to guarantee the effective and safe movement of commodities. This entails choosing the right aircraft depending on the weight, kind of cargo, and size; it also entails planning for required permits and clearances and liaising with ground handling agencies for loading and unloading. To handle non-standard cargo— such as large machinery, live animals, or hazardous materials—cargo charters sometimes call for specific tools and handling techniques.

When time is of the essence or regular scheduled services are not accessible, cargo charters are quite flexible and responsive. For example, cargo charters can rapidly arrange to provide needed goods and relief to impacted areas during natural disasters or humanitarian crises. Likewise in the automobile and aerospace sectors, where just-in-time delivery is vital, cargo charters guarantee that components and parts arrive at their destinations without delay, therefore avoiding expensive manufacturing stoppages.

Role of Logistics in Supply Chain Management

Integration of air cargo into the larger supply chain depends critically on logistics, which guarantees the flawless flow of commodities from source to target. Coordinating several activities—including transportation, warehouse, inventory control, and distribution—effective logistics management ensures that items and information flow across the supply chain as best as possible.

For sectors that depend on quick and consistent delivery, air freight logistics offers great benefits in terms of speed and dependability. It is therefore a necessary part. Using air cargo services helps companies keep lean inventory levels, lower lead times, and react fast to market needs. Industries include electronics, pharmaceuticals, and fashion, where product life cycles are short and market responsiveness is crucial, benefit especially from this agility.

Including air cargo into supply chain management also requires strategic planning and cooperation among several stakeholders—including airlines, goods forwarders, customs officials, and ground handling agencies. To guarantee that shipments are handled effectively and satisfy legal criteria, good communication and coordination among various parties are absolutely crucial. Enhanced visibility, increased efficiency, and lower risk of disruptions depend critically on advanced technology including supply chain management software and automated tracking systems.

Third-Party Agencies

Third-party logistics companies (3PLs) have a major influence on the air freight sector since they provide specialized services improving supply chain flexibility and efficiency. These companies let companies outsource their logistics activities and concentrate on their main business by offering a spectrum of services including transportation, warehouse, goods forwarding, customs brokerage, and distribution.

In air cargo, 3PLs serve to manage intricate logistical networks, maximize travel paths, and guarantee compliance with international trade rules. Using their skills and experience, 3PLs may offer scalable, reasonably priced solutions catered to the particular demands of their customers. Improved service levels, lower running costs, and more supply chain resilience can all follow from this.

Small and medium-sized businesses (SMEs) who might lack the means or knowledge to run their logistics operations on their own find especially great value in 3PLs. Working with 3PLs helps SMEs to access industry knowledge, global networks, and modern logistical capabilities, helping them to compete more successfully in the worldwide market. Furthermore, 3PLs' capacity to offer end-to- end logistics solutions guarantees that companies can keep high degrees of dependability and service quality all along the supply chain.

Warehousing and Inventory Management

Warehousing

Essential to air cargo operations, warehouses offer a safe and regulated space for commodities before, during, and after transit. Receiving, storing, inventory control, order fulfillment, and commodities dispersion to their ultimate destination define warehousing's main purposes. From general warehouses to bonded warehouses to temperature-regulated warehouses, several kinds of warehousing facilities meet the particular needs of air cargo.

General Warehouses: These facilities store a wide range of goods that do not require special handling or storage conditions. Usually including sophisticated racking systems and automated material handling equipment, they are made to maximize storage space and efficiency.

Bonded Warehouses: Bonded warehouses are customs-regulated facilities where imported goods can be stored without paying duties until they are cleared for domestic use. This lets companies more properly control their cash flow and postpone duty payments. Goods that are re-exported especially benefit bonded warehouses since duties are paid only upon domestic market entry.

Temperature-Controlled Warehouses: These facilities are essential for storing perishable goods, pharmaceuticals, and other temperature-sensitive items. Refrigeration and climate control systems help them to keep the necessary temperature and humidity levels, guaranteeing the quality and safety of the kept goods.

Costing and Material Handling Systems

A major factor of warehouse operations is cost issues since they directly affect the general profitability and efficiency of air freight operations. Rent, labor, utilities, equipment maintenance, and security comprise the expenses connected to warehousing. Companies have to carefully review these charges to maximize their warehouse plans and reduce costs without sacrificing the quality of their goods or services.

The effectiveness of warehouse activities depends much on material handling systems. These systems comprise a range of tools and technologies meant to move, store, and control products within the warehouse. Among the common material handling tools used in air cargo warehouses are pallet jacks, conveyor belts, automated storage and retrieval systems (AS/RS), and forklifts.

In terms of speed, accuracy, and labor savings, advanced material handling systems including AS/RS and automated guided vehicles (AGVs) really have great advantages. These systems boost general productivity, lower the danger of human mistake, and manage repetitive jobs by means of robots and automation. Faster order processing times, lower labor costs, and improved inventory accuracy can all follow from using these technologies.

Inventory Management

Air cargo operations depend on efficient inventory control to guarantee that the correct products are always available to satisfy consumer needs. Technologies and inventory control strategies enable companies to lower carrying costs, maximize their stock levels, and lower their risk of stockouts or overstocking.

Just-In-Time (JIT) Inventory: JIT inventory management aims to minimize inventory levels by receiving goods only as they are needed for production or sale. Although this strategy lowers obsolescence risk and carrying costs, it depends on exact supplier and logistics provider cooperation to guarantee timely delivery.

ABC Analysis: ABC analysis is a technique used to categorize inventory based on its value and turnover rate. Three categories define items: A (high value, low turnover); B (moderate value, moderate turnover); and C (poor value, high turnover). This kind of classification enables companies to better spend their resources and prioritize their inventory control initiatives.

Inventory Management Software: Advanced inventory management software provides real-time visibility into stock levels, locations, and movements. These systems accurately track inventory using barcode scanning, RFID technology, and cloud-based platforms, therefore optimizing warehouse operations. Combining inventory control tools with other supply chains systems helps companies to improve general efficiency, lower lead times, and anticipate better.

Unit Load Device (ULD)

Standardized pallets and containers, Unit Load Devices (ULDs) are used to air-transport goods. Their design aims to maximize aircraft space usage, guard cargo during transit, and enable effective loading and unloading practices. Offering various advantages in terms of safety, security, and operational efficiency, ULDs are essential in handling air goods.

Types of ULDs: There are various types of ULDs, including containers and pallets, each serving different purposes. Enclosed items called containers—also called cans or pods—protect goods from environmental elements and harm. Their several sizes and layouts help to suit different kinds of products. Conversely, pallets are level platforms used for cargo stacking and netting or strap security. For delivering big or oddly shaped objects, they are perfect.

Purpose of ULDs: The primary purpose of ULDs is to streamline the handling and transportation of cargo. ULDs help to maximize airplane space by standardizing cargo unit size and shape, therefore saving time and effort needed for loading and unloading. By giving a firm and safe platform for transportation, they help improve cargo safety and security.

Equipment and Devices: The use of ULDs requires specialized equipment and devices for handling and securing cargo. ULDs are moved within the airport and warehouse by ground handling agents using forklifts, pallet jacks, and conveyor systems. Mechanized loaders and motorized rollers among other aircraft loading technologies help to transfer ULDs between the ground and the aircraft smoothly. To guarantee visibility and responsibility, ULD monitoring systems also monitor the position and status of ULDs all through the supply chain using RFID technology and GPS.

Cargo Operations

Air Cargo Sales and Uses

Sales of air goods entail several procedures and techniques meant for marketing and consumer sales of air goods. This covers seeing possible customers, knowing their shipping requirements, and providing customized solutions to fit those requirements. Building connections with shippers, freight forwarders, and logistics providers depends on the sales team, who guarantees efficient use of the aircraft cargo capacity.

From contract negotiations and rate negotiations to operations and customer service teams coordination, air cargo sales serve a variety of purposes. Salespeople have to be well-versed in the air cargo sector, market trends, and competing offers in order to provide clients insightful analysis and recommendations. They also closely coordinate teams on revenue management to increase profitability and control pricing.

Marketing plans for air cargo operations center on highlighting the airline's value-added services, dependability, and capacity. This covers internet marketing initiatives, trade show and industry event attendance, and working with logistics partners and goods forwarders. Airlines may improve their market position, raise their awareness, and draw fresh business by using several marketing methods.

GSA - Cargo Bookings

Acting as representatives for airlines in particular areas or markets, General Sales Agents (GSAs) are absolutely essential in the air cargo business. Promoting and selling the airline's cargo services, handling customer relations, and booking and shipment coordination fall to GSAs.

By offering a useful extension of their sales personnel, they help airlines to enter new areas and increase their clientele.

In cargo bookings, GSAs handle queries, process reservations, and guarantee effective scheduling and management of shipments. Working directly with shippers, cargo forwarders, and other stakeholders, GSAs help to grasp their needs and offer tailored solutions. They also work with the operations team of the airline to guarantee that goods are delivered on schedule and that cargo capacity is best used.

Using their local market knowledge and industry experience, GSAs may efficiently highlight the airline's offerings and create fresh business prospects. They also give the airline insightful comments on consumer preferences, market trends, and competition dynamics, thereby guiding strategic decisions and enhancing the services offered.

Cargo Loading/Unloading Procedures

Safe and effective handling of air goods depends on the loading and unloading processes, which are therefore vital. These operations comprise a sequence of actions meant to maximize the utilization of aircraft space, guard cargo from damage, and uphold safety criteria by means of their implementation.

Loading Procedures: The loading process begins with the preparation of cargo for transport. This covers confirming documentation, checking the state of the products, and pallet or ULD security of them. Ground handling machinery like conveyor belts and forklifts then moves cargo to the airplane. Carefully loading the cargo into the aircraft, ground handling agents guarantee that it is equally distributed to preserve the balance and stability of the aircraft.

Specialized loading systems help to transfer ULDs and pallets between the ground and the aircraft by use of powered rollers and mechanical loaders. These methods increase general efficiency, aid to lower manual effort, and minimize damage risk. Once loaded, the cargo is kept in position to stop movement during flight by netting, straps, or other restraints.

Unloading Procedures: The unloading process begins as soon as the aircraft arrives at its destination. Ground handling agents remove the restraints and gently transport the cargo off the aircraft to ground handling machinery. Depending on the needs of the shipment, the goods are then moved to the consignee straight or to the warehouse.

Verifying the condition of the goods and looking for any evidence of damage or manipulation is crucial throughout the unloading process. Ground handling companies also guarantee that all paperwork is accurate and comprehensive, therefore enabling the seamless flow of goods through customs and on towards their ultimate destination.

Offload Due to Load Restrictions

Load limits often cause cargo to need to be offloaded. Load restrictions might arise for weight restrictions, aircraft balance concerns, or operational restrictions including technical problems or bad weather circumstances.

Cargo offloading can have major logistical and operational effects. Offloaded goods could have to be rebooked on a later aircraft, causing delays and maybe supply chain interruptions. Sometimes alternate transportation options—such as moving the cargo to another flight or mode of delivery—may be needed.

Usually working with ground handling agents and cargo forwarders, the operations staff of the airline makes the decision on unloading of cargo. Managing client expectations and reducing the effect of the offload depend on open communication with them. Working together, airlines and goods forwarders can identify the best methods for rebooking and delivering the offloaded goods as fast and effectively as feasible.

Impact on Offloaded Cargo

Among the difficulties offloaded goods can encounter include delays, more handling, and even damage. Different elements affect the effect on offloaded cargo: the kind of the commodities, the length of the delay, and the availability of substitute means of transportation.

For perishable or time-sensitive products, delivery delays could have major repercussions. For instance, if drugs, fresh food, and other perishable goods are not delivered right away, their shelf life or quality could degrade. In such situations, it is imperative to give the rebooking and transportation of these items top priority in order to reduce their impact on their condition and worth.

Furthermore endangering the cargo's integrity and security is increased handling throughout the offload and rebooking procedure. Every more touchpoint raises the possibility of harm, loss, or manipulation. Ground handling officials have to follow rigorous handling protocols and utilize suitable tools to reduce these hazards and guarantee that the cargo is safeguarded all through the process.

Managing the effects of offloaded goods depends on good coordination and communication among all the engaged parties. This covers keeping clients updated on the state of their shipments, giving quick updates on rebooking plans, and working cooperatively to fix any problems that develop. Airlines and cargo forwarders may develop confidence and guarantee customer satisfaction—even in trying circumstances—by keeping openness and responsiveness.

Ultimately, important elements of the air freight sector are cargo operations, warehousing and inventory control, air cargo handling and logistics, The complexity and difficulties of properly managing air goods are highlighted by the competitive environment for air goods forwarders, the value of cargo charters, and the integration of air cargo into the larger supply chain. While ULDs are absolutely important in maximizing aircraft space and safeguarding cargo, warehouse facilities, material handling systems, and inventory management techniques guarantee the effective storage and flow of goods. At last, air cargo sales, GSA duties, loading and unloading practices, and load constraints highlight the need for cooperation, communication, and flexibility in providing dependable and premium air cargo services.

Chapter-7

Airline Marketing & Sales

Airline Business & Its Customers

From low-cost carriers to full-service airlines, the dynamic and competitive sector of airline business is defined by a wide range of participants. Among other major carriers, Delta, Emirates, and Lufthansa rule different areas and market niches. Constant difficulties for the sector include changing fuel prices, legislative changes, and effects of world events as political unrest or pandemics. Through technology developments, widening paths, and better consumer experiences, it also offers chances for expansion, nevertheless.

Customer Demographics: The aviation sector boasts a varied clientele including several demographic groups with different demands and interests. The main groups are business, leisure, and luxury consumers. Efficiency, regular flight schedules, and loyalty programs providing extra convenience rank highest among the priorities for business travelers. They anticipate great standards of service and facilities and generally fly in premium categories. Though direct flights and in-flight entertainment also affect their decisions, leisure tourists are more price-sensitive and give cost first priority above comfort. Often flying in first or business class, premium consumers—who might cross business and leisure travel—search the best in luxury and customized services. Airlines that want to properly customize their offers and marketing plans must first understand these groups.

Customer Expectations and Preferences: Today's passengers expect more than just a means to get from one point to another; they seek a comprehensive travel experience. This covers simple booking systems, seamless check-in procedures, cozy seating, first-rate in-flight services, and effective handling of delays. Time efficiency and connectivity are absolutely vital for business travelers. To remain efficient, they appreciate services such rapid security checks, priority boarding, and consistent Wi-Fi. Conversely, leisure visitors search for reasonably priced entertainment choices, family-friendly services, and low rates. Exclusive lounges, gourmet cuisine, lie-flat seating, and individualized treatment are expected by premium patrons. Airlines have to keep changing to fit these changing expectations if they are to keep consumer loyalty and draw fresh travelers. Meeting these several needs depends on providing a flawless travel experience from booking to baggage claim.

Impact of Technological Advancements: Technological advancements have significantly impacted the airline industry, transforming how airlines interact with customers and manage operations. Online booking systems, mobile apps, and automated check-in kiosks among other innovations have simplified the consumer trip. Convenience and efficiency these technologies provide let travellers easily book flights, check in, and handle their trip schedule. Furthermore improving the whole travel experience are digital payment choices, Wi-Fi access, and in-flight entertainment systems. Big data and artificial intelligence are additional tools airlines are using to examine consumer preferences, streamline flight itineraries, and raise operational effectiveness. Data analytics-driven loyalty programs and tailored marketing efforts enable airlines to develop closer bonds with their consumers.

Challenges and Opportunities: Despite the numerous opportunities, the airline industry faces several challenges. Changing fuel prices can have a major effect on running expenses, hence good fuel management and hedging techniques are rather important. Compliance with international aviation standards and legislative changes demand ongoing attention and adaptation. Travel demand and income can be disrupted by world events such pandemics or geopolitical concerns. These difficulties, meantime, also offer chances for development and creativity. To lower their environmental impact, airlines could investigate new markets, increase their route networks, and make investments in sustainable technologies. Airlines can set themselves apart in a crowded industry by welcoming digital revolution and improving consumer experiences.

Market Segmentation

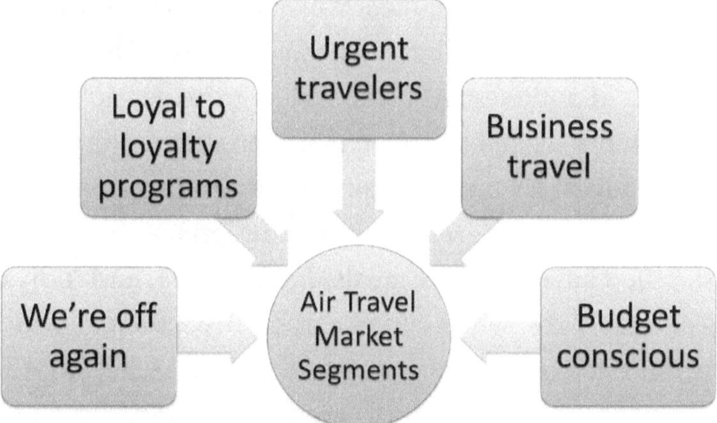

In the aviation sector, market segmentation is the division of the large market into smaller, more controllable customer groups with like wants and preferences. By customizing their offerings to fit the particular needs of various consumer categories, this strategic strategy helps airlines maximize income and customer happiness.

Segmentation Criteria: Airlines typically use various criteria to segment the market, including geographic, demographic, psychographic, and behavioral factors. Geographic segmentation helps airlines to meet local tastes and modify their offerings by separating the market depending on regions, cities, or countries. To fit regional interests, airlines could provide several flight schedules, languages, and in-flight meals. Demographic segmentation is grouping consumers according to age, gender, income, occupation, family size, and so forth. Younger passengers might choose low-cost flights, for instance, whereas those with more money might choose first class. By means of lifestyle, socioeconomic class, and personality qualities, psychographic segmentation enables airlines to target particular groups including adventure seekers, luxury travelers, or environmentally conscientious passengers. By examining consumer behavior—including booking trends, loyalty, and travel frequency—behavioral segmentation helps airlines create focused discounts and loyalty programs.

Examples of Segmentation: Real-world examples of market segmentation in the airline industry highlight its effectiveness. Offering low-cost, basic amenities, Southwest Airlines targets price-sensitive passengers. Their simple and reasonably priced marketing efforts draw consumers on a tighter budget. By contrast, Singapore Airlines seeks after luxury patrons with first-rate facilities and first-rate service. To appeal to high-end guests, they have gourmet meals, lie-flat seats, and individualized service. Delta Air Lines, which serves corporate passengers with its large flight schedule and first-class options including Delta Sky Clubs and priority boarding, is another illustration. Understanding and meeting the particular needs of every segment helps these airlines to efficiently capture and keep their different client groups.

Benefits of Market Segmentation: Market segmentation provides several benefits for airlines. Emphasizing the most profitable client categories, it helps them to better manage resources. Airlines can raise customer loyalty and satisfaction by customizing services and marketing initiatives to particular groups. Segmentation also enables airlines to spot fresh market prospects and create focused campaigns to draw in various clientele. For instance, providing family-friendly packages during holidays for schools can draw more leisure visitors. Moreover, segmentation helps airlines to maximize pricing policies by knowing the price sensitivity of several groups. This strategy guarantees that airlines may satisfy the several wants of their clients and maximize income.

Challenges in Market Segmentation: While market segmentation offers numerous advantages, it also presents challenges. Effective segmentation depends on accurate data collecting and analysis, so major technological and analytical investment is necessary. To keep their segmentation tactics current, airlines have to be constantly observing consumer preferences and market changes. Furthermore, challenging and resource-intensive are creating customized services and marketing strategies for various niches. Another difficult task is ensuring consistency in brand message and service quality over all divisions. Notwithstanding these obstacles, the advantages of market segmentation in raising consumer pleasure and streamlining income must exceed the difficulties.

Marketing Principles to Airline Management

Using the marketing mix—also known as the 4 Ps—Product, Price, Place, and Promotion—applying marketing concepts to airline management is This structure enables airlines to strategically plan and carry out their marketing operations in order to fulfill consumer wants and match corporate objectives.

Marketing Mix (4 Ps): In the context of the airline industry, the Product encompasses the various services offered, including seat classes (economy, business, first), in-flight amenities, and additional services like baggage handling and meal options. Airlines keep developing their products to improve consumer experience: they provide gourmet meals, in-flight Wi-Fi, and lie-flat seats. Price is the pricing schemes airlines apply to draw in various clientele and maximize income. This covers specials deals, discounts, and dynamic pricing. Particularly for low-cost airlines depending on large volume and low margins, competitive pricing is absolutely vital. Place refers to the several ways tickets are sold—that is, via travel agencies, airline websites, mobile apps, and worldwide distribution systems (GDS). Attract and keep clients depend on effective and easy booking systems. Promotion covers all the events meant to convey the value proposition of the airline to the intended market. This can call for loyalty programs, public relations, social media marketing, and advertising.

Product Strategy: Developing a robust product strategy is essential for airlines to meet customer expectations and differentiate themselves in a competitive market. To serve a range of clientele, airlines provide several seat categories: economy, premium economy, business, first class. Every class provides differing degrees of facilities, comfort, and service. For instance, while first class offers opulent seating, gourmet cuisine, and individualized attention, economy class could offer simple seating and minimal amenities. Airlines keep improving their products by including consumer comments and market trends. Airlines improve the travel experience with inventions such lie-flat chairs, in-flight entertainment systems, and connectivity choices. Airlines often provide auxiliary services to increase customer happiness and provide extra income including extra baggage, seat choice, and priority boarding.

Pricing Strategy: Pricing strategies are critical for airlines to attract and retain customers while maximizing revenue. The airline sector makes extensive use of dynamic pricing—that which changes prices depending on demand, competition, and other elements. By billing more during peak times and providing discounts during off-peak hours, this strategy lets airlines maximize income. Early bird discounts encourage customers to book well in advance, therefore guaranteeing better load factors right from start. Last-minute sales appeal to impulsive bargain seekers for travel. To optimize reservations, seasonal deals lineup with peak travel times—that is, holidays and summer vacations. Airlines might also grant discounts to particular groups, like elders, military personnel, students, and members of loyalty programs. Good pricing policies enable airlines strike a balance between consumer satisfaction and profitability.

Place Strategy: The place strategy involves the distribution channels through which airline tickets are sold. Among direct sales channels include call centers, smartphone apps, and airline websites. By avoiding outside commissions, these channels let airlines manage the consumer experience and keep more of the income. Convenient booking, check-in, and customer service choices abound from airline websites and applications. Direct sales also allow airlines to gather priceless consumer information, which can be applied to customize offers and enhance services. Travel agencies, internet travel agencies (OTAs), and global distribution systems (GDS) are among the indirect sales channels. These outlets increase an airline's reach and serve consumers who would rather book via middlemen. Attracting a sizable client base, OTAs such as Expedia and Booking.com provide competitive rates and wide search capability. GDS, like Amadeus and Sabre, link airlines with travel agents and other third parties, therefore enabling bookings and real-time inventory control. Indirect channels are necessary to reach larger markets and boost sales volume even if they entail commission payments.

Promotion Strategy: Effective promotion strategies are crucial for airlines to communicate their value proposition and attract customers. Airlines advertise their offerings using digital marketing, social media, advertising, and public relations among other avenues. Modern campaigns heavily rely on digital marketing—including email newsletters, social media ads, and online travel agency (OTA) listings. Especially for large-scale campaigns, traditional media including print ads, radio, and television can also be rather successful. Limited-time deals and flash sales generate urgency and can cause notable reservations to increase. To increase the impact of their offers, airlines might potentially combine with travel bloggers or other brands. Another important marketing strategy used to keep consumers and promote return business are loyalty programs. For every trip taken, frequent flier programs (FFPs) award points or miles that can be exchanged for various benefits such as future flights and upgrades. Higher degrees of elite membership offer further advantages including greater baggage allowance, lounge access, and priority boarding. To let members earn and spend points across a spectrum of services, loyalty programs can involve alliances with credit card issuers, hotels, and auto rental firms. Customized incentives depending on travel experience and preferences help to increase the value of loyalty programs for consumers even more.

Brand Positioning: Brand positioning is crucial for airlines to differentiate themselves in a crowded market. It entails developing in consumers' thoughts a clear picture and identity. For instance, Ryanair is well-known for its low-cost, no-frills travel choices whereas Emirates bills itself as a premium airline with first-rate comfort and service. Good brand positioning calls for both a thorough awareness of the target market and a consistent message sent across all marketing outlets. By forging an emotional link and a feeling of loyalty, developing a strong brand identity helps draw in and keep consumers. This covers elements like catchphrase, color scheme, and logo that ought to be consistent across all marketing products. Whether the airline's goal is luxury, economy, innovation, or first-rate service, the brand identity should capture that goal.

Customer Relationship Management (CRM): CRM strategies in the airline industry focus on building and maintaining strong relationships with customers. Gathering and evaluating consumer data is part of this process in order to personalize services, raise customer satisfaction, and strengthen loyalty. By tracking consumer interactions, preferences, and comments via CRM systems, airlines enable customized marketing, quick resolution of problems, and a flawless travel experience. CRM is fundamentally based on programs like frequent flier campaigns and special membership incentives, which build loyalty over time and repeat business. Airlines can provide tailored marketing campaigns and customized experiences via better understanding of consumer behavior and preferences obtained by using CRM technologies. Good CRM practices enable airlines to increase customer retention, develop confidence, and stimulate income generation.

Airline Strategies - Fleet Schedule

Crucially important for airline operations and marketing, fleet scheduling affects customer happiness as well as cost effectiveness. Good fleet management guarantees that the correct aircraft are on hand for the correct paths at the correct times.

Fleet Management: Fleet management involves selecting and maintaining a diverse range of aircraft to meet varying operational requirements. From big wide-body jets for long-haul flights to tiny narrow-body planes for regional routes, airlines have to strike a balance between the need for many kinds of aircraft. Fleet choice is much influenced by elements including passenger capacity, maintenance costs, and fuel economy. Safety, dependability, and efficiency depend on regular maintenance as well as timely improvements. Investing in newer, more efficient aircraft helps airlines save costs and environmental impact while constantly evaluating their fleet makeup to fit operational goals and market needs. Using hybrid or electric aircraft technologies can also help with sustainability objectives by lowering the carbon footprint of the airline and drawing in ecologically minded consumers.

Route Planning and Scheduling: Route planning and scheduling are about optimizing flight paths and timetables to maximize revenue and meet customer demand. To map their paths, airlines examine information on passenger flows, market trends, and competitor actions. Scheduling has to take into account seasonal fluctuations, peak travel times, and connecting flights to provide consumers easy choices. Modern software technologies enable airlines to replicate several situations and select the most profitable and effective paths. Airlines may save running costs, boost on-time performance, and raise customer happiness by besting flight schedules. Dynamic scheduling also relies on real-time data analytics and artificial intelligence, which let airlines modify routes and schedules in response to shifting circumstances including disruptions in the weather or unanticipated demand spikes.

Capacity Management: Managing seat capacity is vital for maximizing load factors and profitability. Revenue management systems let airlines dynamically change seat availability and price depending on demand trends. Though contentious, overbooking techniques are used to guarantee that planes run at maximum capacity given the possibility of no-show customers. Good capacity control enables airlines to maximize income and lower the empty seat related expenses. Airlines also use last-minute discounts and frequent flier upgrades to cover remaining seats, therefore guaranteeing best use of the capacity at hand. Good capacity control also entails adjusting seat layouts to suit several passenger types and their differing demand levels.

Sustainability and Innovation: Scheduling and fleet management are starting to give sustainability more significance. To reduce their environmental effect, airlines are funding alternative fuels, carbon offset initiatives, and fuel-efficient aircraft. Aircraft technological innovations including lighter materials and more effective engines help to support environmental efforts. To lower emissions even farther, airlines are also investigating hybrid and electric planes. Airlines not only help to preserve the environment by giving sustainability first priority but also satisfy regulatory needs and attract environmentally minded passengers.

Travel Agency Collaboration

Serving as middlemen between airlines and customers, travel agencies are absolutely vital in the airline business. They book, give travel tips, and sometimes offer combined services including flights, lodging, and other travel-related services. Working with travel agencies will help an airline's reach and sales to be much improved.

Role of Travel Agencies: Travel agencies help airlines by reaching a broader audience, particularly those travelers who prefer booking through a third party rather than directly with the airline. They can improve the client experience by offering individualized services, meeting challenging travel needs, and helping with trip planning. By encouraging these choices to their customers, agencies also assist airlines to fill tickets on less popular routes or during off-peak hours. For many consumers, particularly those organizing intricate itineraries or group travel, travel agents serve as reliable consultants. Travel agencies also add value to the consumer experience by offering auxiliary services including local tour plans, travel insurance, and visa help.

Partnership Models: Airlines can partner with travel agencies through various models. Under conventional commission-based agreements, airlines pay travel companies a percentage of each ticket sold. This motivates organizations to aggressively advertise the airline's offerings. The net fare agreement is another strategy whereby airlines give travel companies discounted net fares so that they may mark-up before offering to consumers. In return for committed sales campaigns, several airlines also form exclusive alliances with a small number of agencies, giving them access to premium services and discounted pricing. These alliances could comprise collaborative promotional events and co-branded marketing initiatives. Airlines may also sign preferred partner agreements, in which case travel agents promise to reach specific sales targets in return for increased commissions or special advantages.

Commission Structures: Travel agency commission structures can differ greatly. Usually ranging from 5% to 10% of the ticket price, standard commissions might rise depending on premium services or group bookings. Performance-based incentives—that is, larger commissions or bonuses depending on sales volume or target attainment—may also be available by airlines. This arrangement helps travel agencies give the airline's offerings top priority over rivals. Performance-based incentives could be tie-red commission rates, bonuses for meeting sales targets, and special benefits for top-performing agencies. Airlines may also provide agencies marketing support cash to help them advertise their offerings, therefore deepening the relationship.

Benefits for Travel Agencies and Airlines: Cooperation between them benefits both of them. Working with travel agents can help airlines boost bookings, particularly in markets where the airline has no direct presence. Access to a greater spectrum of airline choices for their customers helps travel firms to be able to provide more complete travel packages. By using travel agency marketing reach and client relationships, this cooperation helps airlines also improve their brand visibility and market penetration. Travel agents then benefit from the credibility and confidence connected with reputable airlines, which facilitates client attraction and retention. Airlines and travel companies can also together create loyalty programs, providing combined advantages that improve consumer happiness and retention.

Technological Integration: With the advent of digital platforms, airlines and travel agencies are increasingly integrating their systems to streamline bookings and improve customer service. This integration is much enhanced by global distribution systems (GDS), which give real-time access to aircraft itineraries, availability, and pricing. Airlines and travel firms may provide flawless booking experiences, lower running inefficiencies, and improve data exchange for improved consumer insights by using GDS and other digital tools. Offering consumers the ease of comparing and buying flights from many airlines on one platform, online travel agents (OTAs) have likewise transformed the travel booking process.

Group Bookings

Representing a sizable portion of airline revenue, group bookings serve corporate passengers, sports teams, tour groups, and other sizable events. These arrangements include particular considerations and procedures to guarantee a seamless and quick travel experience for every group member.

Definition and Benefits: Group bookings are typically defined as bookings made for ten or more passengers traveling together on the same flight. For airlines, the main advantage is the certain sale of a significant number of seats—often months in advance—which facilitates revenue control and planning. Group bookings give consumers financial savings through discounts and the convenience of well planned travel. Events like conferences, family get-togethers, and school trips—where the practicalities of handling individual bookings might be challenging— group travel is especially appealing. Group bookings' predictability helps airlines to better plan their capacity and allocate their resources.

Booking Process: The group booking process begins with a request for a quote, detailing the number of passengers, travel dates, and specific requirements. Usually giving individualized help and terms, airlines have a specialist group booking crew to address these requests. Once a quote is approved, the group booking is verified with a deposit, and the last passenger information is sent more to the departure date. Often given to suit group planners are flexible payment periods and deadlines. This procedure guarantees that groups have the required cooperation and assistance to move together perfectly. To improve the trip experience, the group booking staff may also help with unique needs such meal preferences, seating choices, and baggage limitations.

Group Travel Packages: Airlines offer various group travel packages tailored to different needs. These packages could call for extra services such as baggage handling, priority boarding, and specialized check-in counters. Packages could provide corporate groups improved conveniences including inflight services and lounge access. Bundled offers including ground transportation and lodging, coordinated through hotel and travel agency relationships, could help tour companies. Customizable packages guarantee a customized travel experience by letting group planners choose the services most fit for their needs. Student groups might have instructional trip packages, for instance, while sports teams can have specific baggage allowances for their gear.

Challenges and Opportunities: Managing group bookings can present challenges, such as coordinating multiple itineraries, handling last-minute changes, and ensuring that all group members receive consistent service. Group bookings, however, also give airlines chances to establish close links with travel brokers, business customers, and event planners. Airlines may raise customer satisfaction and loyalty by offering first-rate service and assistance for group travel, therefore fostering repeat business and good referrals. Group bookings also enable airlines to fill tickets during off-peak, therefore optimizing capacity utilization and income control.

Technology in Group Bookings: The way group bookings are handled using technology has greatly expedited the process. Online tools let group planners easily make payments, handle passenger information, and ask for rates. These systems let airlines interact with group planners, give updates, and offer help all through the booking process. Complicated group travel plans can be handled by advanced booking systems, therefore guaranteeing that every passenger is accommodated effectively and that any adjustments go without incident.

These technological solutions improve the whole experience for the passengers and the airlines, thereby facilitating group travel and management of it.

Discounts & Offers

One of the main ways airlines draw in and keep passengers is by running discounts and special offers. These incentives can support new routes, help to fill seats during off-peak, and foster customer loyalty.

Types of Discounts: Airlines offer a range of discounts to appeal to different customer segments. Early bird discounts encourage customers to book well in advance, therefore guaranteeing better load factors right from start. Last-minute sales appeal to impulsive bargain seekers for travel. To optimize reservations, seasonal deals lineup with peak travel times—that is, holidays and summer vacations. Airlines might also grant discounts to particular groups, including elders, military personnel, students, and loyalty program members. For corporate clients and frequent visitors, special offers could also be accessible, offering further incentives for returning business. To meet the several needs of guests, other discount forms include family packages, weekend trips, and special event promos.

Promotional Campaigns: Effective promotional campaigns combine various marketing channels to reach potential customers. Modern campaigns heavily rely on digital marketing—including email newsletters, social media ads, and online travel agency (OTA) listings. Especially for large-scale campaigns, traditional media including print ads, radio, and television can also be rather successful. Limited-time deals and flash sales generate urgency and can cause notable reservations to increase. To improve the reach and effect of their offers, airlines might potentially combine with other businesses or travel bloggers. Credit card firms, hotels, and auto rental businesses working together can give consumers more value and boost the appeal of the offerings.

Loyalty Programs: Loyalty programs are a cornerstone of airline marketing strategies, designed to retain customers and encourage repeat business. For every trip taken, frequent flier programs (FFPs) award points or miles that can be exchanged for various benefits such as future flights and upgrades. Higher degrees of elite membership offer further advantages including greater baggage allowance, lounge access, and priority boarding. To let members earn and spend points across a spectrum of services, loyalty programs can involve alliances with credit card issuers, hotels, and auto rental firms. Customized incentives depending on travel experience and preferences help to increase the value of loyalty programs for consumers even more. Airlines can create closer bonds and boost long-term profitability by honoring consumer loyalty.

Impact of Discounts on Revenue Management: While discounts and offers can attract more customers, they must be carefully managed to ensure they do not negatively impact overall revenue. Revenue management systems enable airlines to maximize income by helping them to balance the demand to fill seats with their needs. To maximize the availability and price of discounted fares, these systems examine demand estimates, booking trends, and competitive pricing. Airlines can increase their profitability and market share by carefully controlling discounts, so preserving consumer pleasure. Good utilization of discounts also entails segmenting offers to target particular client groups, so guaranteeing the relevance and attraction of promotions.

Case Studies and Examples: Practical knowledge of effective discount techniques could be rather insightful. For instance, Southwest Airlines frequently employs flash discounts to rapidly fill tickets, therefore inducing consumer urgency. Conversely, Emirates provides users of its Skywards loyalty program special discounts and advantages, thus building enduring customer ties. By means of analysis of these case studies, airlines can better grasp the finest methods in applying discounts and promotional offers, thereby guaranteeing their desired results.

Technology in Managing Discounts: Management and optimization of discounts depend much on advanced technology. To examine data, forecast demand, and dynamically change pricing, airlines employ complex revenue management systems. These systems let airlines provide individualized discounts and promotions depending on booking patterns and consumer preferences. Furthermore, digital marketing channels let airlines use tailored offers to reach a large audience, therefore improving the success of their promotional operations.

Combining artificial intelligence and machine learning improves the capacity to customize offers to certain consumers, hence boosting interaction and conversion rates.

Brand Building Strategies

Differentiating themselves in a very competitive industry requires airlines to develop a strong brand. By establishing an emotional connection and loyalty, a well-defined brand identification helps draw in and keep consumers.

Brand Identity: Developing a brand identity involves defining what the airline stands for, its core values, and its unique selling propositions. This covers elements like the catchphrase, color palette, and logo—all of which should be consistent throughout all marketing tools. Whether the airline's goal is luxury, affordability, innovation, or first-rate service, the brand identity should capture that. For instance, Ryanair is well-known for its low-cost, no-frills travel choices; Emirates is associated with luxury and first-rate service. Furthermore included in a good brand identity are the airline's principles and culture, which should appeal to consumers as well as staff.

Marketing Communications: Effective marketing communications are critical to building and maintaining a strong brand. Airlines convey their brand message via direct marketing, social media, public relations, and advertising among other methods. Consistent, interesting material helps to maintain brand identification top-of-mind for consumers and reinforce it. Using client testimonials, behind-the-scenes films, and striking images to craft a compelling tale, storytelling may be especially potent. Furthermore improving company trust and visibility is cooperation with travel bloggers and celebrities. Content marketing techniques include blogs, travel guides, and location highlights can assist the airline project travel industry authority.

Customer Experience: The customer experience is a key component of brand building. From booking to boarding and beyond, every contact with the airline should represent the brand values and fulfill the brand promise. This covers easy-to-use websites and applications, quick check-in and boarding procedures, cozy seating, first-rate in-flight services, and prompt customer service. Airlines who regularly offer a good customer experience develop great brand loyalty and gain from good word-of-mouth and repeat business. Maintaining and improving the customer experience depends on constant development grounded on user comments. By means of staff training and development, one guarantees that staff members represent the brand values and provide outstanding service at every level of interaction.

Community Engagement and Corporate Social Responsibility (CSR): Engaging with the community and demonstrating corporate social responsibility are important aspects of brand building. By helping social issues, attending community activities, and using sustainable methods, airlines can strengthen their brand reputation. Customers find resonance in initiatives like lowering carbon emissions, helping nearby businesses, and advancing diversity and inclusion, therefore strengthening brand relationships. To further JetBlue's dedication to social responsibility, the "JetBlue For Good" program, for instance, emphasizes young people and education, community, and the environment.

Consistency Across Touchpoints: Consistency is crucial in brand building. From commercials to in-flight announcements, every point of contact with a customer should transmit a consistent brand message. This guarantees that, independent of their interaction with the airline, consumers view the brand in one whole. Customers know what to anticipate from the brand, hence consistency also fosters trust. For example, Singapore Airlines is well-known for its first-rate service and opulent experience; it consistently meets its brand promise in every customer contact.

Selling & Distribution Channels

Airlines must optimize sales by reaching their target market by means of efficient selling and distribution policies. Using a multi-channel strategy guarantees that airlines can satisfy the several tastes of their clients.

Direct Sales Channels: Direct sales channels include airline websites, mobile apps, and call centers. By avoiding outside commissions, these channels let airlines manage the consumer experience and keep more of the income. Convenient booking, check-in, and customer service choices abound from airline websites and applications. Direct sales also allow airlines to gather priceless consumer information, which can be applied to customize offers and enhance services. For consumers who would want to speak with an agent or who need help with complicated itineraries, call centers offer a personal touch. Airlines can improve the booking process and establish direct contacts with their consumers by providing flawless and easy digital platforms.

Indirect Sales Channels: Indirect sales channels include travel agencies, online travel agencies (OTAs), and global distribution systems (GDS). These outlets increase the reach of an airline and serve those who would rather book via middlemen. Attracting a sizable client base, OTAs such as Expedia and Booking.com provide competitive rates and wide search capability. GDS, like Amadeus and Sabre, link airlines with travel agents and other third parties, therefore enabling bookings and real-time inventory control. Although indirect channels pay commission fees, they are necessary for reaching larger customers and raising sales volume. Further driving notable business travel reservations are alliances with corporate travel agencies.

Global Distribution Systems (GDS): GDS are critical tools for airlines, enabling them to distribute their inventory to a wide range of travel agents and OTAs globally. By giving flight schedules, availability, and pricing real-time access, these systems enable travel agencies to give consumers reliable information. To further improve the whole booking experience, GDS also assists with auxiliary services including seat choice, baggage options, and in-flight entertainment. Airlines can reach more people and simplify their distribution systems by combining with GDS. Moreover, GDS systems include analytics and reporting capabilities to enable airlines track performance and maximize their distribution plans.

Dynamic Packaging and Ancillary Revenue: Dynamic packaging, which allows customers to bundle flights with other travel services such as hotels and car rentals, is an effective strategy to increase sales and enhance customer convenience. To present appealing package offers, airlines can team with hotels, car rental firms, and other travel agencies. This improves sales as well as offers consumers a flawless travel experience. An airline's profitability is much enhanced by auxiliary income sources such luggage fees, seat choices, in-flight purchases. Offering a range of auxiliary services will help airlines optimize income and satisfy varied consumer tastes.

Channel Management and Optimization: Effective channel management involves balancing the use of direct and indirect sales channels to optimize revenue and customer reach. Airlines have to keep assessing every channel's success under consideration of cost, reach, and customer happiness. By means of a strong channel management strategy, airlines may guarantee efficient distribution of their goods and services while preserving control over price and client contacts. Using data analytics to grasp consumer preferences, track industry trends, and modify plans is how one optimizes channel performance.

Technology and Innovation in Distribution: Technological developments have completely changed airline policies. Airlines are improving their distribution procedures by using big data, machine learning, and artificial intelligence. Airlines can provide their consumers customized solutions by means of predictive analytics, dynamic pricing and personalized marketing. Blockchain technology is also becoming a possible fix for security and openness in the distribution process. Airlines can keep ahead of the competitors and provide first-rate consumer experiences by using creative technologies. For instance, virtual assistants and chatbots offer 24/7 customer service, therefore improving the booking process and instantly answering questions.

Challenges and Future Trends: While effective distribution strategies offer numerous benefits, they also present challenges. Control of several distribution channels can be challenging and resource- demanding. Maintaining constant price and availability across all media calls for advanced systems and coordination. Besides, the emergence of digital channels and shifting consumer behavior need for constant adaptation and creativity. Rising use of mobile platforms, integration of augmented reality for improved customer experiences, and more attention on sustainability in travel options define future trends in airline distribution.

Airlines who aggressively adopt these trends and make technological investments will be more suited to satisfy changing expectations of their clients.

GSA - Structure & Functions

Particularly in areas where airlines have no direct presence, General Sales Agents (GSAs) are absolutely vital in the aviation sector. Dealing with sales, marketing, and customer service, GSAs represent airlines. By using an alliance, airlines can increase their sales efforts and reach without paying the expenses related to creating and preserving a full-scale operational presence.

Definition of GSA: A General Sales Agent (GSA) is an independent entity that acts on behalf of an airline in a specific region or country. Promoting the airline's offerings, ticket sales, and customer service fall to GSAs. Operating under a contractual arrangement with the airline, they have obligations, commission structures, and performance goals defined. Usually established travel agencies with great awareness of the local market and solid ties to travel brokers, corporate clients, and other stakeholders, GSAs are well-known travel organizations.

Functions of GSA: The primary functions of a GSA include sales, marketing, and customer support. Regarding sales, GSAs are in charge of reaching the airline's specified targets. They actively advertise the airline's offerings to corporate clients, travel agents, and individual passengers. Development and execution of marketing initiatives to raise brand recognition and generate bookings constitute part of marketing activities. This covers using many promotional outlets, running roadshows, and attending travel fairs. Customer service covers answering questions, fixing problems, and offering details on policies, rates, and travel itineraries. Along with doing administrative chores such ticket issuing, payment processing, and record keeping, GSAs also oversee

Sales and Marketing: In their respective areas, GSAs are quite helpful for motivating sales and marketing initiatives. They aggressively advertise the airline's offerings using their established networks and local market expertise. This entails developing customized marketing plans that appeal to local consumers and leverage regional travel patterns. Negotiating contracts with corporate clients and travel agencies also heavily relies on GSAs to guarantee reasonable terms and competitive rates that increase sales. Through planning advertising campaigns and attending trade shows, GSAs increase the airline's profile and encourage direct interaction with possible consumers.

Customer Support and Service: Providing excellent customer support is a critical function of GSAs. Customer initial point of contact, they answer questions, handle complaints, and provide bookings and other travel-related help. By guaranteeing accurate and timely knowledge of the airline's offerings, GSAs help to increase customer loyalty and satisfaction. To guarantee a flawless travel experience for every traveler, they also manage unique needs including group bookings, special meals, and accessibility services.

Administrative and Operational Functions: GSAs handle various administrative and operational tasks to support the airline's operations in their region. This covers keeping thorough records of transactions, handling returns, and ticket sales management. For strategic decisions, GSAs also track consumer preferences, competition behavior, and market situations, therefore offering the airline insightful information. They also guarantee industry standards and local rule compliance, therefore preserving the operational integrity and reputation of the airline.

Benefits of Using GSA: For airlines, working with GSAs presents a number of advantages. It lets airlines enter new markets without having to physically be there, so lowering administrative load and expenses. Local market knowledge and established ties with travel agencies and corporate clients enable GSAs to improve sales and customer service by means of their expertise. GSAs also give airlines flexibility so they may vary their operations depending on demand in the market. To maximize bookings, GSAs can, for example, intensify advertising campaigns and boost sales activity during busiest travel seasons.

Challenges and Best Practices: While GSAs offer numerous advantages, managing GSA relationships can be challenging. Clear communication, frequent performance assessments, and good teamwork will help the airline to be in line with the actions of the GSA. Airlines have to provide GSAs the tools, knowledge, and support they need to properly and powerfully represent the brand. Setting clear performance criteria, providing incentives for either meeting or surpassing goals, and keeping open lines of contact to quickly handle any problems help to best manage GSA partnerships.

Revenue Sharing Between GSA and Airline

A major component of their relationship is the financial arrangement between airlines and GSAs, which influences operational efficiency as well as income generating. Good performance-based incentives and revenue-sharing systems guarantee that both sides gain from the cooperation.

Revenue Models: Different revenue-sharing models are used in GSA agreements, depending on the airline's strategy and market conditions. The most often used model is the commission-based one in which the GSA gets paid a percentage of the sales they bring about. The type of service—economy vs. business class—and the volume of sales will affect this commission. Another approach is the fixed fee schedule, in which case the GSA gets a set amount for their work independent of sales volume. For airlines, this approach offers cost stability; nevertheless, it does not encourage the GSA to optimize sales. To balance risk and reward, some airlines utilize a hybrid model—that is, a base price combined with performance-based commissions.

Commission-Based Models: In commission-based models, the GSA's earnings are directly tied to their performance, aligning their incentives with the airline's sales objectives. Often granted for meeting or surpassing sales targets, higher commissions inspire GSAs to give the airline top priority. Bonuses for reaching particular benchmarks and performance-based incentives help GSAs be even more motivated to boost sales and enhance customer service. A GSA might, for instance, get more commissions for selling premium tickets or for reaching a specific percentage increase in sales over last year.

Fixed Fee Models: Fixed fee models provide stability and predictability for both the airline and the GSA. Under this approach, independent of sales volume, the GSA gets a flat price for their services. In markets with erratic or challenging to forecast revenues, this strategy can help. It might not, however, encourage the GSA to optimize sales or follow bold marketing plans. Airlines could thus include performance bonuses or other incentives into the fixed fee schedule to guarantee that GSAs stay motivated to reach high sales success.

Hybrid Models: Hybrid models combine elements of both commission-based and fixed fee arrangements, offering a balanced approach to revenue sharing. Under a hybrid arrangement, the GSA pays a flat fee to cover running expenses and gets extra commissions contingent on sales performance. This approach motivates the GSA to accomplish performance goals and boost sales while yet giving them financial stability. In markets with changing demand, hybrid models can be especially successful since they guarantee both the airline and the GSA gain from high sales performance while reducing financial risks during slower times.

Performance-Based Incentives: Performance-based incentives are designed to reward GSAs for exceptional performance and achieving strategic goals. Based on criteria including sales volume, market share, and customer happiness, these incentives could be extra commissions, bonuses, and other financial benefits. Performance-based incentives help to drive a proactive, results-oriented approach to sales and marketing by matching the incentives of the GSA with the goals of the airline. GSAs might, for example, get bonuses for introducing new paths or having excellent customer satisfaction ratings.

Challenges in Revenue Sharing: Revenue-sharing arrangements can present challenges, including disputes over commission rates, performance metrics, and payment terms. Preventing misunderstandings and guaranteeing flawless cooperation depend on clear, open agreements. Open communication and frequent performance reviews enable quick resolution of any problems and preservation of a friendly working relationship. Furthermore, both sides have to be adaptable and ready to amend the terms of the agreement depending on the state of the market so that the cooperation stays mutually advantageous.

Best Practices for Revenue Sharing: Effective revenue-sharing models require careful planning and management. Clear, quantifiable performance benchmarks, competitive commissions and incentives, and open, timely payment systems are among best practices. Regular feedback and support from airlines should help GSAs to raise their performance and meet their goals. Using data analytics will also enable both sides to monitor performance, spot areas needing work, and make wise judgments. Developing a cooperative and encouraging relationship with GSAs guarantees long-term success for the airline as well as for the GSA and builds trust.

Case Studies and Examples: Examining actual cases of successful GSA alliances can help one gain important understanding about appropriate revenue-sharing strategies. In certain areas, for example, British Airways has effectively teamed with GSAs utilizing a mix of fixed fees and performance-based incentives to increase sales and improve customer experience. Likewise, Emirates has used its GSA network to increase its worldwide presence by providing appealing commissions and support meant to guarantee robust sales success. These case studies show how important adaptable and orderly revenue-sharing systems are to reaching shared success.

Chapter 8

Frequent Flier Program

Membership Benefits

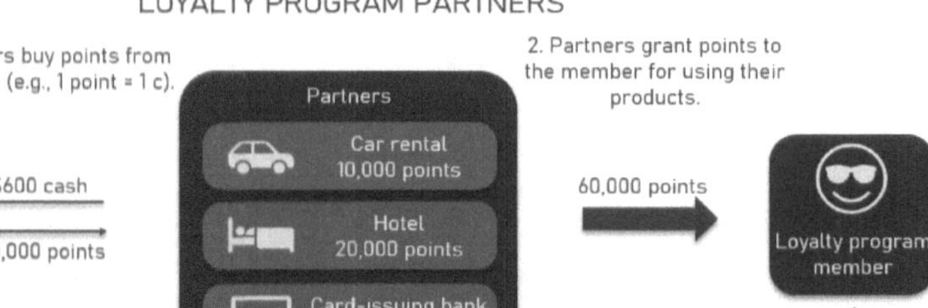

Frequent Flier Programs (FFPs) are designed to reward loyal customers and encourage repeat business. These programs offer a range of benefits that enhance the travel experience and provide added value to members. Membership benefits vary depending on the airline and the tier of membership, with higher tiers offering more exclusive perks. This section explores the various membership tiers, the benefits associated with each level, the enrollment process, and the value these benefits bring to members.

Introduction to Membership Tiers: Most FFPs have multiple membership tiers that reflect the loyalty and travel frequency of the member. Common tiers include Silver, Gold, and Platinum, although the names and number of tiers can vary by airline. Entry-level members typically start at the base tier, with opportunities to progress to higher tiers through accumulated travel miles or points.

For example, an airline might structure its FFP as follows:

- **Silver Tier:** The entry-level tier, accessible to all new members upon signing up.

- **Gold Tier**: A mid-level tier, attainable after accruing a certain number of miles or segments flown.

- **Platinum Tier**: The highest standard tier, reserved for the most frequent travelers with the airline.

Higher tiers often come with increasing benefits, encouraging members to maintain their loyalty to the airline to achieve and retain these status levels.

General Benefits: All members of frequent flier programs, regardless of tier, enjoy a range of basic benefits designed to enhance their travel experience. These can include priority check-in, which lets members avoid typical check-in lines, therefore saving airport time. Extra baggage allowances that members get help them to travel with more bags without paying extra fees. Common exclusive discounts on flights, hotel stays, car rentals, and other travel-related charges also abound, so saving money and offering further convenience.

Access to exclusive member-only specials, early notice of sales, and the option to accumulate points or miles not only on flights but also on purchases made through partner businesses such hotels, car rental companies, and retail stores would be other overall advantages. Members of this extensive network of partners can earn a range of benefits and rapidly collect points.

Tier-Specific Benefits: As members advance to higher tiers within an FFP, they gain access to more exclusive and valuable benefits. Every level builds on the benefits of the one before it offers more incentives for regular passengers.

- **Silver Tier Benefits**: Besides the general benefits, Silver tier members might receive modest upgrades such as complimentary seat selection and priority boarding, allowing them to board the aircraft earlier than standard passengers and secure their preferred seats and overhead bin space.

- **Gold Tier Benefits**: Gold members typically enjoy enhanced benefits, such as access to airport lounges, which offer a comfortable and quiet environment to relax or work before a flight. They may also receive additional baggage allowances, expedited security screening, and priority boarding and check-in, further streamlining their airport experience. Moreover, Gold members often have access to a dedicated customer service line for quicker and more personalized support.

- **Platinum Tier Benefits**: Platinum members receive the highest level of service and benefits. These may include guaranteed seat availability on fully booked flights, complimentary upgrades to premium cabins, and invitations to exclusive events hosted by the airline. Platinum members often enjoy the highest priority for check-in, boarding, and baggage handling, ensuring a seamless travel experience. Additionally, they may receive substantial bonuses on miles earned per flight, accelerating their accumulation of points for future rewards.

Enrollment Process: Joining an FFP is typically straightforward and free. Prospective members can sign up at the airport, via a smartphone app, or on the airline website. The enrollment process calls for simple personal data including name, phone number, and passport information. Members who enroll get a special membership number, which they have to use when making airline bookings to guarantee they accrue points for their trip.

Members must accumulate a designated amount of miles or segments flown inside a calendar year to advance through the membership levels.

Certain airlines also take flight expenditure into account overall. Every airline has rules and thresholds for moving up to more elite levels. Through the airline's website or app, members can monitor their development by seeing their present tier, total miles, and eligibility for the next tier.

Value of Membership Benefits: FFPs give members real savings and improve their whole travel experience, therefore adding great value. While greater luggage allowances remove the anxiety of overpacking and additional expenses, priority check-in and boarding help to save time at the airport. Often with free food, beverages, and Wi-Fi, lounge access offers a pleasant and efficient setting.

Special discounts and promotions help to make travel more reasonably priced; meanwhile, the option to accumulate points on different purchases speeds up the benefits accumulation. Members save significantly by redeeming their points for free flights, seat upgrades, hotel stays, car rentals, and other travel-related expenses.

Higher tiers—such as faster security, dedicated customer service, and assured seat availability—translate into a better, more efficient, more fun travel experience for regular travelers. Long-haul flights are more pleasant when complementary improvements to premium cabins provide more comfort and luxury.

Enhanced Customer Loyalty: Frequent flier programs are designed not only to reward travelers but also to foster customer loyalty. Flights inspire consumers to consolidate their travel with one carrier or alliance instead of distributing their travel among several flights by offering a defined road of increasing perks. The airline gains from repeat business and the client gets a progressively improved travel experience; both of which depend on this loyalty.

Airlines heavily fund their FFPs since devoted consumers often spend more, are less price-sensitive, and offer priceless word-of-mouth advertising. Additionally more likely to engage in extra revenue-generating activities are loyal members who buy ancillary services, book through travel partners connected to airlines, and renew annual memberships for further perks.

Additional Perks for Long-term Members: Airlines often recognize and reward long-term loyalty by offering special perks to members who have been with the FFP for many years. Among these benefits could be lifetime elite status, extra bonus miles, and exclusive invites to airline events. Since it ensures that members retain their elite advantages independent of their travel frequency in next years, lifetime status is very useful.

Customized Benefits and Personalization: With the advent of big data and advanced analytics, airlines are increasingly able to offer personalized benefits and promotions to their FFP members. Airlines can customize their offers to particular members by examining travel habits, preferences, and purchasing history, improving the relevance and appeal of the rewards. For instance, a member who regularly visits a given location might get discounts on nearby hotels or special offers on flights to that site.

Customized messages, such as birthday wishes and unique holiday incentives, can help to create a closer emotional link between the user and the airline, therefore supporting loyalty.

Integration with Airline Alliances: Many airlines are part of global alliances, such as Star Alliance, Oneworld, and SkyTeam. Usually spanning the whole alliance network, membership in an FFP gives members consistent experience and access to rewards when flying with partner airlines. This integration provides a greater spectrum of locations, more chances to earn and redeem points, and access to lounges and amenities across several airlines, therefore improving the value of the FFP.

When flying with any of the Star Alliance member airlines, a Platinum member of an airline in the network can, for instance, receive priority services, lounge access, and other exclusive advantages. This increases the attraction of the FFP and motivates members to select alliance partners depending on their travel requirements.

Case Studies of Successful FFPs: Examining successful FFPs provides insights into best practices and the benefits of well-designed programs. For example, Delta Air Lines' SkyMiles program is much praised for its tier-specific incentives that improve the travel experience, thorough partner network, and generous earning and redemption rules. Comparably, the Emirates Skywards program is well-known for its opulent offerings, which include free chauffeur services, large lounge access, and valuable redemption choices.

These case examples underline the need of adaptability, customer-centric design, and ongoing improvement in building a successful FFP. They also show how effectively well-executed FFPs may support revenue development, brand distinctiveness, and customer loyalty.

Future Trends in FFPs: FFPs are adjusting to fit evolving consumer expectations and technology improvements as the airline sector develops. More dynamic and flexible redemption choices will be part of future FFP developments so members may utilize their points for a greater spectrum of services and experiences. For members, integrating with digital wallets and mobile payment systems helps to simplify the earning and redemption procedure, therefore increasing their convenience.

Many tourists are starting to give sustainability first priority, hence FFPs could include environmentally friendly projects including letting members utilize points for carbon offset programs or supporting environmental causes. Using artificial intelligence and machine learning can also improve personalization and provide members highly customized rewards and promotions suitable for their tastes and activities.

Ultimately, frequent flier programs are mostly based on membership advantages, which greatly value passengers and promote customer loyalty. FFPs inspire recurring business and a strong emotional link between the airline and its patrons by providing a disciplined road of rising advantages. Airlines will remain a key instrument for increasing customer interaction, contentment, and long-term loyalty as they keep innovating and improving their FFPs.

Airline Services for FFP Members

Frequent Flier Programs (FFPs) cover a wide range of services meant to improve the travel experience for devoted consumers, not only about accumulating miles and redeeming incentives. These companies provide efficiency, comfort, and convenience tailored especially for the demands of regular passengers. This part looks at the special deals, priority services, committed customer support, and promotions accessible to FFP members.

Dedicated Customer Service: One of the key benefits of being an FFP member is access to dedicated customer service. Airlines know that frequent travelers often need rapid and effective help to handle their intricate travel plans. FFP members—especially those at higher levels—are thus given special customer service lines that give their calls top priority and guarantee speedier response times. Customized assistance with booking flights, itinerary changes, and problem resolution constitutes part of dedicated client care. FFP members can get in touch with well-trained dedicated service agents to meet the particular needs of regular travelers. This tailored approach covers help with missing bags, priority wait-listing for completely booked flights, and quick management of travel interruptions. Airlines make sure that their most devoted passengers get quick and effective help by offering this degree of care, therefore lowering stress and improving the whole trip experience.

Priority Services: Priority services are a hallmark of FFP membership, offering significant advantages in terms of convenience and time-saving. Designed to simplify frequent passengers' travel experience, these services include priority check-in, priority boarding, and priority baggage handling. By using dedicated check-in counters, priority check-in lets FFP members fast complete the check-in process and avoid waits. During busy travel times when airports are packed and wait times are lengthy, this advantage is especially appreciated. In addition to saving time, priority check-in helps to lower stress and guarantees a better beginning of the trip. By allowing FFP members to board the aircraft ahead of other passengers, priority boarding guarantees that they have plenty of time to settle into their seats, store their carry-on bags, and get ready for the journey free from the rush and inconvenience of general boarding. Priority boarding for business or first class generally consists in dedicated boarding lanes, therefore improving the convenience and uniqueness of the experience. Priority baggage handling is among the most valued conveniences for frequent travelers. The checked bags of FFP members are tagged for quick handling, therefore making sure they are among the first to arrive at the baggage claim area. Particularly helpful for business visitors who must swiftly move to their next activities, this service greatly lowers waiting time at the destination.

Special Offers and Promotions: Airlines frequently extend special offers and promotions exclusively to FFP members. These deals are meant to add more value and boost frequent passengers' loyalty. Discount airfare, bonus miles, and special access to limited-time deals can all be part of special promotions. Many times, discounted flights are given to FFP members so they might cut travel expenses. For devoted travelers, these savings apply to both domestic and foreign flights, therefore making travel more reasonably priced. Another frequent incentive are bonus miles, which let members achieve reward levels sooner and quickly collect miles. Exclusive sales provide FFP members early access to unique offers and promotions before they are made public. Early access guarantees members' favorite travel dates and destinations can be secured as well as their benefit from the greatest offers.

Enhanced In-Flight Services: FFP members often enjoy enhanced in-flight services that make their journey more comfortable and enjoyable. These services can call for extra baggage allowances, unique meal options, and free upgrades. A very appreciated advantage are complimentary upgrades, which let FFP members enjoy the comfort and luxury of higher-class cabins without paying extra for them. Higher tiers of members often have access to these upgrades, which are subject to availability. Special meal options guarantee that FFP members' dietary preferences and demands are met, therefore assuring a customized and pleasurable in-flight dining experience. Greater baggage allowances give members the freedom to travel with larger bags, therefore meeting their demands for both short and long travels.

Access to Exclusive Airport Lounges: One of the most coveted benefits of FFP membership is access to exclusive airport lounges. Before their trip, members of these lounges can relax, work, or enjoy a meal in a peaceful and opulent surroundings. Usually including business centers, fast Wi-Fi, comfortable seating, and a range of food and drinks, lounges are Certain lounges may have extras including private conference rooms, showers, and spa treatments. Usually restricted for members in higher categories or those boarding premium cabins, lounge access is Although airport and airline will determine their availability, lounges are usually found at important hubs and main points of interest.

Priority for Improvements and Award Seats: FFP members frequently get first choice for improvements and award seats. This implies, particularly in busy travel times, customers are more likely to get an award seat or an upgrade to a higher-class cabin using their miles. Usually allocating a specific number of seats for upgrades and award travel, airlines assign more priority to FFP members in higher tiers. This advantage guarantees that devoted consumers enjoy a better travel experience and have access to the most desired benefits.

Additional Partner Benefits: Many FFPs have partnerships with other airlines, hotels, car rental companies, and various service providers. These alliances give members a complete variety of privileges, therefore transcending the advantages of FFP membership beyond air travel. Members might get, for instance, free car rental days, reduced hotel prices, and retail partner special offers. These extra advantages increase the whole value of the FFP and attract more frequent visitors looking for savings and convenience all through their travel experience.

Personalized Services and Benefits: Airlines are increasingly leveraging technology to provide personalized services and benefits to FFP members. Airlines can customize their products to particular consumers by examining information on travel habits, preferences, and buying behavior. Targeted promotions, birthday wishes, and special offers—personalized communications—help you establish a more interesting and significant relationship with members. This personalization also applies to in-flight services, whereby the cabin crew may provide customized greetings and service upon learning of a member's preferences.

Expedited Security Screening: Another valuable service for FFP members is expedited security screening. This advantage lets members pass security checkpoints faster, therefore cutting the time spent in line and improving the general trip efficiency. Dedicated lanes or trusted traveler programs like TSA PreCheck in the United States or like systems in other nations allow expeditious security screening. Business visitors and frequent passengers who must save travel time and prevent delays will notably benefit from this service.

Customer Loyalty Programs Integration: Airlines often integrate their FFPs with other customer loyalty programs, such as credit card rewards programs. This connection gives members more freedom and value by letting them accumulate and redeem miles or points on several platforms. Members might be able to transfer points from a hotel loyalty program to their airline FFP or earn airline miles when using a co-branded credit card for regular transactions. This perfect integration of loyalty programs improves the whole client experience and motivates members to stick to the airline and its partners.

Exclusive Member Events and Experiences: To further engage and reward their most loyal customers, some airlines host exclusive events and experiences for FFP members. Private concerts, VIP access to athletic events, behind-the-scenes tours, and unique meet-and-greet chances with celebrities or airline officials can all fall under these activities. For members, these unusual encounters produce unforgettable events that deepen their emotional bond to the airline. Offering special events allows airlines to set their FFPs apart from rivals and provide value beyond standard travel incentives.

Comprehensive Travel Insurance: Many FFPs offer comprehensive travel insurance as part of their membership benefits. This insurance can cover a wide range of travel-related risks, including trip cancellations, medical emergencies, lost luggage, and travel delays. For FFP members, included travel insurance guarantees protection and peace of mind by shielding them from unanticipated circumstances that can throw off their vacation plans. Frequent travelers who are more prone to have travel interruptions will especially find this advantage very useful.

Community and Social Responsibility: Some airlines incorporate community and social responsibility initiatives into their FFPs, allowing members to use their miles or points to support charitable causes. Members could be allowed to contribute their miles, for instance, to groups offering travel for educational initiatives, disaster relief, or medical treatment trips. This integration of social responsibility into FFPs not only helps the community but also improves the brand image of the airline and conforms with the values of environmentally concerned tourists.

In conclusion, the range of services offered to FFP members significantly enhances the travel experience, providing convenience, comfort, and efficiency. While priority services simplify the travel procedure, dedicated customer care guarantees that regular travelers get individualized and quick help. Value and elegance abound in the travel experience from special discounts and promotions, improved in-flight services, and access to private airport lounges. Further motivating loyalty and involvement are priority for upgrades and award seats, extra partner incentives, and customized services. Round out the whole array of features that make FFP membership particularly appealing for regular travelers with accelerated security screening, integrated loyalty programs, special events, thorough travel insurance, and community projects. Airlines can build great customer loyalty and stand out in a crowded industry by always improving and inventing these offerings.

Lounge Access & Other Add-ons

With access to exclusive airport lounges among the many advantages frequent flier programs (FFPs) offer to their members. Apart from lounge access, airlines provide several add-ons meant to improve the flying experience for their devoted patrons. This part explores the facilities offered by airport lounges, the rules controlling lounge entry depending on membership levels, and various extras enabling pleasant and joyful frequent flight.

Lounge Access: Access to airport lounges is a significant benefit for FFP members, particularly those in higher tiers. These lounges provide a peaceful haven free from the bustle of the airport where guests may work, unwind, or eat before their departure. Comfortable seating, fast Wi-Fi, business centers, and a variety of complimentary food and drinks abound in lounges. During layovers or before long-haul flights, some lounges additionally provide extra conveniences including showers, spa treatments, and private conference rooms, enabling guests to relax.

Usually serving several purposes, airport lounges have quiet areas for relaxation, office areas with workstations and printers, and dining facilities with buffet-style meals or a la carte menus. Although lounge and airline will determine the availability of these facilities, the main objective is to create a premium experience that improves travel comfort and convenience. Often with attractive décor, gentle lighting, and relaxing music, Lounges have elegant interiors that contrast strongly with the packed and chaotic public areas of the airport.

Policies Governing Lounge Access: Lounge access policies vary depending on the airline and the member's tier within the FFP. Usually reserved for members in higher grades, such Gold or Platinum, as well as those in premium cabins, entrance to airport lounges is restricted. Certain airlines also give mid-tier passengers lounge access in recognition of meeting specific program benchmarks.

For example, a typical airline might structure its lounge access policy as follows:

- **Silver Tier**: Limited or no lounge access. Some airlines might offer access to select lounges or during specific off-peak times as a special promotion.

- **Gold Tier**: Access to the airline's lounges, as well as those of its partners within an airline alliance. This tier might also include access to domestic and international lounges.

- **Platinum Tier**: Unrestricted access to all lounges in the airline's network and its partners, including first-class lounges and flagship locations with enhanced amenities.

Some airlines let members purchase annual lounge memberships or single-visit permits in addition to tier-based access. For those who might not fly enough to reach higher-tier classification but still want to take advantage of lounge access, these choices give flexibility.

Guest Policies: Lounge access policies also define the rules for bringing guests. Higher-tier members sometimes get the honor of bringing one or more visitors inside the lounge with them. Families traveling together or business travelers who could be flying with colleagues will especially find this advantage helpful. While airlines and lounges have different specific guest regulations, generally they allow a set number of gratis visitors; more guests are paid for.

Lounge Networks and Partnerships: Many airlines are part of global alliances such as Star Alliance, Oneworld, and SkyTeam, which means FFP members can access lounges operated by partner airlines. By extending the advantages of lounge access to a larger spectrum of locations, this network of lounges gives visitors all around the globe a consistent and first-rate experience. For example, a member of a Star Alliance airline's FFP can access lounges run by any other Star Alliance member airline, therefore guaranteeing a high degree of service and comfort independent of the carrier they are flying with.

Apart from airline alliances, some airlines teamed with independent lounge networks to provide their passengers even more choices. These alliances can involve access to lounges at airports where the airline does not run its own facilities. International visitors especially benefit from this increased access since they can find themselves in airports without a lounge run by their main airline or alliance partner.

Additional Add-ons: Beyond lounge access, frequent flier programs offer a variety of add-ons designed to enhance the travel experience for their members. Complementary improvements, priority services, and luxury-oriented special privileges abound among these add-ons.

Complimentary Upgrades: One of the most attractive add-ons for FFP members is the possibility of complimentary upgrades to higher cabin classes. Higher level members generally get first priority for business or first class upgrades either with their accrued miles or via airline complimentary offers. These improvements give the travel experience a major boost in comfort, service quality, and other conveniences.

Usually prioritized depending on the member's tier level, complimentary upgrades are provided depending on availability. Platinum members might, for instance, be first in line for upgrades, then Gold members. Different airlines allow members to request upgrades in advance or bid for them through an auction system; some provide automatic upgrades at check-in.

Priority Services: Priority services are a key component of the add-ons provided to FFP members. These offerings comprise luggage handling, security screening, boarding, and priority check-in. Airlines make sure their most devoted passengers have few waiting periods and a simpler travel experience by offering these advantages.

By using dedicated counters, priority check-in lets members escape the usually huge lineups at regular check-in stations. When airports are busiest and travel is most intense, this accelerated service is very helpful. Priority security screening similarly gives access to speedier lanes, therefore saving time spent in line and enabling members to go swiftly to their gate or lounge.

Priority boarding guarantees that FFP members may board the aircraft before other passengers, therefore allowing plenty of time for them to settle into their seats and arrange their carry-on baggage. Those who fly with big carry-ons or those who would want to escape the hurry and stress of general boarding will find this advantage very helpful. Priority baggage handling guarantees that members' checked bags arrive among the first to be transported to the baggage claim area upon arrival, therefore saving significant time and lowering wait times at the destination.

Special Privileges: Frequent flier programs often include special privileges that add a touch of luxury and exclusivity to the travel experience. From access to luxury airport transfer services to free hotel stays and automobile rentals, these benefits may span anything.

For their most elite customers, certain airlines provide chauffeur services—door-to--door travel to and from the airport. By removing the stress of planning transportation, this service not only improves convenience but also the whole travel experience. Likewise, members with long layovers or in circumstances when their flights are greatly delayed or canceled can be provided complimentary hotel stays.

Another popular add-on are car rental alliances, which give members discounts or free upgrades when leasing cars from affiliated businesses. These alliances guarantee that, when planning ground transportation, FFP members have extra advantages and preferential treatment.

Exclusive Member Events and Experiences: To further engage and reward their most loyal customers, some airlines host exclusive events and experiences for FFP members. Private concerts, VIP access to athletic events, behind-the-scenes tours, and unique meet-and-greet chances with celebrities or airline officials can all fall under these activities. For members, these unusual encounters produce unforgettable events that deepen their emotional bond to the airline. Offering special events allows airlines to set their FFPs apart from rivals and provide value beyond standard travel incentives.

Personalized Services and Benefits: Airlines are increasingly leveraging technology to provide personalized services and benefits to FFP members. Airlines can customize their products to particular consumers by examining information on travel habits, preferences, and buying behavior. Targeted promotions, birthday wishes, and special offers—personalized communications—help you establish a more interesting and significant relationship with members. This personalization also applies to in-flight services, whereby the cabin crew may provide customized greetings and service upon learning of a member's preferences.

Expedited Security Screening: Another valuable service for FFP members is expedited security screening. This advantage lets members pass security checkpoints faster, therefore cutting the time spent in line and improving the general trip efficiency. Dedicated lanes or trusted traveler programs like TSA PreCheck in the United States or like systems in other nations allow expeditious security screening. Business visitors and frequent passengers who must save travel time and prevent delays will notably benefit from this service.

Customer Loyalty Programs Integration: Airlines often integrate their FFPs with other customer loyalty programs, such as credit card rewards programs. This connection gives members more freedom and value by letting them accumulate and redeem miles or points on several platforms. Members might be able to transfer points from a hotel loyalty program to their airline FFP or earn airline miles when using a co-branded credit card for regular transactions. This perfect integration of loyalty programs improves the whole client experience and motivates members to stick to the airline and its partners.

Exclusive Member Events and Experiences: To further engage and reward their most loyal customers, some airlines host exclusive events and experiences for FFP members. Private concerts, VIP access to athletic events, behind-the-scenes tours, and unique meet-and-greet chances with celebrities or airline officials can all fall under these activities. For members, these unusual encounters produce unforgettable events that deepen their emotional bond to the airline. Offering special events allows airlines to set their FFPs apart from rivals and provide value beyond standard travel incentives.

Comprehensive Travel Insurance: Many FFPs offer comprehensive travel insurance as part of their membership benefits. Trip cancellation, medical emergencies, missing bags, and travel delays are just a few of the travel-related hazards this insurance can cover. For FFP members, included travel insurance guarantees protection and peace of mind by shielding them from unanticipated circumstances that can throw off their vacation plans. Frequent travelers who are more prone to have travel interruptions will especially find this advantage very useful.

Community and Social Responsibility: Some airlines incorporate community and social responsibility initiatives into their FFPs, allowing members to use their miles or points to support charitable causes. Members could be allowed to contribute their miles, for instance, to groups offering travel for educational initiatives, disaster relief, or medical treatment trips. This integration of social responsibility into FFPs not only helps the community but also improves the brand image of the airline and conforms with the values of environmentally concerned tourists.

Future Trends and Emerging Technologies: FFPs' future resides in their capacity to adapt to changing travel needs and in their incorporation of new technologies. Personalizing the travel experience for FFP members is being done in great part by artificial intelligence (AI) and machine learning. From trip choices to in-flight conveniences, artificial intelligence can examine enormous volumes of data to forecast member preferences and provide customized recommendations. This degree of customizing improves the member experience and strengthens closer allegiance.

Another developing development that might completely change FFPs is blockchain technology. Blockchain can track miles and points transparently and securely, therefore lowering the risk of fraud and strengthening airline-member confidence. Blockchain might also help different loyalty programs to easily trade miles and points, therefore enhancing their flexibility and value.

Many tourists now also give sustainability first priority, and FFPs are probably going to feature more environmentally friendly projects going forward. Airlines might give members who choose more environmentally friendly travel choices—direct flights or carbon offset programs—incentives. Airlines can attract ecologically minded passengers and support more general environmental initiatives by matching FFPs with sustainability goals.

Case Studies of Successful Lounge Access Programs: Examining successful lounge access programs provides insights into best practices and the benefits of well-designed FFPs. For example, the Emirates Skywards program is quite well-known for its opulent lounges, which provide a spectrum of first-rate conveniences including private rooms, fine dining, and spa treatments. These lounges offer a first-rate pre-flight experience, therefore supporting the airline's standing for luxury and first-rate service.

Another instance is the United Club, a component of United Airlines MileagePlus scheme. Comfortable seats, workstations, free snacks and drinks, and access to corporate facilities such printers and conference rooms abound in United Club lounges. United Club lounges at major airports all over guarantee that MileagePlus members may enjoy a premium experience anywhere they are traveling to.

These case studies underline the significance of offering first-rate facilities, keeping constant standards across sites, and always improving the lounge experience to satisfy changing expectations of guests. They also show how much customer loyalty and brand uniqueness can be greatly enhanced by properly run lounge access policies.

In essence, frequent flier programs depend on lounge access and other add-ons, which offer great value and improve the travel experience for devoted consumers. While laws controlling access guarantee that perks are fairly distributed depending on membership tiers, exclusive airport lounges provide a refuge of comfort and elegance. Complimentary upgrades, priority services, and unique privileges among other add-ons improve the travel experience and help frequent flying to be more handy and fun. With even more personalizing, flexibility, and sustainability as airlines keep innovating and including new technologies, FFPs have bright future prospects. Airlines can build great customer loyalty and stand out in a crowded market by always improving these offerings.

Mileage Points & Upgradation

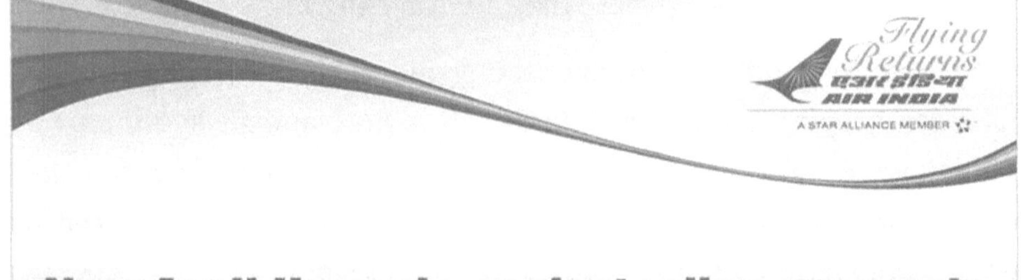

Two of the most important incentives provided by frequent flier programs (FFPs) are mileage points and the capacity to upgrade to better class services. These special qualities not only honor devoted consumers but also inspire them to keep selecting the same airline for next trips. This part looks at mileage points gained, used, and tracked as well as the procedures and advantages of upgrades.

Earning Points: Earning mileage points is the cornerstone of any frequent flier program. Usually, points are calculated depending on the distance flown, the fare class, and the member's tier level inside the FFP. A flight from New York to London, for instance, might have a base amount of miles that could be multiplied by a factor based on the ticket class (economy, business, first) and member level (Silver, Gold, Platinum). Because of their loyalty, higher-tier members sometimes receive extra bonus points, which lets them quickly acquire points.

Different partner activities—such as staying in associated hotels, leasing automobiles from partner companies, and using co-branded credit cards for purchases—also count points. These alliances let members accumulate points from a variety of regular activities, therefore extending the earning possibilities beyond only flights. Airlines also regularly conduct specials with double or triple points on some routes or during particular times, therefore creating even more chances to increase point balances.

Redeeming Points: Redeeming mileage points is one of the most appealing aspects of FFPs, as it allows members to use their accumulated points for free flights, upgrades, and other rewards. Although each airline has different redemption policies, normally members may explore available alternatives by logging into their FFP accounts online or via a mobile app. Points can be used for free flights, cabin upgrades, hotel stays, vehicle rentals, and even merchandise.

The most often used redemption option is free flights; the points needed depend on the destination, kind of fare class, and booking time. A domestic flight might, for example, ask for less points than an international one, while flights reserved well in advance usually call for less points than last-minute bookings. Many times, airlines publish award charts showing the points required for different itineraries and price classes, which promotes openness and enables members to schedule their redemptions.

Mileage points are also quite used for upgrades. Members greatly improve their travel experience by using their points to move from economy to business class or from business to first class. The points needed for upgrades also change usually based on the route and availability. Certain airlines let members bid for upgrades, combining points and money to guarantee a higher-class seat.

Managing Points: Effective management of mileage points is crucial for maximizing their value. Airlines use online account dashboards and smartphone apps among other tools and resources to enable users to track their points. Members of these systems can examine their point balance, follow their earning and redemption actions, and obtain comprehensive statements displaying point accumulation and expenditure.

Members should be informed of the policies regarding point expiration. Most airlines have expiration policies whereby points must be used within a given period, usually one to three years. Many airlines, however, provide methods to keep points active—such by frequently earning or redeeming points or by using a co-branded credit card. Members who keep informed about expiration dates and carefully manage their points will help to prevent losing priceless benefits.

Upgrading with Points: Upgrading to a higher class using points is a major incentive for frequent travelers. Airlines vary in their upgrading procedures, but generally speaking, an eligible flight is booked and then points are used to seek an upgrade. Usually subject to availability, members can ask for upgrades during the booking process, at check-in, or even at the gate.

A route, fare class, and member status all affect the points needed for an upgrade. Higher-tier members can have first preference for upgrades; some airlines give free upgrades to their most devoted passengers. Usually restricted, particularly on busy routes and at peak travel hours, the availability of upgrade seats makes it advantageous for members to ask early on.

Airlines also run upgrade auctions when members may bid for upgrades using a mix of points and cash. These auctions give users a flexible approach to get improvements without having to use a lot of points, and they liven the upgrading process.

Benefits of Upgrades: Upgrading to a higher class offers numerous benefits, significantly enhancing the travel experience. Often with lie-flat beds, which let for peaceful slumber on long-haul flights, business and first-class cabins offer more roomy and comfortable seating. Improved dinner service with gourmet cuisine and fine beverages gives the voyage some elegance.

With less seats and more customized cabin staff service, upgraded accommodations also provide more privacy and exclusiveness. The experience is improved even more by other conveniences as priority boarding, extra baggage allowance, and access to luxury lounges. Working comfortably in-flight, with power outlets, bigger tray tables, and better lighting, may be a big benefit for business travelers.

Tier Status and Upgrades: Frequent flier programs often tie upgrade benefits to the member's tier status, with higher-tier members receiving more generous upgrade opportunities. A Platinum member might, for instance, get free upgrades on domestic flights and top priority for upgrades on foreign routes. Although they could have less priority or need to use more points, lower-tier members may nonetheless be qualified for improvements.

Moreover affecting the success rate of upgrade requests is tier status. Usually depending on the member's situation, airlines give upgrades top priority; then, the fare class and the timing of the request are of second importance. This strategy guarantees that most devoted consumers get the best possible service and incentives, therefore strengthening their allegiance to the airline.

Promotions and Special Offers: Airlines frequently run promotions and special offers related to mileage points and upgrades. These specials can call for cheaper upgrade rates, bonus points for booking within a given period, or double or triple points on particular paths. Emails, the airline's website, and the FFP's mobile app all alert members of these specials.

Promotions provide members great chances to get extra points and guaranteed upgrades at lowered costs. Using these deals will help members improve their travel experience and hasten their approach toward reward targets. To guarantee best capacity usage and consumer involvement, airlines also run promotions to encourage new routes or to reward bookings during off-peak times.

Mileage Runs and Strategies for Earning Points: Some frequent travelers engage in mileage runs—flights taken specifically to earn points and achieve or maintain elite status within an FFP. Usually featuring complicated itineraries with many parts and layovers, mileage runs are designed to maximize the number of points gained for the least cost.

Strategic earning also entails selecting airlines and partners with most generous point accruing rates. Members could choose longer routes, premium pricing classes, or flights via partner airlines with extra points. Taking advantage of partner offers and using co-branded credit cards for regular purchases help to increase point balances.

Maximizing Redemption Value: Members should be deliberate in their redemption decisions to best value the points they have earned. Particularly on long-distance and international flights, award flights and upgrades typically offer the highest value per point. Members should also take into account the time of their redemptions since booking far in advance or during promotions will greatly cut the necessary points.

Online travel communities and award calculators among other tools can assist members in determining the best redemption choices and maximize their point use. Members may get most use from their mileage points by keeping educated and carefully scheduling their redemptions.

Challenges and Best Practices: While mileage points and upgrades offer significant benefits, there are challenges associated with managing and redeeming them. Particularly during busy travel seasons, availability of reward seats and upgrade options may be restricted. Expiration policies call on members to remain alert regarding their point balances and redemption dates.

Regular account activity, setting reminders for point expiration dates, and keeping current on specials and offers help to best manage mileage points. To keep a consistent point flow, members should also vary their point-earning activities using co-branded credit cards and partner possibilities.

In essence, frequent flier programs depend on mileage points and upgrades, which offer great value and improve the travel experience for devoted consumers. Effective point earning, redeeming, and managing will help FFP members utilize the advantages of their membership and enjoy a more pleasant and fulfilling travel experience by using upgrades and incentives.

Chapter-9

Airline Operation & Scheduling

Airline Schedule Planning

Season	Airline	Flt. no	Sch. time	Route	Weekdays	Total Records	Period star
W20	SK	9595	04:04	CPH	M T W Th F Sa S	60	16DEC20 01:
W20	SK	3209	05:55	CPH - IST	M T W Th F Sa S	4	10JAN21 01:
W20	SK	1419	10:00	ARN - CPH	M T W Th F Sa S	9	03JAN21 01:
W20	SK	1455	10:15	OSL - CPH	M T W Th F Sa S	5	03JAN21 01:
W20	SK	1455	10:15	OSL - CPH	M T W Th F Sa S	9	31DEC20 01:
W20	SK	1420	10:40	CPH - ARN	M T W Th F Sa S	2	09JAN21 01:
W20	SK	1420	10:40	CPH - ARN	M T W Th F Sa S	2	13JAN21 01:
W20	SK	1420	11:00	CPH - ARN	M T W Th F Sa S	2	10JAN21 01:
W20	SK	406	13:05	CPH - ARN	M T W Th F Sa S	4	12JAN21 01:
W20	SK	458	13:20	CPH - OSL	M T W Th F Sa S	2	10JAN21 01:

A basic element of airline operations, airline schedule planning is essential for operating efficiency, meeting market demand, and best use of resources. This part explores the nuances of schedule planning, investigates the elements affecting it, the tools and methods used, and actual case studies showing its use.

Introduction to Schedule Planning: Determining the frequency and scheduling of flights on several paths to maximize efficiency, profitability, and customer satisfaction is known as schedule planning. It entails a complicated interaction among market demand, aircraft availability, personnel scheduling, and legal limitations. Good schedule planning guarantees airlines' ability to maximize income and keep operational dependability while nevertheless providing competitive services.

Developing a flight plan that satisfies market demand while best using the airline's fleet and crew is the main goal of schedule planning.

This entails juggling the demands of several markets, matching flight plans to times of maximum travel, and guaranteeing effective aircraft and staff deployment. An airline's market position, profitability, and customer loyalty can all be much improved by effective schedule planning.

Factors Influencing Schedule Planning: Several factors influence the schedule planning process, each playing a critical role in shaping the final flight schedule. One of the most important considerations is market demand since airlines have to match their schedules to the choices and travel habits of their patrons. By means of historical data, seasonal trends, and competitive actions, airlines can project demand and modify their plans.

Another absolutely important consideration in schedule planning is aircraft availability. Airlines have to make sure they have the correct kind and count of aircraft ready to run their scheduled flights. This entails weighing elements including fleet development plans, lease agreements, and aircraft maintenance schedules. Maximum income and lowest running costs depend on effective fleet use.

Another absolutely important component of schedule planning is crew scheduling. Airlines have to make sure their cabin crew and skilled pilots count for enough operations of their flights. This entails handling crew availability and preferences as well as following rules on crew duty hours and rest times. Good crew scheduling guarantees safe and effective operation of aircraft free from needless expenses.

Schedule planning is significantly influenced by regulatory limitations since airlines have to follow certain rules and regulations set by aviation authorities. These can comprise air traffic control rules, curfews and noise restrictions, and slot distribution guidelines at crowded airports. Airlines have to negotiate these limitations when they create their plans to guarantee compliance and prevent operational interruptions.

Tools and Techniques: The complexity of schedule planning necessitates the use of advanced tools and techniques to analyze data, optimize resources, and develop efficient flight schedules. Several programs and techniques are used to assist in the scheduling planning process.

A main instrument used in schedule planning is network planning software. These programs assist airlines in traffic forecasts, market demand analysis, and evaluation of several scheduling options. They let designers replicate, on the flight schedule, the effect of several elements, including changes in market conditions, rival actions, and regulatory limitations. Network planning software guides airlines in making wise judgments and schedule optimization by offering thorough insights and predictive analytics.

Furthermore, extensively applied in schedule planning are optimization techniques. These systems find the most effective approach to distribute resources and create flight plans by using mathematical models. To create best plans that maximize income and save expenses, they take into account several elements like demand patterns, aircraft availability, and crew scheduling restrictions. The process of scheduling planning can be much improved by optimization techniques.

Another crucial part of schedule planning are simulation instruments. These instruments let airlines replicate several scheduling situations and assess how they affect operations. Simulation tools enable airlines to evaluate the viability and efficiency of several schedules by simulating several elements, such as passenger demand, aircraft performance, and airport congestion. They help designers to see possible problems and make corrections to guarantee a dependable and seamless running.

Scheduling also depends critically on tools for corporate information and data analytics. These instruments enable airlines to examine past performance of their schedules, track industry trends, and assess historical data. Data analytics and business intelligence technologies let airlines make data-driven choices and always maximize their schedules by offering real-time insights and actionable intelligence.

Case Studies: Real-world case studies provide valuable insights into the application of schedule planning tools and techniques in airline operations. These cases show how well schedule planning could maximize profitability, satisfy market demand, and improve operational efficiency.

One notable case study involves Delta Air Lines, which has successfully implemented advanced schedule planning techniques to optimize its operations. Delta develops effective flight plans, analyzes market demand, and forecasts traffic using complex network planning tools and optimization algorithms. Delta has been able to raise income, enhance customer satisfaction, and change its market posture by using these instruments.

Another example is Southwest Airlines, which has implemented innovative schedule planning practices to achieve operational efficiency and maintain its competitive edge. Southwest models several scheduling possibilities and assesses their effects on operations using simulation tools and data analytics. With this strategy, Southwest has been able to maximize its flight plans, reduce running interruptions, and provide its clients with a consistent and handy service.

Market Demand Analysis: Understanding market demand is essential for effective schedule planning. To properly estimate demand, airlines have to consider a lot of elements like past performance, seasonal trends, and competition behavior. Data on passenger travel trends, preferences, and behaviors is gathered and examined in market demand analysis.

Market research surveys provide one method of market demand analysis. These polls compile passenger travel choices including preferred trip times, destinations, and service expectations. Through survey data analysis, airlines can spot patterns and preferences that guide their choices on schedule development.

Examining booking and ticket data is yet another approach. By means of previous booking data, airlines can spot trends in demand including those pertaining to popular routes, peak travel times, and ticket preferences. This information enables airlines to project demand going forward and modify their plans to fit passenger wants.

Analysis of market demand also depends critically on competitive analysis. Airlines have to keep an eye on the activities of their rivals including price policies, new route launches, and scheduling adjustments. Understanding the competitive scene helps airlines create plans with a competitive edge that draw more customers.

Aircraft Utilization: Efficient utilization of aircraft is a key objective of schedule planning. Airlines have to make sure their fleet is used wisely to maximize income and cut running expenses. This entails juggling the necessity for enough capacity to satisfy demand with the aim of reducing empty time and optimizing aircraft output.

Hub-and--spoke networks are one approach for best use of airplanes. Under a hub-and-spoke arrangement, aircraft are directed via central hub airports from which passengers may connect to other flights. This approach gives passengers easy connections to a vast spectrum of locations and lets airlines combine demand on key routes and reach better load factors.

Point-to-- point networks—where aircraft run straight between origin and destination airports without passing via a hub—are another strategy. For some paths, especially those with great demand and little connecting traffic, point-to- point networks can be more efficient. Airlines can maximize their timetables to satisfy varying market needs by combining point-to--point networks with hub-and-spoke systems.

A crucial component of aircraft use is also aircraft maintenance scheduling. Airlines have to organize their flights around necessary maintenance inspections and checks to guarantee aircraft availability for operation. This entails timing repair operations with flight operations to reduce disturbance and optimize aircraft availability.

Crew Scheduling: Crew scheduling is an integral part of the schedule planning process. Airlines have to make sure they have enough qualified pilots and cabin staff to run their flights in addition to following laws on crew duty hours and rest times.

One of the challenges in crew scheduling is managing crew availability and preferences. When choosing crew members for flights, airlines have to take into account things such as crew qualifications, seniority, and personal choices. This entails juggling the necessity for operational effectiveness with the objective of preserving crew morale and satisfaction.

To address these challenges, airlines use advanced crew scheduling software that automates the scheduling process and optimizes crew assignments. To create compliant and effective crew rosters, these software programs take into account many elements like crew qualifications, duty time constraints, and flight schedules. Airlines can guarantee that they have the correct personnel on hand to run their flights safely and effectively by using crew scheduling systems.

Regulatory Constraints: Compliance with regulatory constraints is a critical consideration in schedule planning. Airlines have to negotiate several laws and restrictions set by aviation authorities like curfews, slot allocation policies, noise limits, and air traffic control systems.

Rules on slot allocation decide when airlines may run flights at crowded airports. Through complicated and competitive slot allocation procedures, airlines have to guarantee spaces for their flights. Maintaining the intended network and ensuring that flights run on time depend on efficient slot management, hence the airline can keep it.

Some airports set noise limits and curfews to reduce the effect of aircraft activity on nearby populations. Airlines have to plan their flights to fit these limits, which can limit the availability of some paths or flying hours. Navigating these restrictions calls for careful communication with airport authorities and preparation.

Aircraft routing and separation within an airspace are controlled by air traffic control rules. Airlines have to follow these rules to guarantee the effective and safe aircraft movement. Developing flight plans that fit airspace capacity and routing criteria requires working with air traffic control authorities.

Case Studies and Examples: Examining real-world case studies and examples provides valuable insights into the application of schedule planning tools and techniques in airline operations.

One particularly good example of careful timetable planning is Delta Air Lines. Delta forecasts traffic, analyzes market demand, and creates effective flight schedules using sophisticated network planning tools and optimization algorithms. Delta has been able to strengthen customer satisfaction, raise income, and change its market posture by using these instruments. Delta's data-driven strategy, constant market trend monitoring, and proactive schedule changes help to explain its effectiveness in schedule planning.

Another creative schedule design is that of Southwest Airlines. Southwest models several scheduling situations and assesses their effects on operations using simulation tools and data analytics. By use of this strategy, Southwest has been able to maximize its flight plans, eliminate operational interruptions, and provide a consistent and handy service to its patrons. Southwest's emphasis on efficiency and simplicity in its scheduling technique has helped to establish its operational excellence and customer satisfaction reputation.

In essence, airline schedule planning is a complicated and multifarious process requiring careful attention to several elements, including market demand, aircraft availability, personnel scheduling, and legal limitations. Airlines may create effective flight plans that improve operational efficiency, satisfy market demand, and maximize revenue by using cutting-edge tools and technologies, therefore enhancing operational effectiveness. Real-world case studies show how critical proactive changes, constant optimization, and data-driven decision-making are to properly schedule planning. Effective schedule planning helps airlines to better their market position, boost income, and provide their clients with a first-rate travel experience.

Time-Space Networks

Crucially important instruments for optimizing airline operations and scheduling are time-space networks. By use of these networks, which offer a disciplined approach to depict and examine the movements of aircraft, crew, and passengers over time and place, airlines may make well-informed decisions on operational efficiency, schedule planning, and resource allocation. The concept and significance of time-space networks, their constituents, their application in scheduling, and the difficulties and remedies related with their implementation are investigated in this part.

Definition and Importance: A time-space network is a graphical depiction of resource movement (such as that of aircraft and crew) across time and space. Whereas the arcs show the movement between several points—e.g., a flight segment from one airport to another—each node in the network represents a distinct position in time and space—e.g., an airport at a certain moment. Time-space networks enable airlines to maximize their resources and schedule by showing the intricate interactions and interdependence across several flights, aircraft, and crew.

For numerous purposes, time-space networks are absolutely vital. They first offer a detailed, all-encompassing perspective of the whole process, stressing any congestion, inefficiencies, and areas for development. Second, they let airlines assess several scheduling choices and how they affect operations, therefore guiding their data-driven judgments. Time-space networks last but not least help to coordinate and synchronize several resources so as to guarantee timely and effective operation of aircraft.

Components of Time-Space Networks: The primary components of a time-space network include nodes, arcs, and timelines. Every one of these elements is absolutely important in depicting and evaluating resource movement.

Nodes define certain spots in space and time. Within airline scheduling, nodes usually relate to events like arrivals and departures at airports. Every node links to a certain airport and a given time, therefore offering a comprehensive picture of the operations at that very moment. A node might symbolize, say, the arrival of a flight at JFK Airport at 10:00 AM.

Arcs show how resources flow between nodes. Arcades in airline scheduling relate to flight segments, ground operations, and other activities involving aircraft, crew, or passenger movement. Every arc corresponds to a particular resource and a duration, therefore indicating the time needed for the movement. An arc might show, for instance, a five-hour travel from JFK to LAX.

Timelines give the network a chronological framework, grouping nodes and arcs in line with their historical order. Timelines let airlines monitor the development of events and activities over time, therefore helping them to spot dependencies, overlaps, and possible conflict. Through timeline analysis, airlines can guarantee that their plans are realistic and that resources are applied wisely.

Application in Scheduling: Time-space networks are widely used in airline scheduling to optimize the allocation of resources and develop efficient flight schedules. They give airlines a disciplined framework for examining the intricate relationships across several flights, aircraft, and crew, therefore guiding their decisions on resource allocation and schedule.

Time-space networks find great use in flight scheduling among other areas. Airlines can assess many scheduling options and find the best flight sequence by viewing flights as arcs in the network. Analyzing elements including demand trends, aircraft availability, and crew scheduling restrictions helps one create plans that optimize income and reduce running expenses.

Additionally utilized to maximize aircraft navigation are time-space networks. Airlines can find the most effective paths for their fleet by showing the flight of planes between nodes. This entails juggling the necessity for direct flights with the aim of reducing idle time and optimizing aircraft output. Time-space networks enable airlines to assess several routing choices and choose the ones that offer the optimum mix of cost-effective efficiency.

Still another important use of time-space networks is crew scheduling. Airlines can guarantee sufficient trained pilots and cabin crew to run their flights by showing the mobility of crew between nodes. This entails handling crew availability and preferences as well as following rules on crew duty hours and rest times. Time-space networks enable airlines to create compliant and effective crew schedules guaranteeing the dependability and safety of their flights.

Challenges and Solutions: Time-space networks in aircraft scheduling provide a number of difficulties. These include the difficulties of maintaining data accuracy and consistency, the need of integrating several data sources, and the complexity of depicting and analyzing vast-scale networks. Still, many approaches and solutions can help to solve these problems and improve the efficiency of time-space networks.

Representing and analyzing big-scale time-space networks is one of the main difficulties since it is complicated. Operating vast networks of flights, aircraft, and staff, airlines run thousands of nodes and arcs. Representing and evaluating such big networks calls for advanced computational resources and techniques. Modern optimization methods and machine learning tools enable airlines to control this complexity and create effective plans. These systems can spot trends and patterns in the data, therefore offering information to guide scheduling decisions.

Including several data sources presents still another difficult task. Data from several sources—including flight schedules, aircraft performance records, crew availability records, and market demand forecasts—forms time-space networks. Effective scheduling depends on accurate, consistent, current data that is also reliable. Strong data integration and management systems help airlines to solve this difficulty. These systems can provide constant updating and accessibility, evaluate its accuracy, and combine data from several sources.

Time-space networks' efficacy depends critically on data correctness and consistency. Incorrect or inconsistent data might cause operational interruptions and less than ideal scheduling choices. Rigid data validation and quality control procedures help airlines improve data accuracy and consistency. These procedures entail routinely looking over the data for mistakes and inconsistencies, fixing any problems, and changing the data as appropriate.

Real-world case studies and examples offer insightful analysis of how time-space networks could be used in airline scheduling. These cases show how well airlines have applied time-space networks to maximize their operations and raise performance.

American Airlines is one such example as it has improved its scheduling process by cleverly leveraging time-space networks. Analyzing its vast fleet of flights, aircraft, and personnel, American Airlines applies sophisticated optimization algorithms and machine learning tools. Using time-space networks, American Airlines has been able to create successful flight plans, maximize aircraft routing, and guarantee crew member efficient use. Significant operational improvements—including improved on-time performance, lower running costs, and more customer satisfaction—have come from this strategy.

Lufthansa is another example; it has put time-space networks into use to maximize its long-distance operations. Time-space networks allow Lufthansa to examine the flight path of its wide-body aircraft and create effective plans maximizing aircraft output. Lufthansa may assess several scheduling possibilities and choose the one that offers the best combination of efficiency and cost-effectiveness by modeling flights and ground operations as nodes and arcs in the network. By using this strategy, Lufthansa has been able to lower delays, increase operational dependability, and enhance customer travel experience generally.

Future Trends and Innovations: Advances in technology and growing data availability will probably help to define the future of time-space networks in airline scheduling. Blockchain and artificial intelligence (AI) among other emerging technologies could transform airline schedule development and management.

Techniques for artificial intelligence and machine learning can improve time-space network analysis and optimization. Airlines can create predictive models using artificial intelligence that estimate demand trends, spot possible interruptions, and suggest best timing changes. By means of constant learning from operational performance and historical data, machine learning techniques help airlines to optimize their schedules and thereby increase efficiency over time.

Blockchain technology can improve the security and openness of data applied in time-space networks. Blockchain notes data changes and transactions on a distributed, unchangeable ledger. Blockchain lets airlines guarantee that their data is safe, consistent, and correct. This helps time-space networks to be more dependable and supports better choices of scheduling.

Another important factor influencing the direction of time-space networks is the growing availability of data. From several sources— including flight operations, market demand, and customer behavior— airlines have access to enormous volumes of data. Airlines may create more sensible timetables and have a better understanding of their operations by combining and examining this data. By means of advanced data analytics and business intelligence instruments, airlines may make data-driven decisions and ongoing schedule optimization is facilitated.

In order to maximize airline operations and scheduling, time-space networks are therefore important instruments. They give airlines a disciplined framework for showing and evaluating the flow of resources, therefore helping them to decide on operational efficiency, schedule development, and resource allocation. Time-space networks—which include nodes, arcs, and timelines—have fundamental elements that help to depict and examine the intricate relationships across several flights, aircraft, and crew.

Using time-space networks in airline scheduling means maximizing flight plans, aircraft routing, and crew scheduling. Airlines may create effective schedules that improve operational efficiency, satisfy market demand, and optimize revenue by using cutting-edge tools and technologies, therefore enhancing operational performance. Time-space networks provide various difficulties, too, including the complexity of big-scale networks, the necessity to combine several data sources, and the need for data accuracy and consistency. Advanced optimization algorithms, data integration systems, and strict data validation procedures among other methods and approaches help to solve these problems and improve the performance of time-space networks.

Case studies from the actual world, such those of American Airlines and Lufthansa, show how well time-space networks are used to maximize airline operations. These illustrations show the need for proactive changes, ongoing optimization, and data-driven decision-making in reaching effective schedule planning.

Looking ahead, developments in technology and the growing availability of data will probably help time-space networks to become even more successful. Blockchain technology, artificial intelligence, and machine learning have the ability to completely transform airline scheduling by offering improved data protection, predictive power, and deeper understanding. Airlines that embrace these technologies will be able to keep streamlining their operations, raising efficiency, and giving their passengers first-rate travel experience.

Multi-Commodity Flow Models

Powerful methods applied in airline operations and scheduling to maximize the distribution of several resources over a network are multi-commodity flow models. These models help airlines to simultaneously control the flow of several goods, including passengers, cargo, aircraft, and staff, so optimizing operating efficiency and assuring effective use of resources. The idea of multi-commodity flow models, their components, optimization methods, useful applications, and the difficulties and remedies related with their execution are explored in this part.

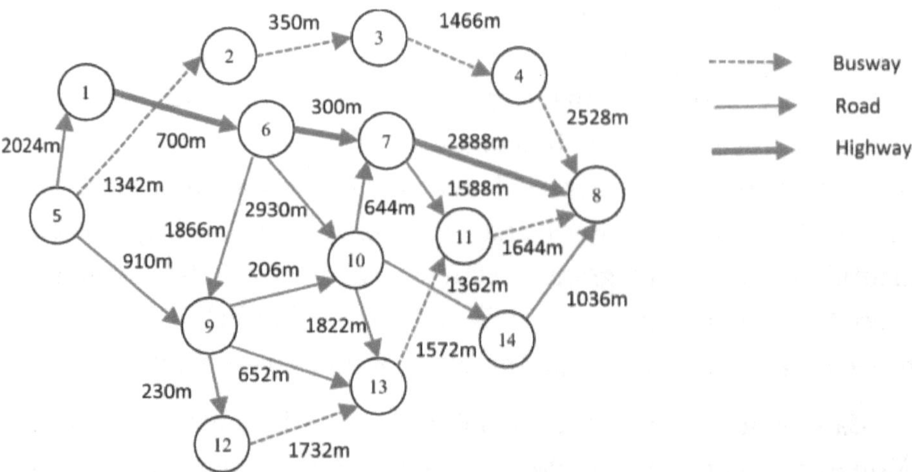

Concept Overview: Multi-commodity flow models are mathematical models used to optimize the allocation of multiple resources across a network. Within the framework of airline operations, these elements comprise passengers, cargo, aircraft, and staff. Given restrictions like capacity, demand, and operational needs, the model seeks to identify the most effective path of routing these resources over the network.

A multi-commodity flow model's main goals are to minimize costs, satisfy demand, and follow operational restrictions while nevertheless allowing for This entails harmonizing the flow of several goods to guarantee efficient use of resources and operation of aircraft. In complicated and dynamic settings where several resources have to be handled concurrently, multi-commodity flow models are especially helpful.

Model Components: The main components of a multi-commodity flow model include commodities, flows, nodes, arcs, and constraints. Every one of these elements is absolutely important for best representing and distributing resources.

Commodities are the several varieties of resources under management. In airline operations, commodities usually comprise passengers, goods, aircraft, and personnel. Every good has unique qualities that the model has to take into account including capacity, demand, and routing choices.

Commodities move throughout the network in flows. Within the framework of airline operations, flows relate to the distribution of passengers, goods, aircraft, and crew to several flights and paths. The approach seeks to ascertain the ideal flow of every good to reduce expenses and maximize effectiveness.

Nodes, which stand for certain sites in the network—such as airports, repair shops, and crew bases—represent Every node is connected to particular capacities and limitations including crew rest needs, gate availability, and airport slots. Nodes define the points at which goods may be routed and provide the network its framework.

Corresponding to flight segments, ground operations, and other activities, arcs show the links between nodes. Every arc has unique characteristics that affect the routing choices including capacity, cost, and length. Arcs define the interactions between several nodes and offer the routes via which goods move.

Constraints are the guidelines and restrictions controlling the commodity movement over the network. Among these limitations are operational constraints, demand criteria, capacity restraints, and legal ones. Constraints guarantee that the model generates workable and pragmatic answers and follows actual conditions.

Optimization Techniques: Various optimization techniques are used to solve multi-commodity flow models and determine the optimal allocation of resources. These methods examine the network and pinpoint the most effective answers using computational tools and mathematical algorithms.

Linear programming is one of the primary techniques used in multi-commodity flow models. Formulating the optimization problem as a series of linear equations and inequalities helps linear programming to reflect the objective function and constraints. By determining the values of the decision variables that either maximize or reduce the objective function while satisfying the constraints, one finds the solution. Particularly useful for large-scale optimization challenges and able to manage several commodities concurrently, linear programming is

Another method applied in multi-commodity flow models, especially when the decision variables have to adopt integer values, is integer programming. Though it adds the requirement that the decision variables must be integers, integer programming is like linear programming. When dealing with discrete resources—such as aircraft and crew—where fractional values are not practical, this method helps.

Designed for flow problems in networks, network flow algorithms are specialized optimization methods. These techniques effectively tackle the optimization problem using the network's structure. Examples of network flow algorithms include the Ford-Fulkerson algorithm, the Edmonds-Karp algorithm, and the push-relabel algorithm. Optimizing the movement of goods over vast and intricate networks calls especially for these algorithms.

Metaheuristic algorithms, such as genetic algorithms, simulated annealing, and ant colony optimization, are also used in multi-commodity flow models. Through iteratively improving the solutions and exploring the solution space, these algorithms are meant to find approximative answers to difficult optimization problems. Problems with huge and complicated solution spaces where accurate solutions may be computationally impossible benefit especially from metaheuristic techniques.

Practical Applications: Multi-commodity flow models have a wide range of practical applications in airline operations and scheduling. These uses cover cargo management, aircraft routing, crew scheduling, and flight schedule optimization.

Multi-commodity flow models are applied in flight scheduling to ascertain the best distribution of aircraft to several paths and times slots. The model creates schedules that maximize income and reduce running expenses by considering elements such passenger demand, aircraft availability, and legal restrictions. Airlines can better their market position, raise load factors, and raise customer happiness by streamlining flight plans.

Another important use for multi-commodity flow models is aircraft navigation. Given elements including fuel costs, maintenance needs, and airport capacity, the model helps the airline choose the most effective paths for its fleet. Airlines can save fuel usage, guarantee efficient use of aircraft, and minimize delays by besting aircraft routing.

Allocating pilots and cabin crew to several flights while following legal criteria and operational restrictions is the difficult and demanding work that is crew scheduling. Crew schedules are optimized using multi-commodity flow models, therefore guaranteeing that aircraft are manned with the correct crew and that crew duty hours and rest periods are controlled efficiently. Airlines can increase operational effectiveness, lower costs, and guarantee compliance with safety rules by besting personnel schedules.

Another significant use of multi-commodity flow models is cargo management. With regard to cargo capacity, demand, and delivery dates, the model helps to maximize the distribution of goods to several flights and routes. Through better on-time delivery, cargo management optimization will help airlines optimize income from cargo operations and raise customer satisfaction.

Challenges and Solutions: Implementing multi-commodity flow models in airline operations presents several challenges. These difficulties include the complexity of the models, the need for reliable and timely data, and the difficulty of including the models with current systems and procedures. Nonetheless, different approaches and solutions can solve these difficulties and improve the performance of multi-commodity flow models.

The difficulty of multi-commodity flow models is among the main ones. These models are computationally difficult to solve and involve several commodities, constraints, and decision factors. By effectively tackling broad-scale optimization problems and offering high-quality solutions, advanced optimization algorithms and computational tools can help to handle this complexity.

Multi-commercium flow models cannot be effective without accurate and timely data. Data from many sources—including flight schedules, aircraft performance records, crew availability records, and cargo demand projections—forms the foundation for the models. Effective optimization depends on this data being correct, consistent, and up to current. By putting strong data integration and management systems that combine data from many sources, confirm its accuracy, and guarantee that it is regularly updated and available into use, airlines may solve this problem.

Another major difficulty is adding multi-commodity flow models into current systems and procedures. For flight scheduling, aircraft routing, crew scheduling, cargo management, airlines have often developed systems and procedures. Including the optimization models into these systems and processes calls for careful coordination and preparation. By using modular and flexible optimization solutions easily connected with current systems and procedures, airlines may solve this difficulty. This method guarantees that the optimization models enhance rather than disturb current activities, therefore complementing them.

Case Studies and Examples: Real-world case studies and examples provide valuable insights into the application of multi-commodity flow models in airline operations. These cases show how well airlines have applied these ideas to maximize their operations and raise effectiveness.

FedEx is one prominent example as it has efficiently applied multi-commodity flow ideas to maximize its freight operations. Advanced optimization techniques allow FedEx to control cargo movement across its vast network of delivery hubs, airports, and distribution locations. FedEx has been able to raise on-time delivery, lower running expenses, and raise customer satisfaction by using multi-commodity flow models. FedEx's freight operations show how well multi-commodity flow models might maximize dynamic and sophisticated networks.

Another such is British Airways, which has used multi-commodity flow ideas to maximize aircraft routing and flight scheduling. British Airways examines its network of routes, aircraft, and staff using linear programming and network flow methods. British Airways has been able to raise load factors, boost market position, and lower running costs by besting flight scheduling and aircraft routing. The effectiveness of British Airways' scheduling and routing optimization shows how crucial modern optimization methods and data-driven decision-making are to airline operations.

Future Trends and Innovations: Advances in technology and the growing availability of data will probably help to define multi-commodity flow models in airline operations. Blockchain and artificial intelligence (AI) among other emerging technologies could transform airline schedule development and management.

Techniques like artificial intelligence and machine learning can improve the analysis and optimization of multi-commercium flow models. Airlines can create predictive models using artificial intelligence that estimate demand trends, spot possible interruptions, and suggest best schedule changes. By means of constant learning from operational performance and historical data, machine learning techniques help airlines to optimize their schedules and thereby increase efficiency over time.

Blockchain technology can improve the security and openness of data applied in models of multi-commodity flow. Blockchain notes data changes and transactions on a distributed, unchangeable ledger. Blockchain lets airlines guarantee that their data is safe, consistent, and correct. This helps multi-commodity flow models to be more reliable and supports better choices of scheduling.

Another important factor influencing the direction of multi-commodity flow models is the growing data accessibility. From several sources—including flight operations, market demand, and customer behavior— airlines have access to enormous volumes of data. Airlines may create more sensible timetables and have a better understanding of their operations by combining and examining this data. By means of advanced data analytics and business intelligence instruments, airlines may make data-driven decisions and ongoing schedule optimization is facilitated.

In order to maximize airline operations and scheduling, multi-commodity flow models are therefore indispensable instruments. They give airlines a disciplined framework for showing and evaluating the distribution of several resources over a network, therefore helping them to make judgments on operational efficiency, schedule planning, and resource allocation. Representing and optimizing the allocation of resources depends critically on the main constituents of multi-commodity flow models—including commodities, flows, nodes, arcs, and limitations.

Multi-commodity flow models are applied in airline operations to maximize flight schedules, aircraft routing, personnel scheduling, and cargo management. Airlines can create effective plans that improve operational efficiency, satisfy market demand, and optimize profitability by using cutting-edge optimization strategies by means of which to Implementing multi-commodity flow models, however, offers a number of difficulties including the complexity of the models, the requirement for reliable and timely data, and the difficulty of combining the models with current systems and procedures. Advanced optimization algorithms, data integration systems, and modular optimization solutions among other methods and approaches can help to solve these difficulties and improve the performance of multi-commodity flow models.

Real-world case studies including those of FedEx and British Airways show how effectively multi-commodity flow models are applied to maximize airline operations. These illustrations show the need for proactive changes, ongoing optimization, and data-driven decision-making in reaching effective schedule planning.

Looking ahead, developments in technology and growing data availability will probably help multi-commodity flow models to become even more effective. Blockchain technology, artificial intelligence, and machine learning have the ability to completely transform airline scheduling by offering improved data protection, predictive power, and deeper understanding. Airlines can keep maximizing their operations, increasing efficiency, and giving their passengers a first-rate travel experience by adopting these advancements.

Pax Mix Model

Airlines employ a sophisticated instrument called the Pax Mix Model, sometimes known as Passenger Mix Model, to maximize their operational plans and schedules. This approach enables airlines to maximize income and raise customer happiness by helping them to grasp and control the passenger mix on their flights. The definition and relevance of the Pax Mix Model, its elements, use in schedule planning, advantages and drawbacks of its use are examined in this part.

Introduction to Pax Mix Model: Airlines use this structure to examine and control the passenger mix on their flights. It entails grouping travellers according to several characteristics like fare class, trip intent, booking behaviour, and loyalty status. Understanding the makeup of a passenger base helps airlines to customize their offerings of services, pricing policies, and schedules to more satisfy various groups, hence improving profitability and customer satisfaction.

The Pax Mix Model's value resides in its capacity to offer thorough understanding of consumer preferences and behavior. Making wise decisions about route planning, pricing, and service offers depends on knowing this data. Airlines can maximize load factors and guarantee effective use of resources by using the Pax Mix Model to optimize their operations so attracting and retaining high-value customers.

Pax Mix Models consist of multiple components, each reflecting a unique facet of passenger segmentation. These elements enable airlines to properly classify and examine their passenger load in all around perspective.

Defining passenger segments depending on different criteria forms the initial element of the Pax Mix Model. Fare class (economy, premium economy, business, first), trip purpose (business, pleasure, VFR - visiting friends and relative), booking behavior (early bookers, last-minute passengers), and loyalty status (frequent fliers, occasional traveler). Airlines can better know passenger preferences, wants, and behavior by separating them.

The second element emphasizes on examining the income contribution of several passenger groups. This entails figuring each segment's average fare as well as their whole portion of the airline's overall income. Knowing the income contribution of various departments enables airlines to prioritize their marketing and service initiatives, therefore guaranteeing that they satisfy the needs of their most important clients.

Load factors, which show the proportion of filled available seats on a flight, Load factors for several passenger groups are analyzed in the

Pax Mix Model to offer understanding of the occupancy rates of several price levels and routes. While low load factors may call for changes in price, scheduling, or capacity allocation, high load factors indicate great demand.

Analyzing the booking behavior of several passenger groups, the component on booking patterns helps This covers the booking preferences (e.g., direct flights, connecting flights), the channels used for booking (e.g., online, travel agents, corporate travel offices), and the timing of bookings—that is, early bookings against last-minute bookings. Knowing booking trends lets airlines maximize their pricing policies and inventory control.

Crucially important to the Pax Mix Model is customer happiness. To evaluate their degree of satisfaction with many facets of the travel experience, including check-in, boarding, in-flight services, and post-flight operations, airlines gather and examine comments from consumers in many segments. Knowing customer satisfaction levels helps airlines to pinpoint areas needing work and customize their offerings to optimize the whole passenger experience.

Implementation in Schedule Planning: Helping airlines maximize their flight schedules to satisfy various passenger segments, the Pax Mix Model is absolutely essential in schedule planning. Airlines can create schedules that maximize income, increase load factors, and raise passenger satisfaction by using the knowledge acquired from the Pax Mix Model into their scheduling systems.

Route planning is one of the main uses for the Pax Mix Model in schedule design. Airlines can find the most lucrative routes and distribute capacity by use of demand pattern analysis and preference identification for several passenger groups. If the model shows, for instance, substantial demand from business travelers on a given route, the airline might plan more flights during the busiest business travel times and provide other services to serve this market.

The Pax Mix Model also guides airlines in deciding the ideal frequency and time for flights. Understanding the booking trends and preferences of various segments helps airlines to plan flights at times that meet the demands of the passengers. Business travellers could choose early morning flights, for example; leisure travellers might want mid-morning or afternoon departures. Changing flight times and frequencies depending on consumer choices helps airlines raise load factors and enhance the travel experience.

The Pax Mix Model offers understanding of the demand for various fare levels on particular paths. This data enables airlines to distribute the suitable number of seats to every tariff class, therefore optimizing income and satisfying passenger needs. If demand for premium economy on a given route is strong, for instance, the airline might allot additional seats to this price class and modify pricing policies in accordance.

Airlines can create focused marketing plans using the knowledge from the Pax Mix Model. Understanding the interests and booking patterns of various segments helps airlines design offers appealing to particular customer groups. For early bookers, for instance, they might provide lower rates; for frequent fliers, loyalty awards; or package discounts for leisure tourists. Targeted campaigns enable airlines to draw in and keep customers, hence increasing load factors and income.

Benefits of the Pax Mix Model: Airlines may maximize their operations and improve their competitiveness in the market by means of various advantages this model presents.

Improved Revenue Management: Airlines can create more successful revenue management plans knowing the income contribution of various passenger groups. To maximize income from high-value sectors, this entails modifying pricing, capacity allocation, and promotional activities. Improved financial performance and preservation of profitability in a competitive market depend on improved revenue management for airlines.

Enhanced Customer Satisfaction: The Pax Mix Model helps airlines to customize their offers and services to fit several customer groups. Airlines may raise customer happiness and loyalty by offering individualized experiences and attending to the particular preferences of every group. Contented consumers are more likely to select the airline for next travel, suggest it to friends, and take advantage of reward schemes.

The Pax Mix Model guides airlines in best using their aircraft, personnel, and ground services among other resources. Airlines may guarantee effective use of their resources by matching flight plans, ticket class distribution, and service offers with passenger demand. Reduced cost, better operational efficiency, and better service quality follow from optimized use of resources.

Analysis of load factors for various passenger groups helps airlines to find chances to raise occupancy rates on their flights. To more closely fit passenger demand, this could entail changing flight frequencies, schedules, or price policies. Higher income, better use of aircraft capacity, and more profitability follow from increased load factors.

Using the Pax Mix Model brings various difficulties like data collecting and analysis, interaction with current systems, and handling passenger segmentation complexity. Still, many approaches and ideas can help to solve these problems and improve the model's performance.

Data collecting and analysis for the Pax Mix Model calls for access to precise and thorough knowledge on passenger behavior, preferences, and satisfaction. By putting strong data collecting systems—including surveys, feedback forms, and loyalty program data—into place, airlines may meet this difficulty. Modern data analytics tools and methods include artificial intelligence and machine learning enable airlines to examine vast amounts of data and provide insightful analysis.

Effective application depends on combining the Pax Mix Model with current systems including revenue management, inventory control, and customer relationship management (CRM) systems. Using modular and adaptable software solutions that may be readily combined with current systems can help airlines meet this difficulty. Data integration systems and APIs—application programming interfaces—can help to enable flawless data flow and system interoperability.

Managing Complexity: Particularly for big airlines with varied passenger bases, the complexity of passenger segmentation and analysis can be taxing. By using cutting-edge segmentation strategies including predictive modeling and clustering algorithms to properly classify passengers, airlines can meet this difficulty. Frequent changes and evaluations of segmentation criteria guarantee the model's continued accuracy and relevance.

Real-world case studies and examples give important new perspectives on the effective application of the Pax Mix Model.

One such example is Singapore Airlines, which has improved revenue management and schedule planning using the Pax Mix Model rather successfully. Based on fare class, travel goal, booking behavior, and loyalty level, Singapore Airlines divides its customers. Through segment-specific analysis of preferences and behavior, the airline has refined its flight plans, fare class distribution, and marketing tactics. Higher revenue, better load factors, and more customer happiness are outcomes of this strategy.

Another such is Southwest Airlines, which has customized its offers to fit its varied customer base by using the Pax Mix Model. Southwest Airlines divides its customers according to travel goal, booking patterns, and loyalty level. These revelations help the airline create focused promotions, change flight frequency, and improve in-flight offerings. Southwest has thereby attained better load factors, more income, and great customer loyalty.

Advances in technology and the growing availability of data will probably help to define the Pax Mix Model in airline operations going forward. Emerging technologies including blockchain and artificial intelligence (AI) might completely change how airlines handle passenger segmentation.

Methods of artificial intelligence and machine learning can improve Pax Mix Model analysis and optimization. Airlines may create predictive models using artificial intelligence that predict passenger behavior, spot new trends, and suggest best pricing and scheduling policies. By constantly learning from operational performance and past data, machine learning techniques help airlines to enhance efficiency over time by means of better segmentation.

Blockchain technology might improve the security and openness of data applied in the Pax Mix Model. Blockchain notes data changes and transactions on a distributed, unchangeable ledger. Blockchain lets airlines guarantee that their data is safe, consistent, and correct. This helps the Pax Mix Model to be more dependable and facilitates more wise decision-making.

Another important aspect influencing the Pax Mix Model's future is the growing data accessibility. From several sources—including flight operations, market demand, and customer behavior— airlines have access to enormous volumes of data. Airlines may better understand their passenger base and create more sensible segmenting plans by combining and evaluating this data. Business intelligence technologies and advanced data analytics can enable airlines to make data-driven decisions and ongoing operational optimization is made possible.

In essence, the Pax Mix Model is a great tool for scheduling and streamlining airline operations. Airlines can customize their services, pricing policies, and timetables to fit the demands of various passenger segments by grouping them into distinct segments and evaluating their preferences, behaviors, and degrees of satisfaction. Representing and evaluating the makeup of the passenger base depends much on the main elements of the Pax Mix Model— Passenger segments, revenue contribution, load factors, booking patterns, and customer satisfaction.

Using the Pax Mix Model in schedule planning means maximizing route planning, airline frequency, fare class distribution, and promotional tactics. Airlines can improve revenue management, raise customer satisfaction, maximize resource use, and raise load factors by using the insights acquired from the model. Using the Pax Mix Model does, however, provide a number of difficulties including data collecting and analysis, interaction with current systems, and handling of passenger segmentation complexity. Advanced data analytics, modular software solutions, and sophisticated segmentation techniques among other solutions and approaches help to solve these problems and improve the model's performance.

Real-world case studies including those of Southwest Airlines and Singapore Airlines show how well the Pax Mix Model is applied to maximize airline operations. These illustrations show the need of proactive changes, ongoing optimization, and data-driven decision-making in reaching effective schedule planning.

Looking ahead, data availability and technological developments will probably help the Pax Mix Model to become even more effective. Blockchain technology, artificial intelligence, and machine learning offer deeper insights, predictive capabilities, and improved data security, hence transforming passenger segmentation and airline scheduling. Airlines that embrace these technologies will be able to keep streamlining their operations, raising efficiency, and giving their passengers first-rate travel experience.

Chapter-10

Fleet Assessment Problems

Galley Equipment and Preflight Checks

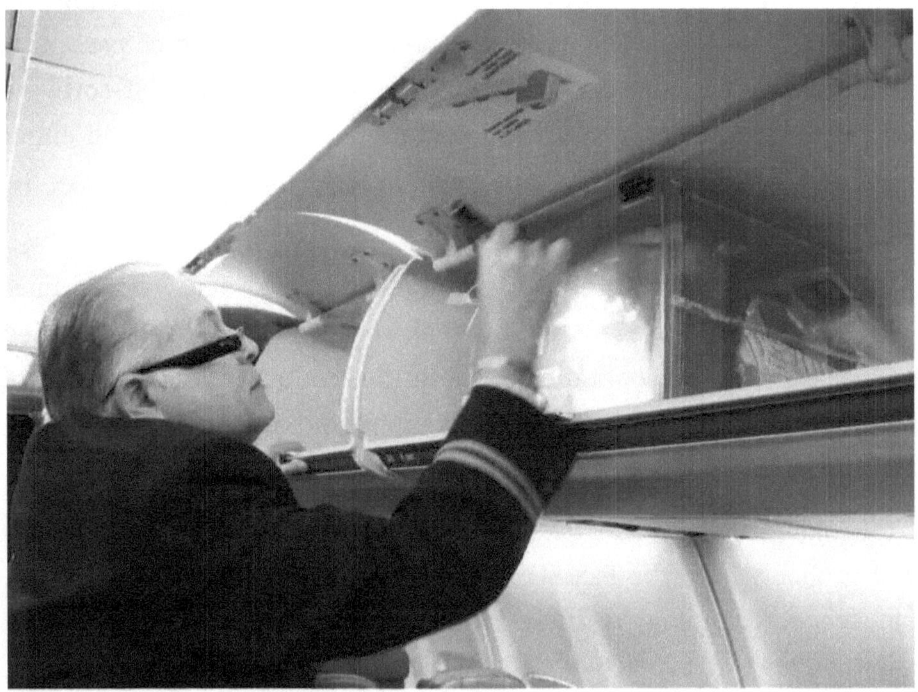

Airline catering, one of the important components of in-flight service, begins with a detailed grasp of the galley and its equipment. The galley is the kitchen of an airplane, and while it could be substantially smaller in size than a regular kitchen, it is filled with equipment that is crucial for ensuring that passengers receive their meals and beverages in a timely and efficient manner. Galleys are built to maximize space, with equipment such as ovens, refrigeration units, beverage dispensers, trolleys, and storage facilities meticulously organized to simplify the crew's work during flights. Understanding how to correctly handle and maintain these tools is vital for a seamless food service experience in the air.

Introduction to Galleys and Equipment

Galleys come in numerous forms based on the type of aircraft and the airline's business model. Larger aircraft, such as the Boeing 777 or Airbus A380, have vast galleys that accommodate a full variety of meal and beverage services, but smaller regional jets may have more limited galley space. Despite the size, every galley is outfitted with critical tools that allow the crew to cook and serve meals efficiently.

Key equipment in galleys includes ovens, which are used to cook pre-prepared meals; refrigerators to store perishable products like dairy, salads, and desserts; and coffee makers, which are critical for creating hot beverages for passengers. The galley also has compartments for storing dry items like snacks, bread, and packaged foods. Other critical equipment includes trolleys for food and beverage service, secure storage rooms for glassware, cutlery, and dishes, and safety equipment like fire extinguishers. Each piece of equipment is built to endure turbulence and assure safety while operating during the trip.

Preflight Galley Checks: Food and Nutrition Essentials

Before any aircraft takes off, the cabin crew undertakes crucial preflight checks to verify that the galley is adequately stocked and all equipment is functioning properly. These preflight tests are crucial for the success of the meal service and to accommodate the different dietary preferences of passengers. The checks begin with an inventory of all the food and beverages that have been put onboard the aircraft. Since many airlines provide numerous food options, including vegetarian, gluten-free, and other special dietary needs, it is crucial that the crew confirms that the correct amount and types of meals are onboard.

In addition to the usual meals, the crew must also ensure that the galley is stocked with snacks, bottled water, and beverages, including juices, soft drinks, and alcohol. The preflight checklist also involves an inspection of the ovens and refrigerators to ensure they are working correctly. Faulty equipment could result in food not being adequately heated or kept, which could lead to food safety problems or a bad in-flight dining experience for passengers.

Nutritional considerations are also part of the preflight tests. Airlines are increasingly focusing on delivering nutritious meal alternatives to cater to the growing number of health-conscious travelers. The crew must check that meals match the airline's nutritional rules, which frequently include balanced servings of proteins, carbohydrates, and vegetables, and account for various dietary restrictions like low-sodium or low-fat requirements. Preflight checks, therefore, serve a key role in ensuring that passengers not only receive meals but also that these meals are healthy, fresh, and safe to ingest.

Proper Handling Techniques of Galley Equipment

Handling galley equipment involves a combination of technical understanding, safety awareness, and efficiency. The tight space of the galley implies that crew members must be well-trained in utilizing the equipment without compromising safety or the quality of the service. For instance, the ovens used onboard are specialized devices designed to swiftly reheat food. These ovens can become extremely hot, therefore safe handling, including the wearing of protective gloves and ensuring the doors are securely closed during usage, is vital to avoid burns or injuries.

Refrigerators and coolers in the galley also require correct management to ensure food safety standards. It's crucial to ensure that cold items like dairy products, salads, and desserts are stored at the optimum temperatures. Opening and closing the refrigerator doors frequently might elevate the inside temperature, which could affect the freshness of perishable contents. Therefore, cabin crew members must be cautious of minimizing how often they open these units to ensure appropriate temperatures for the stored food.

Another crucial part of handling galley equipment is the control of beverage machines. Hot beverage dispensers for coffee and tea are in regular use during flights, and crew members must be adept at operating them without causing spills or mishaps. This requires not only understanding the technical functions of these machines but also ensuring that cups, lids, and condiments are readily available and appropriately stored for easy access during meal service. Furthermore, these machines must be cleaned and maintained periodically to prevent any contamination or malfunction during the flight.

Equally crucial is the handling of trolleys utilized for meal and beverage service. Trolleys are the lifeline of in-flight catering, since they enable the crew to convey meals and beverages quickly from the galley to passengers seated throughout the aircraft. These trolleys must be loaded appropriately, ensuring that heavier products are placed at the bottom and lighter items on top to prevent tipping during turbulence. The trolleys are equipped with brakes to prevent them from moving while not in use, and the crew must constantly ensure that the brakes are applied when the trolleys are stationary.

Crew members must also handle all galley equipment with an emphasis on hygiene. Since the galley is a high-traffic area where food and beverages are frequently produced and served, keeping cleanliness is vital. This includes regular sanitization of counters, equipment, and utensils to prevent cross-contamination between different food items, especially those containing allergens. Proper hygiene techniques are a crucial element of the training for airline crew members, as they directly effect the quality and safety of the food service.

Food Service Equipment Maintenance

The efficient operation of galley equipment is not only crucial for offering high-quality food service but also a question of safety. Routine maintenance checks guarantee that all equipment is in good functioning order before and during flights. This involves evaluating ovens, refrigerators, and beverage machines for any evidence of malfunction, such as inconsistent temperature control, malfunctioning heating elements, or broken components. Should any issue emerge, it must be notified to the maintenance personnel immediately so that repairs or replacements can be completed before the next trip.

In addition to maintenance checks performed by ground crews, flight attendants are trained to identify potential faults with galley equipment during the flight. For example, if an oven fails to heat properly or a refrigerator stops cooling, the crew must take prompt action to mitigate the problem. This may include changing the meal service, notifying the cockpit crew, and ensuring that any contaminated food items are destroyed to prevent serving spoiled food to passengers.

Another crucial part of equipment maintenance is the storage and handling of emergency supplies. Galleys are equipped with fire extinguishers, smoke detectors, and other safety measures in case of fire or smoke in the kitchen area. Proper maintenance and checks of these equipment are vital to ensure the safety of the crew and passengers. Additionally, the galley must have proper signage and training materials readily available so that crew members may rapidly access safety protocols in case of an emergency.

To conclude, the galley is a critical component of airline catering operations, and understanding the equipment and handling practices is fundamental to providing quality in-flight service. Preflight tests, proper handling practices, and the maintenance of equipment guarantee that the food service runs smoothly, passengers receive nutritious and well-prepared meals, and safety standards are upheld throughout the flight. For airline crew members, learning the galley and its operations is vital for delivering a high-quality, safe, and efficient food service that satisfies the different needs of customers.

Food Service and Hygiene Standards

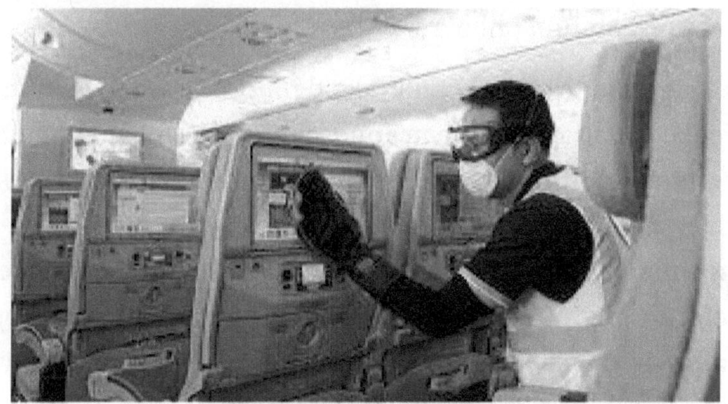

The in-flight food service experience is a vital feature of airline operations. Beyond the logistics of making and delivering meals to hundreds of passengers each day, airlines must ensure that food safety, cleanliness, and quality standards are kept at all times. This demands a carefully coordinated effort between ground-based catering companies and in-flight cabin crew, ensuring that all meals not only fulfill strict health criteria but are also provided with an emphasis on passenger happiness. As airlines serve millions of passengers with various dietary demands, they must achieve a delicate balance between taste, nutrition, and convenience. This section discusses the fundamental components of food service and hygiene, highlighting the necessity of safe food handling, meal diversity, specific dietary accommodations, and the mechanisms in place to ensure food quality at cruising altitude.

Food Handling and Safety: Ensuring Safe Preparation and Delivery

Food safety is one of the most critical areas of airline catering. Serving meals at 35,000 feet comes with unique problems, since food must be cooked, kept, and served in settings that differ greatly from those of a regular restaurant or catering service. The necessity of safe food handling practices cannot be emphasized, as a single case of foodborne illness onboard an aircraft can have significant ramifications. To avoid such mishaps, airline caterers must adhere to strict food safety requirements, starting from the production of meals on the ground to their final presentation onboard.

On the ground, caterers undertake tight processes to guarantee that food is cooked in a safe and clean atmosphere. This includes maintaining adequate temperature controls throughout the cooking process, from the refrigeration of raw ingredients to the preparation of meals and the subsequent storage of finished dishes. Meals are sometimes made hours before a flight departs, meaning that maintaining the optimum temperature is crucial to prevent bacterial growth. To achieve these standards, caterers utilize specialized equipment, like as blast chillers and insulated containers, that maintain food at safe temperatures during delivery to the aircraft.

Once the meals get onboard, the responsibility transfers to the cabin staff to ensure that food handling practices continue to exceed safety regulations. Meals must be kept refrigerated until they are ready to be heated and served. When using galley ovens, crew members must ensure that food reaches the necessary temperature to destroy any hazardous bacteria before serving. Additionally, they must take steps to avoid cross-contamination between different food components, particularly when working with special dishes that cater to allergies or specific dietary requirements. Hygiene is crucial, and crew members are educated to use gloves and sanitizing wipes when handling food, utensils, and serving trays.

The need of hygiene extends beyond food preparation to the cleaning and upkeep of galley equipment. Surfaces, utensils, and storage locations must be cleaned periodically to avoid the growth of germs or other impurities. Ovens and refrigeration machines must be wiped out after each usage, while trolleys and serving trays must be sterilized between meal services. These sanitary standards ensure that food is not only safe to eat but also of the highest possible quality when it reaches the passenger.

Menu Planning and Quality Control: Balancing Taste and Nutrition

The process of preparing an in-flight menu is a highly skilled endeavor that goes beyond merely choosing meals that taste well. Airlines must consider numerous variables when planning their menus, including passenger preferences, dietary requirements, cultural differences, and the logistical obstacles of supplying meals at high altitudes. Additionally, dishes must be designed to keep their quality when reheated, ensuring that passengers enjoy a dining experience that rivals that of a regular restaurant.

One of the important issues in menu preparation is the impact of altitude on passengers' taste senses. At cruising altitude, the cabin's low humidity and pressured air degrade the sense of taste, making food seem less tasty. To compensate for this, aircraft caterers typically add extra seasoning to their dishes, utilizing bolder flavors, such as herbs, spices, and umami-rich products, to ensure that meals stay palatable even at high altitudes. Sauces and gravies are also routinely used to keep dishes from drying up when reheated in the galley ovens.

Nutrition is another key component in menu planning. As passengers become increasingly health-conscious, airlines have responded by delivering meals that are not only delicious but also nutritionally balanced. Meals are often structured to contain a balance of proteins, carbs, and vegetables, with an emphasis on fresh, whole products. Airlines may also offer lighter, healthier options, such as salads, fruits, and low-calorie snacks, to cater to passengers who are aware of their diet while traveling.

Quality control is an ongoing process in aircraft catering, and airlines work closely with their caterers to ensure that all meals satisfy their requirements for flavor, appearance, and safety. Before a meal is certified for onboard service, it undergoes extensive testing, including taste tests at simulated altitudes to ensure that the flavors are appropriate for in-flight eating. Meals are also examined for their appearance and texture, as these variables can influence passengers' overall happiness. Airlines constantly update their menus to reflect seasonal foods and regional flavors, ensuring that customers have a choice of meal options to select from.

Types of Meals and Special Meals: Catering to Diverse Dietary Needs

One of the most problematic elements of in-flight catering is satisfying the different dietary preferences of passengers. Airlines serve individuals from all over the world, each with their own food preferences, restrictions, and cultural or religious constraints. To accommodate these expectations, airlines offer a wide array of meal options, including ordinary meals, special meals for dietary restrictions, and meals suited to certain religious or cultural customs.

Regular meals often provide a choice between a meat-based entrée and a vegetarian option, allowing passengers to select the meal that best meets their preferences. These meals are designed to be nutritionally balanced and delectable, with an emphasis on delivering diversity throughout multiple courses, such as appetizers, main dishes, and desserts.

In addition to ordinary meals, airlines also offer a choice of customized meals to satisfy passengers with unique dietary needs. These meals are classified using standard meal codes, which enable both caterers and cabin staff guarantee that the correct meal is provided to the right passenger. Some frequent special meal codes include:

VGML (Vegetarian Meal): A meal that does not contain any meat, poultry, or fish, and is often based on vegetables, grains, and legumes.

LSML (Low-Sodium Meal): A meal developed for travelers who need to reduce their salt intake, incorporating low-sodium products and seasonings.

GFML (Gluten-Free Meal): A meal that excludes gluten-containing components, such as wheat, barley, and rye, for passengers with celiac disease or gluten intolerance.

HNML (Hindu Meal): A meal that follows to Hindu dietary customs, omitting beef and often containing vegetarian foods.

MOML (Muslim Meal): A meal that follows to Islamic dietary regulations, omitting pork and alcohol and using halal foods.

KSML (Kosher Meal): A meal prepared in conformity with Jewish dietary restrictions, approved by a kosher body and often sealed to assure compliance.

Airlines frequently offer meals for passengers with specific sensitivities, such as nut-free or dairy-free meals, to guarantee that they can eat safely throughout the journey. The preparation of these meals takes special attention to avoid cross-contamination, and airlines must work closely with their caterers to verify that all ingredients and preparation processes meet the necessary standards.

The ability to meet such a wide diversity of food preferences is a testament to the complexity of airline catering. Meals must be made in enormous quantities, often in a short amount of time, and yet they must still fulfill the particular needs of each passenger. This involves meticulous coordination between the airline, caterers, and cabin staff to guarantee that every passenger receives the correct meal, whether it's a conventional meal or a specific dietary requirement.

Introduction to Cheese: A Delicate Addition to In-Flight Dining

Cheese has become an increasingly popular addition to in-flight menus, particularly in premium cabins where passengers anticipate a more sophisticated meal experience. Offering a selection of cheeses allows airlines to upgrade their meal service, presenting customers with a premium delicacy that matches nicely with wine or as part of a dessert course. However, serving cheese onboard comes with its own set of issues, as the texture and flavor of cheese can be influenced by the cabin environment and the manner of preservation.

There are many various varieties of cheeses that can be offered onboard, ranging from soft cheeses like Brie and Camembert to hard cheeses like Cheddar and Parmesan. The type of cheese supplied often depends on the airline's menu and the location in which it operates. For example, European airlines may serve a selection of French or Italian cheeses, while airlines headquartered in Asia may offer kinds more typical in their native cuisine.

When serving cheese onboard, it is crucial to consider how it will be preserved and presented. Cheese must be kept at the appropriate temperature to maintain its flavor and texture, which implies that refrigeration is necessary. However, cheese should be brought to room temperature before serving to allow the tastes to fully develop. This involves careful planning and coordination between the catering team and cabin crew, ensuring that cheese is provided at the right time during the meal service.

In addition to supplying a range of cheeses, airlines may also give accompaniments such as crackers, bread, and fruit. These innovations enhance the cheese-tasting experience and offer travelers a more comprehensive and pleasant dinner. Airlines may also offer wine pairings with their cheese selection, further improving the in-flight eating experience for passengers in premium cabins.

Special Handling for Food Service: Maintaining Hygiene and Food Quality

In-flight food service involves rigorous handling skills to ensure that meals are provided safely and hygienically. The intimate quarters of the airplane galley, combined with the fast-paced nature of food delivery, provide a particular challenge for cabin crew personnel. To maintain the highest standards of food safety and hygiene, airlines adopt tight rules for handling and serving food throughout the flight.

One of the most crucial parts of food handling onboard is preventing cross-contamination. Cabin crew workers must take care to prevent mixing different food items, particularly when dealing with special meals for customers with allergies or dietary restrictions. This may require utilizing distinct utensils and serving trays for special meals or designating certain areas of the galley for cooking these meals. Crew members are trained to handle food with gloves, and sanitizing wipes are utilized to sanitize surfaces and equipment between usage.

Proper handling practices also apply to the storage of food onboard. Refrigerators and coolers must be maintained at the correct temperature to ensure that perishable items, including as dairy products and salads, remain fresh during the journey. Hot meals, on the other hand, must be reheated to the optimum temperature to guarantee that they are safe to eat. Crew members are instructed to monitor the temperature of ovens and refrigerators routinely and to report any failures that could threaten food safety.

Hygiene is a primary priority in the galley, and cabin crew workers are expected to observe strict cleanliness regulations. This includes regularly washing their hands, using gloves while handling food, and cleaning all equipment and surfaces after each meal service. Additionally, crew members must ensure that any remaining food or waste is disposed of appropriately to avoid attracting bugs or producing unpleasant aromas in the galley.

Finally, airlines also take steps to ensure that food is presented in an appealing manner. Even though meals are pre-prepared on the ground, they must still be served and presented in a way that appears attractive to passengers. This takes meticulous attention to detail, as the appearance of a meal can significantly influence passengers' opinions of its quality. Cabin crew workers are trained to arrange meals neatly on trays, ensuring that all components are in the correct order and that the meal is visually appealing.

In conclusion, the food service and hygiene standards onboard an aircraft are crucial to ensuring a high-quality eating experience. From the thorough preparation and management of meals to the fastidious attention to hygiene and presentation, airlines go to considerable lengths to ensure that customers have safe, nutritious, and enjoyable meals during their journey. The complexity of airline catering, along with the specific problems of providing food at high altitudes, makes it one of the most intricate components of in-flight operations, yet when done effectively, it contributes greatly to customers' overall happiness with their voyage.

Airline Catering and Delivery Onboard

The flawless delivery of food services onboard an airplane is one of the most crucial parts of delivering a comfortable and joyful flying experience for passengers. Airline catering entails not simply the preparation of meals but also the logistics of delivering, storing, and serving them in a high-altitude environment. The coordination required between the ground-based catering teams, airline crew, and cabin attendants is considerable, and every element must be properly prepared to assure a seamless meal service. This section dives into the logistical problems of catering, the unique handling techniques needed for food preparation, and the in-flight protocols that assure passengers receive their meals safely and quickly.

Catering Logistics: Coordinating Between Ground and Air

The voyage of an in-flight meal begins long before passengers board the plane. Airlines engage with professional catering firms to plan, produce, and deliver meals that satisfy high quality and safety criteria. The process starts with menu planning, as stated in earlier sections, but the logistical difficulty of ensuring that these meals are produced and carried in time for the flight adds another layer of complication.

Airline catering facilities, frequently located near major airports, are intended to manage the large-scale manufacturing of meals for several flights. These facilities must run with military-like precision, as every meal must be cooked, packaged, and delivered within a fixed time window. The timing is crucial: meals must be fresh and ready to be served onboard, but they also need to be delivered to the aircraft well before boarding begins. Depending on the airline and the amount of passengers, catering businesses may produce thousands of meals daily, ensuring that each aircraft receives the necessary quantity and varieties of meals, including those catering to special dietary needs.

Once the meals are produced, they are properly packaged and placed onto temperature-controlled trucks for transfer to the aircraft. During travel, it is necessary to maintain the right temperature for both hot and cold meals to ensure food safety. Cold storage units guarantee that perishable items like salads and desserts are kept fresh, while precooked hot meals are stored in insulated containers to keep them warm until they can be reheated onboard.

Upon arriving at the aircraft, the catering team works with ground staff to carry the meals and beverages into the galley. This operation must be conducted swiftly and safely, as it frequently takes place while other pre-flight preparations are continuing. Trolleys with the meals, beverages, and snacks are loaded into the galley, and the cabin crew takes responsibility for ensuring that everything is in place and ready for serve.

Special Handling for Food Service: Maintaining Quality During Flight

Once the meals are onboard, the cabin crew plays a crucial role in ensuring that food is provided in a timely and professional way. Unlike a regular restaurant, where food may be made and served promptly, in-flight catering needs the crew to work within the limits of the aircraft's galley equipment. Meals are pre-prepared on the ground and then reheated onboard, which implies that cautious handling is important to maintain the quality and safety of the food.

The initial phase in this process is the reheating of meals. Galley ovens are designed to reheat numerous meals simultaneously, ensuring that they are served hot and fresh. Crew members must be educated to operate these ovens safely and efficiently, monitoring the cooking periods to avoid overcooking or scorching the meals. Additionally, the ovens must be periodically cleaned and maintained to prevent any contamination from prior flights.

Special attention is essential while handling special meals, which must be kept segregated from conventional meals to prevent cross-contamination, particularly in circumstances when passengers have severe food allergies. For example, a gluten-free meal must be kept away from any goods containing wheat or gluten, and vegetarian meals must be stored apart from meat-based dishes. Airlines have special protocols in place to guarantee that these meals are correctly labeled and handled with care, decreasing the chance of errors during meal service.

The mechanics of serving meals on a flight also offer issues. The cabin crew must cross confined aisles with heavy trolleys, ensuring that meals are given quickly and efficiently to all passengers. In addition, they must handle specific requests, such as passengers requesting for additional beverages or snacks, all while maintaining a high level of service. This needs outstanding time management and organization, as meal service must be done within a set schedule to allow for other in-flight activities, such as entertainment or beverage service.

F&B Service: Efficient Delivery of Meals and Beverages Onboard

Food and beverage (F&B) service is one of the most visible components of the passenger experience, and airlines place great attention on ensuring that this service is done smoothly. The quality of the service can considerably influence passengers' opinions of the airline, and as such, cabin crew members are trained extensively in offering a high degree of customer care during the flight.

Meal service often begins with the distribution of beverages, which might include a variety of soft drinks, juices, water, and alcoholic beverages. In premium cabins, guests may be provided a welcome drink, such as champagne or sparkling wine, before the main dinner service begins. The distribution of beverages is often timed with the commencement of the meal service, with crew members offering passengers their choice of drink while delivering the first course of the meal.

In premium cabins, such as business or first class, the dinner service is often more extensive, with many meals served on beautiful china, glassware, and genuine cutlery. Passengers may be provided a choice of appetizers, main dishes, and desserts, along with a selection of wines and liqueurs. The cabin crew in these sections often take on a more personalized role, communicating with customers to ensure that their eating preferences are satisfied and offering drink pairings to enhance the dinner experience. This type of service requires additional training, as crew members must be educated about the menu, including the materials used in each meal and the wines served onboard.

In the economy class, dinner service is often speedier and more streamlined, with pre-packaged meals served on trays. Passengers usually get an option between two main courses, such as a chicken or pasta dish, which are provided alongside a salad, bread, dessert, and beverage. While the service is less formal than in premium cabins, cabin crew members are nevertheless expected to deliver the meals with efficiency and professionalism, ensuring that passengers receive their food in a timely way.

In addition to the normal food service, crew members must also be prepared to address special requests and dietary restrictions. This involves serving customers who require assistance with their meals, such as the elderly or people with disabilities, and ensuring that all special meals are given correctly. Crew members must be careful in verifying the labels of each meal to assure that the correct food is being served to the right passenger.

Liqueur Service: Serving Alcoholic Beverages Onboard

Alcoholic beverages, including wine, beer, and spirits, are a crucial element of the in-flight experience for many customers, particularly those in luxury seats. Airlines offer a range of alcoholic drinks to improve the food service or to assist passengers relax during the journey. However, providing alcohol onboard an airplane needs careful attention to legal requirements, passenger safety, and the potential effects of alcohol use at high altitudes.

When serving alcohol, cabin crew personnel must be conscious of the legal drinking age in the country where the airline is registered, as well as the legislation of the destination country. This means that passengers under the legal drinking age should not be provided alcohol, even if they are traveling to a nation where the legal drinking age is lower. Crew members are instructed to check passengers' identification if necessary and to refuse service to anyone who seems to be underage.

Additionally, the effects of alcohol are accentuated at high altitudes due to the lower quantities of oxygen in the cabin. Passengers may become intoxicated more faster than they would on the ground, thus crew members are trained to monitor alcohol intake and assist if necessary. This could mean refusing to offer extra beverages to passengers who look to be intoxicated or addressing disruptive conduct induced by excessive alcohol use.

Alcoholic beverages are commonly matched with meals to enhance the dining experience. In premium cabins, airlines often offer a selection of wines, including red, white, and sparkling kinds, as well as spirits and liqueurs. Crew members in these cabins are educated to make advice on wine pairings based on the meal being served, and some airlines hire specialist sommeliers or wine consultants to create their onboard wine selection. The idea is to deliver a premium dining experience that rivals that of a fine dining establishment.

In economy class, the alcohol selection is usually more limited, with passengers able to choose from a narrower range of wines, beers, and spirits. While the service is less customized, crew members are still obliged to serve the drinks promptly and ensure that guests have a favorable experience.

Alcohol service is sometimes followed by tiny snacks, such as pretzels or nuts, which assist to balance the effects of the alcohol and offer passengers with something to enjoy between meals. These accompaniments also serve as a method to enhance the overall experience, providing passengers with a sense of pleasure and elegance, even in the budget cabin.

In conclusion, the supply of meals onboard an airplane entails a complex logistical process that requires coordination between ground operations, catering teams, and cabin crew. From ensuring that meals are produced and served on schedule to addressing special requests and supplying beverages, the entire process is meant to offer passengers with a high-quality dining experience. By maintaining stringent sanitary standards, treating food with care, and serving meals swiftly, airlines can ensure that passengers enjoy their in-flight meals and feel pleased during the journey. Liqueur service, a vital aspect of the onboard experience, significantly enriches the whole atmosphere, making the in-flight dining experience one of the pleasures of air travel.

Menu Courses and Cultural Diversity in Airline Catering

In addition to reflecting the technical difficulties of serving meals at 35,000 feet, airline catering is a sophisticated and fascinating aspect of in-flight service that represents the diversity of world cultures and cuisines. In order to give customers an outstanding dining experience, airlines must do more than simply serve food; they must also recognize and accommodate the various dietary requirements, tastes, and culinary customs of its international passengers. This section examines the ways in which airlines offer their services in conjunction with menus from around the world, such as French, Indian, and Asian cuisines. It also explores the art of food and drink matching, the cultural significance of meals in various locales, and how airlines handle passengers' particular dietary needs. Finally, this section discusses the changing trends in airplane food service, including the emphasis on wellness and health, the growing demand for locally and sustainably sourced foods, and the ongoing quest of culinary innovation at altitude.

Menu Items: Asian, French, and Indian Flavors in Airline Catering

Travelers carry their cultural preferences, including eating preferences, on board with them. Airlines have to accommodate a wide range of gastronomic preferences, especially when flying internationally and carrying passengers from different cultural backgrounds. French, Indian, and Asian cuisines are among the most frequently offered on in-flight menus because many airlines understand how important it is to offer menu options that reflect the range of cultures among their customers.

French Food

Due to its historical associations with refinement and elegance, French food is frequently served in premium cabins where airlines strive to offer a gourmet dining experience. The classic French meal plan, which often consists of an appetizer, a main course, cheese, dessert, and coffee, works well for eating on an airplane, especially in first and business class.

Airlines frequently begin creating a French-inspired menu with traditional starters like foie gras, pâté, or smoked salmon served with butter and fresh bread. Among the options for the main course are coq au vin, which is chicken cooked in red wine, beef bourguignon, and seafood dishes like poached salmon. These rich, savory recipes reheat beautifully without sacrificing their texture or flavor, making them ideal for in-flight dining.

French cuisine is known for its rich and delicious desserts, which include crème brûlée, chocolate mousse, and tarte Tatin. Pain au chocolat and croissants are two more popular French pastries that are frequently served for breakfast or as a snack on long-haul flights.

A cheese course is a staple of French cuisine and is frequently included in premium cabins as a post-meal option. A variety of cheeses, including Brie, Camembert, and Roquefort, are usually offered by airlines together with fresh bread or crackers. Passengers may have a typical French meal experience while in flight with this cheese course and wine pairing.

Indian Food

Indian food is renowned for its vivid spices, strong flavors, and extensive culinary history. It is now a standard on a lot of international flights, particularly those operated by airlines that go to and from India or to areas where the Indian population is substantial. Indian cuisine is a great option for in-flight food because of its intricate layers of spices and ingredients that can be maintained while being reheated.

Airlines that provide Indian food usually offer both vegetarian and non-vegetarian alternatives to suit the dietary requirements of their customers. A typical Indian meal served on board can consist of a main course such as lamb biryani, chicken curry, or dal (lentil stew) with an appetizer like samosas or paneer tikka. A variety of tasty vegetable-based meals, like palak paneer (spinach with Indian cheese), chana masala (spicy chickpeas), and aloo gobi (potatoes and cauliflower), are frequently offered as vegetarian options.

Meals are frequently served with a variety of accompaniments, such as rice, naan bread, pickles, chutney, and yogurt, in keeping with Indian culinary traditions. With yogurt acting as a cooling agent to temper the heat of the spices, these side dishes not only improve the flavor of the dinner but also give it a well-rounded appearance.

Indian desserts are usually rich and sugary, such as barfi (a condensed milk-based fudge-like treat), kheer (rice pudding), and gulab jamun (milk-based doughnuts drenched in syrup). These sweets provide a lovely counterpoint to the fiery main meals and round off the dinner in a gratifying way.

Asian-inspired Food

Asian food has a broad variety of culinary traditions, ranging from Southeast Asian dishes that are spicy and aromatic to Japanese cuisine that is light and delicate in flavor. Airlines that serve travelers from Asia or on Asian routes frequently provide menu selections that showcase the variety of the region's culinary customs.

For instance, Japanese food is renowned for its simple presentation and concentration on using only the freshest, highest-quality ingredients. Sushi, sashimi, and tempura are examples of foods that airlines may provide on their in-flight menu. Steamed rice, pickled veggies, and miso soup are frequently served with these dishes. Another well-liked option for Japanese-inspired on-air lunches is a bento box, which serves a variety of miniature items in a single serving.

Chinese food is another well-liked choice because of its strong flavors and array of textures. Foods like sweet and sour chicken, dim sum, and stir-fried noodles may be served on airplanes. Meals are frequently served with classic Chinese sides such spring rolls, dumplings, or steamed buns, and these dishes are usually served with steamed rice or noodles.

Aromatic herbs and spices are widely used in Southeast Asian cuisines, including Thai, Vietnamese, and Malaysian dishes. Dishes like pad Thai, pho, or nasi lemak—which blend fresh ingredients like lemongrass, cilantro, and chili peppers with powerful flavors—may be served aboard airplanes. These dishes are frequently served with rice, noodles, or fresh vegetables along with dipping sauces that improve the dish's flavor profile.

Including International Foods in In-Flight Dining

Airlines collaborate closely with chefs and culinary experts who comprehend the special difficulties involved in preparing meals for air travel in order to include these varied culinary traditions into in-flight menus. These professionals are entrusted with producing meals that preserve the region's culinary legacy while still being delicious and high-quality even after being reheated aboard.

Because taste perception is affected at high altitudes, menu designers must take this into consideration while creating meals. This implies that in order to keep passengers' meals tasty, meals frequently need to be seasoned more heavily or have bold flavors. In order to better fit the in-flight environment, airlines may also alter classic recipes. For example, they may change the moisture level of some foods to keep them from drying out when being reheated.

In order to accommodate ethnic diversity in onboard meals, airlines must also be considerate of the dietary needs and religious beliefs of its patrons. Airlines have an obligation to make sure that its cuisine serves passengers with allergies or food intolerances as well as those who adhere to religious dietary requirements, such halal or kosher diets. To guarantee that meals are properly cooked and served, careful coordination between catering crews, chefs, and flight attendants is needed.

Personalized Dinner Preparation: Meeting Nutritional Requirements

Airlines have additional dietary requirements to meet in addition to providing a variety of menu options depending on ethnic preferences. As was discussed in earlier sections, airlines can identify passengers who need meals that follow specific dietary requirements or preferences by using special meal codes. To guarantee that these special meals fulfill the requisite standards for quality, safety, and health, extra care must be taken in their preparation.

Intolerants and Allergies

Allergies or dietary intolerances are among the most frequent reasons travelers ask for special meals. Airlines are starting to provide allergen-free meal alternatives as a result of growing awareness of the need to accommodate customers with dietary allergies, such as nut or dairy allergies. These dishes are made in kitchens outfitted to manage unique dietary needs, and stringent protocols are in place to avoid cross-contamination.

Airlines provide gluten-free meals that lack any wheat, barley, or rye ingredients for travelers who have celiac disease or gluten intolerance. These meals are cooked carefully to prevent any interaction with gluten-containing components, and they frequently incorporate substitute grains like rice, quinoa, or maize.

Vegan and Vegetarian Diets

Airlines have responded to the growing popularity of plant-based diets among travelers by providing a range of plant-based meal options for vegetarians and vegans. Meat, poultry, and fish are often not included in vegetarian meals, whereas vegan meals do not include any animal products, such as dairy or eggs.

Foods like salads, pasta dishes with plant-based sauces, veggie stir-fries, and grain-based meals like quinoa bowls may be served on airplanes. These dishes are meant to be tasty and nourishing, frequently including a range of fresh veggies, whole grains, and legumes. Airlines make sure that a range of vegetarian and vegan alternatives are offered throughout long-haul flights, where passengers may be served many meals.

Religious Restrictions on Diet

Airlines provide meals that comply with the dietary restrictions that many travelers observe because of their religious convictions. Halal meals are served to Muslim passengers in accordance with Islamic dietary regulations, which specify that particular foods, such alcohol and pig, must be avoided and that meat must be slaughtered in a particular manner. Airlines that serve halal food collaborate with approved vendors to guarantee that every component satisfies halal requirements.

Kosher meals, which are cooked in compliance with Jewish dietary regulations, are available upon request for Jewish travelers. To preserve their integrity, these meals are frequently double-sealed and come with packaging and cutlery that have received kosher certification. Traditional foods like gefilte fish, matzo, or kugel are often served at kosher meals, and airlines collaborate with kosher-certified caterers to guarantee that all meals fulfill the criteria.

Low-Fat and Low-Sodium Meals

Passengers who are concerned about their health might ask for low-fat or low-sodium meals, which are meant to limit the consumption of dangerous fats or salt. Lean proteins, whole grains, and fresh veggies are frequently used in these dishes, which emphasize flavor preservation without the use of excessive amounts of salt or oil. Airlines may serve salads with light dressings, steamed salmon with vegetables, or grilled chicken with quinoa. The purpose of preparing these meals is to offer passengers a wholesome and fulfilling dining experience that complements their objectives for wellbeing and health.

Cheese and Liquor Pairing: Enhancing the Dining Experience While Flying

The ability to match cuisine with drinks, like as wine and liqueurs, is one of the best parts of in-flight meals, especially in premium cabins. As was previously mentioned, cheese is a common ingredient in airline menus, especially on long-haul flights when customers are offered several dishes. Cheese and wine or liqueurs can be paired to improve the whole eating experience and give travelers a little taste of luxury on their travels.

Overview of Cheese Pairing

Cheese is a very adaptable meal that goes well with many different types of drinks, such as liqueurs like port or sherry as well as red and white wines. Cheeses such as soft cheeses like Brie and Camembert, hard cheeses like Cheddar and Parmesan, and blue cheeses like Roquefort or Gorgonzola are usually offered by airlines that serve cheese courses onboard.

The general idea for matching wine and cheese is to match the intensity of the wine with the cheese. For instance, heavier, aged cheeses like Cheddar or Gouda enhance the powerful flavors of a red wine like Cabernet Sauvignon or Merlot, while soft, creamy cheeses like Brie go well with a light, fruity white wine like Chardonnay or Sauvignon Blanc. Because the sweetness of the wine counteracts the saltiness of the cheese, blue cheeses, with their sharp, acidic flavor, go well with sweet wines like Port or dessert wines like Sauternes.

Liqueur Service: Fundamentals of Alcoholic Drinks and Refreshments

Liqueurs are another well-liked choice for travelers seeking an opulent in-flight experience; they are typically provided at the conclusion of a meal. Airlines provide a selection of liqueurs, such as well-known options like Grand Marnier, Baileys Irish Cream, and Amaretto. These liqueurs offer a sweet and decadent way to finish a meal and are frequently served with coffee or tea.

Liquors and desserts or cheese courses go well together and complement each other's flavors. For instance, chocolate-based sweets go well with a rich, creamy liqueur like Baileys, whereas fruit-based dishes or lighter, creamy desserts like panna cotta are enhanced by a citrus-flavored liqueur like Grand Marnier. When combined with biscotti or other nut-based treats, liqueurs like Amaretto, which have an almond flavor, can enhance the richness of the eating experience.

As part of the meal service, airlines may also serve liqueur-based drinks or aperitifs, especially in luxury seats. These beverages, which are frequently offered either before or after the meal, provide travelers a chance to unwind and enjoy their journey. Popular choices include a glass of Champagne to begin the flight on a festive note or traditional cocktails like the Bloody Mary, which is frequently served as a pre-meal beverage.

Fitness and Health Advantages: Encouraging Traveler Well-Being

Airlines have been putting more of an emphasis on encouraging passenger wellness in recent years, especially on long-haul flights where travelers may have to remain in close quarters for extended periods of time. The main elements of this wellness effort are the provision of nutritious meal alternatives and the promotion of frequent movement throughout the trip.

The Importance of Nutritious Food for Passenger Wellbeing

Eating correctly is crucial for maintaining passenger well-being, especially on lengthy flights where there is an increased chance of weariness, bloating, and dehydration. Airlines have started serving meals that are fewer in calories, salt, and harmful fats in response to the increased demand for better eating options. Lean meats, whole grains, and fresh produce are frequently found in these meals, which promote healthy digestion and sustain energy levels while in flight.

Airlines are focusing more on portion control in addition to providing nutritious meals, especially in economy cabins where meal quantities may be bigger than necessary. Airlines may help travelers avoid the pain that comes with overindulging while flying by serving smaller, more balanced meals.

Promoting Exercise and Movement

Airlines urge customers to stand and stretch during the journey because prolonged sitting might raise the risk of blood clots and other health problems. A lot of airlines provide information about easy exercises that travelers can perform in their seats, like neck rotations, leg stretches, and ankle rolls, in their in-flight magazines or safety videos.

Dedicated wellness programs, such as yoga or meditation sessions, have even been introduced by some airlines. These programs can be accessed through in-flight entertainment systems or as part of the onboard experience. These initiatives aim to improve travelers' general well-being by assisting with stress relief, relaxation, and adaptability throughout the journey.

Trends and Innovations in Airline Catering for the Future

The airline catering industry is always changing due to shifting passenger preferences, new technology, and an increasing emphasis on sustainability. Passengers may anticipate much more innovation in the preparation, serving, and eating of meals onboard in the future.

Locally sourced and sustainable ingredients

Airlines are concentrating more on lowering their carbon footprint, especially in their catering operations, as environmental concerns continue to rise. These days, a lot of airlines source their materials locally in order to support regional farmers and producers and lessen the need for long-distance travel. In addition, airlines are switching from using single-use plastics for meals and beverages to reusable or biodegradable packaging.

Plant-Based and Other Protein-Rich Dinners

Airlines are catering to the growing demand for plant-based meals by expanding their menus to include more vegetarian and vegan alternatives. To provide passengers more options for meals, airlines are investigating the use of other proteins in addition to typical plant-based meals, such as plant-based meat alternatives.

Tailored Dining in-Flight

Airlines are starting to provide more individualized dining experiences thanks to technological developments, enabling customers to choose their meals in advance or alter them to suit their tastes. By ensuring that meals are customized to each passenger's preferences, this level of personalization not only improves the traveler experience but also aids airlines in reducing food wastage.

In summary, airline catering is a vibrant, diverse sector that keeps growing in response to passengers' shifting demands and tastes. Airlines often look for new methods to improve the in-flight eating experience, from introducing international cuisines and meeting dietary needs to encouraging wellness and sustainability. Airlines can guarantee that their catering services continue to be an integral element of the overall travel experience, assisting passengers in feeling cozy, well-fed, and taken care of during their voyage, by embracing innovation and placing a high priority on customer happiness.

Chapter-11

Airline Catering – Outline in Four Sections

Galley Operations and Equipment

Catering for passengers in flight starts long before they board the aircraft. The galley, which is the center of in-flight food service, requires a great deal of planning and preparation. The aircraft's galley is a small kitchen where passengers store, cook, and serve food and drinks while in flight. The galley is furnished with specialized machines and tools that enable the cabin crew to effectively serve meals and beverages to hundreds of passengers, while being much smaller and more constrained than a regular kitchen. A seamless, secure, and effective catering service is largely dependent on the layout, design, and equipment employed in the galley. This section will cover a variety of topics related to galley operations, including as the equipment utilized, the layout and design of the galley, food and nutrition preflight checks, and safe handling procedures for galley equipment.

Overview of Equipment and Galleys

Every commercial aircraft must include a galley, which is built to utilize available space and supply the crew with everything they need to serve meals. The galley can be found in the front, center, or rear of the cabin, or it can be dispersed over different areas depending on the size of the aircraft. Larger airplanes, like the Airbus A380 or Boeing 777, may include multiple galleys with trolleys, storage compartments, refrigerators, ovens, and drink dispensers. Even while smaller regional jets might only have one, more constrained galley, the three fundamental concepts of efficiency, safety, and space optimization are still applicable.

Particularly during dinner service, the galley's layout is designed to let cabin crew to carry out their responsibilities with the least amount of disturbance to passengers. The galley needs to hold everything from food and drinks to utensils, trays, and napkins, therefore storage is an essential component. Shelves, cabinets, and trolleys are all made with locking mechanisms to keep belongings from moving or dropping during turbulence. Furthermore, galley surfaces are constructed from materials that are heat- and stain-resistant, making the space hygienic for the duration of the trip.

Coffee machines, beverage dispensers, ovens, and refrigerators are some of the essential appliances in the galley. Pre-made meals that are kept in insulated trays or containers are usually reheated in ovens. These ovens are small in size but strong in capacity, able to reheat several meals at once. For perishable goods like salads, fruits, and sweets to stay fresh, refrigerators and coolers are necessary. They are also used to hold beverages that must be served cold and dairy goods. Serving hot beverages, including as tea, coffee, and hot chocolate, which are highly requested during flights, requires the use of beverage dispensers, which include coffee machines. Ensuring that passengers receive their meals and drinks on time depends on these devices operating efficiently.

Preflight Galley Inspections: Vital Signs of Food and Nutrition

The cabin crew has to carry out a number of preflight inspections to make sure the galley is adequately stocked and prepared for food service prior to the aircraft taking off. Preflight inspections are essential to the effectiveness of in-flight services since broken or missing equipment can cause delays and passenger discontent. An exhaustive inventory of the food, drinks, and equipment on board is the first step in the procedure.

Making sure that all of the meals have been put onto the airplane is one of the first responsibilities in the preflight inspection process. This entails confirming the accurate quantity and kind of meals served, along with any special dietary meals that patrons may have requested. In order to preserve freshness, meals are sometimes made in sizable catering facilities on the ground and then brought to the aircraft in sealed containers. To keep food from spoiling, the crew must make sure that all meals are present and kept at the proper temperature.

The staff is responsible for checking the amount of water, soft drinks, juices, and alcoholic beverages in addition to the meal inventory. It's imperative to make sure there is enough of each beverage to serve every passenger because running out of drinks during a flight can aggravate other travelers. In addition, the staff makes sure the coffee makers and hot water dispensers are working correctly because hot beverages are a crucial component of in-flight amenities, particularly on lengthy flights.

The team needs to make sure that there is enough food and drink, as well as cutlery, trays, napkins, and other service items. This involves making sure there are enough serving trays for each passenger and that all the cutlery, including glasses, forks, knives, and spoons, is available. Usually, during meal service, these products are kept in carts that are rolled down the aisles.

Another crucial factor to take into account during preflight inspections is nutrition. In order to guarantee that all meals supplied on board are safe to consume and fulfill nutritional requirements, airlines must abide by health and safety rules. This is especially crucial for special meals—like gluten-free, vegetarian, or low-sodium meals—that are served to passengers who have dietary limitations. To prevent cross-contamination with conventional meals, the staff needs to make sure that these meals are properly labeled and stored separately. It's also crucial to make sure the meals are maintained at the right temperature because incorrect storage can result in foodborne illnesses.

Techniques for Handling Galley Equipment Correctly

During a flight, the galley is a busy place where crew members are always preparing and serving food and drinks. For this reason, keeping a seamless and secure service depends on knowing how to handle galley equipment. In order to ensure that they can deliver prompt service without sacrificing safety or hygiene, crew members receive efficient training on how to operate galley equipment.

A critical component of managing galley appliances is making sure ovens and freezers are operated properly. Pre-prepared meals are reheated in ovens, and in order to guarantee food safety, meals must be heated to the proper temperature. To prevent overcooking or undercooking food, crew members must keep an eye on cooking times and temperatures. Crew members are instructed to wear protective gloves when handling trays or dishes that have just come out of the oven because ovens get very hot while they are operating. Furthermore, food should never be overcooked in an oven due to the possibility of uneven heating.

To keep perishable goods at the right temperature, refrigerators and coolers need to be treated carefully. Reopening refrigerator doors too often might raise the temperature inside and affect how fresh the food is. Crew members are therefore instructed to restrict how frequently they open the refrigerators and to make sure they are safely closed after each use. To preserve their quality, foods like salads, desserts, and dairy products need to be kept apart from hot food items in storage.

During flights, beverage dispensers—including coffee makers—are always in use. Particularly popular are hot drinks like tea and coffee, which coffee machines are made to manufacture in big amounts with ease. When working with these devices, crew members need to exercise caution because the hot liquids could burn them. Before serving drinks to passengers, they have to make sure that the lids and cups are placed firmly, especially when there is turbulence and there is a greater chance of spills.

Managing trolleys is another essential component of handling galley equipment. Meals and drinks are carried throughout the cabin on trolleys, which are made to be stable and simple to use. When the trolleys are not in use, crew members must make sure they are secured. If not, an unsecured trolley may move suddenly during turbulence, endangering the safety of both passengers and crew. In order to avoid unintentional movement, trolleys come with brakes that must be applied when the cart is stationary.

Lastly, crew members are instructed to adhere to stringent hygiene rules when handling food and equipment because hygienic conditions are of the utmost importance in the galley. To avoid cross-contamination, this entails constantly cleaning surfaces and utensils, using gloves while handling food, and washing your hands frequently. After every meal service, the galley needs to be properly cleaned, paying special care to the ovens, freezers, and beverage dispensers. In order to avoid odors and bugs, crew members are also educated in proper garbage disposal, which includes removing leftover food and packaging from the galley.

Maintenance of Food Service Equipment

Proper maintenance of galley equipment is necessary to guarantee seamless in-flight service. All equipment must be routinely inspected and maintained to avoid problems during flights, as these can cause delays and disrupt the food service. Airlines maintain close working relationships with maintenance teams to guarantee that galley equipment is maintained in optimal operating condition and that issues are immediately resolved.

Ground crew perform preflight maintenance checks to make sure all equipment is operating properly before the aircraft takes off. This include looking for wear or malfunctions on ovens, freezers, and beverage dispensers. For instance, ovens need to be inspected to make sure the heating components are operating correctly and that the oven reaches the required temperature. In order to ensure that they are keeping food at the proper temperature, refrigerators and coolers are examined. Before the flight may take off, any defective equipment must be fixed or replaced.

Members of the cabin crew are taught to recognize possible problems with the galley equipment during the flight in addition to doing preflight inspections. In the event that a refrigerator stops chilling or an oven does not heat up correctly, the crew needs to act quickly to address the issue. This could entail contacting the cockpit crew or modifying the food service so that ground maintenance crews are informed when they arrive. In order to handle little problems that may arise during a flight, crew members are also taught in basic troubleshooting techniques including equipment resets and power connection checks.

Another crucial factor to take into account when maintaining galley equipment is safety. Smoke detectors, fire extinguishers, and other safety equipment are installed in galleys to safeguard passengers and staff in the event of an emergency. To make sure these gadgets are in good functioning condition, regular checks are required. Crew members are taught to adhere to safety procedures, like locking up all equipment during takeoff and landing or shutting off coffee makers and ovens during turbulence.

To sum up, the equipment and operations of the galley are essential to the success of in-flight food. Every aspect of galley operations, from the architecture and design of the galley to the handling of food and equipment, is meticulously designed to guarantee that passengers have safe, delicious meals during their journey. The galley is the hub of airline catering services since it is essential to provide a flawless in-flight eating experience through preflight inspections, appropriate handling procedures, and equipment maintenance.

Catering and Onboard Delivery on Airlines

Ensuring that passengers have a pleasant and comfortable experience on board an airplane depends on the seamless delivery of food services. Every stage of the process, from loading the catering supplies onboard the aircraft to serving the last meal or drink, calls for careful planning, strict observance of hygienic guidelines, and effective use of available space and equipment. This part will address the following topics: airline catering procedures, passenger meal and beverage delivery logistics, the importance of hygiene in food service, and crew member training programs for providing attentive and caring meal service. It will also discuss the value of exercising on lengthy flights, taking into account the wellbeing of the workers as well as the passengers.

Catering on Airlines and Meal Delivery on Board

Long before passengers ever board the flight, catering starts. Meal preparation, packing, and delivery for flights are handled by specialized catering firms that work with airlines. A high degree of coordination is necessary due to the logistical complexity of airline catering in order to guarantee that everything about the meal service operates seamlessly once the aircraft is in the air.

Meals are prepared in spacious, well-kept kitchens that are usually found close to major airports. These catering establishments provide meals according to menus created by airline chefs for hundreds or even thousands of customers every day. Carefully choosing ingredients is the first step in the process. Meals are then prepared and cooked, portioned, wrapped, and sent to the airplane in chilled containers. Meals for premium classes, such business or first class, require special attention because the food's quality and presentation must live up to higher standards.

The crew takes control after the catering supplies board the aircraft. Depending on when they are served, the pre-packaged meals are kept in the ovens or galley refrigerators. Meals that have already been prepared are kept in insulated containers until they are time to reheat, while chilled goods like salads, desserts, and drinks are kept in special chilling sections. The crew makes sure that everything is packed safely, being cautious not to let anything break during takeoff, landing, or turbulence.

Meal service to passengers is provided according to a set schedule that coincides with the flight timetable. Multiple meal services are standard on long-haul flights. Typically, the service begins with a beverage and snack, then moves on to a full dinner and, occasionally, another meal or snack before arrival. While meals in premium class are frequently provided to customers at their seats, meals in economy class are usually served from carts that are wheeled across the aisles.

The cabin crew plays a vital role in meal delivery. When there are several food selections and unique dietary requirements, it can be difficult for them to provide the appropriate meal to the right passenger. Economy class meals are often served on a pre-packaged tray with a main course, salad, bread roll, dessert, and beverage. Meal service is more formal in corporate and first class settings, frequently consisting of several dishes delivered on real plates with real silverware and glasses. Crew members have received training on how to provide this service effectively while upholding the highest levels of client care.

When delivering meals, timing is crucial. Due to the short time between takeoff and landing, meal service on short-haul flights must be prompt and effective. The crew must schedule the meal and relaxation periods on long-haul flights so that passengers don't feel pressured. To maintain a seamless and uninterrupted flight experience, meal service must be synchronized with other in-flight amenities like entertainment or beverage service.

Techniques for Food Service and Hygiene in Quality Control

The food business has some of the tightest hygienic requirements for food service on airplanes. Members of the cabin staff are in charge of keeping the area tidy and making sure that food is handled safely to avoid contamination. This is especially crucial because of the small galley aboard an airplane and the large number of passengers that must be served quickly.

Members of the cabin staff handle food and beverages according to strict rules in order to uphold high standards of hygiene. Hand sanitization and washing on a regular basis rank among the most crucial habits. Before handling food, after touching possibly contaminated surfaces, and in between serving different passengers, crew members are expected to wash their hands. The galley is kept clean by using disinfectant wipes and hand sanitizers.

Apart from personal hygiene, the equipment in the galley needs to be kept spotless. Before and after every meal service, the galley's surfaces, utensils, and equipment need to be thoroughly cleaned and sanitized. To avoid the accumulation of bacteria or food particles, ovens, freezers, and beverage dispensers need to be cleaned. Serving carts also need to be maintained spotless during the trip. To avoid contamination, utensils like spoons, forks, and knives are typically pre-packaged in sealed, sterile containers.

In addition, the staff takes precautions against cross-contamination. To protect travelers with allergies or dietary restrictions from potentially harmful components or allergens, special meals are prepared and served separately. For example, gluten-free food is stored apart from ordinary food, and the equipment necessary for it are not kept in the same area as other food. Meals with clear labels make it easier for the staff to recognize and serve the right meal to the right passenger.

Another important component of food safety is temperature regulation. While hot meals need to be reheated to the proper temperature before serving, cold items, such salads and dairy products, must be stored at the proper temperature to prevent spoiling. Meals are heated rapidly and evenly in the onboard ovens, guaranteeing that they are safe to eat. Members of the crew are taught to keep an eye on the temperature of both hot and cold food to make sure it stays within safe bounds.

Food quality on board is constantly observed. In order to make sure that meals fulfill the required requirements for flavor, freshness, and presentation, airlines regularly conduct taste testing and quality checks. Meals are frequently made to withstand the particulars of air travel, where variations in humidity and pressure can impact the food's flavor and texture. Additionally, airlines value customer feedback and use it to continuously raise the caliber of their in-flight catering offerings.

Exercise and Its Benefits: An Emphasis on Passengers' and Crew Members' Well-Being

Both passengers and crew members can suffer from the cramped quarters, extended sitting, and variations in cabin pressure on long-haul flights, which can cause stiffness, pain, and even serious health problems including deep vein thrombosis (DVT). Airlines are pushing passengers to do easy exercises throughout the flight to improve overall comfort, prevent stiffness, and increase circulation as part of their focus on passenger wellbeing.

One of the main pieces of advice for travelers is to move about frequently while in flight. This could be moving about the store, getting up, or doing exercises like leg lifts, ankle rolls, and neck stretches while seated. Many airlines use in-flight entertainment systems, safety cards, or crew announcements to offer instructions on basic exercises that can be performed while seated. These activities are intended to increase blood flow, lessen the possibility of blood clots, and ease the stiffness that results from prolonged sitting.

Since they are always on their feet serving passengers and maintaining the cabin atmosphere, the cabin crew members' regular mobility is an integral component of their job description. Nonetheless, the physical rigors of their work can wear them out, especially on lengthy flights where the crew must work long hours. To lessen the pressure on their bodies, airlines provide their staff members ergonomic equipment like lightweight trolleys and comfy shoes. Additionally, crew members receive training on how to control their energy levels and stay healthy throughout extended hours.

To enhance customer wellness, airlines have begun to provide healthier meal alternatives in addition to encouraging mobility. Meals with less calories, sodium, and bad fats may be served to passengers on long-haul flights. These meals are meant to be filling and healthy without giving rise to the gas or discomfort that sometimes comes with eating on an airplane. Typically, these healthy meal alternatives include salads, whole grains, lean proteins, and fresh fruits.

Another crucial component of in-flight health is hydration. Passengers who do not drink enough water throughout their journey risk dehydration because the cabin climate is frequently dry. Airlines provide bottled water and serve water throughout meal service to encourage passengers to stay hydrated. In order to preserve their energy levels and avoid exhaustion, crew members are also trained to drink plenty of water during the trip.

Maintaining wellness throughout a trip is about more than just comfort for both passengers and crew; it's about making sure that everyone reaches their destination feeling rejuvenated and prepared to continue traveling. Airlines are improving the overall in-flight experience by encouraging frequent movement, providing healthy meal options, and stressing the value of staying hydrated.

Efficiency, hygienic practices, and meticulous attention to detail are required in the highly coordinated operation of airline catering and meal delivery onboard. Every stage of the dining process, from the galley's meal preparation and storage to the cabin crew's cautious handling and service, is vital to guaranteeing that passengers have a pleasurable mealtime experience at altitude. By providing healthier meal alternatives and promoting frequent activity during flights, airlines are placing a greater emphasis on customer wellbeing in addition to upholding strict standards of food safety and hygiene. Airlines are contributing to the creation of a more pleasant and joyful travel experience by placing a higher priority on both the standard of food and the health of its passengers.

Menu Planning and Special Meals

With airlines working to provide a broad selection of meal options that satisfy the various dietary requirements and tastes of its customers, in-flight eating has emerged as a critical component of the overall travel experience. The days of few options for meals for passengers are long gone. These days, airlines prioritize offering a wide range of meal selections that satisfy passengers' dietary needs as well as their cultural preferences. The process of creating a menu is meticulous and requires consideration of the special conditions found in airplanes, where low cabin pressure and high altitudes can alter the flavors and aromas of food. This section discusses the preparation that goes into the many meal options provided on flights, how airlines handle special meals to satisfy dietary needs and religious observances, and the function of special meal codes in guaranteeing that every passenger gets the right meal. We also examine if cheese is served in premium cabins and how best to store and serve it to preserve quality.

Offering a choice of meals to accommodate a wide range of passengers' dietary requirements is one of the biggest issues airlines confront. Airlines typically provide a variety of standard meal options, including vegetarian and meat-based meals as well as lighter fare for health-conscious passengers. But the most difficult part of menu planning is making accommodations for customers with certain dietary requirements. In order to guarantee that every customer may have a meal that meets their needs, airlines must plan and serve meals that adhere to dietary, medical, and religious limitations.

Planning a menu usually starts months in advance and is revised often to take into account seasonal ingredients, customer input, and shifting preferences. The impact of dry air and cabin pressure on taste senses is one of the main obstacles to meal planning on airplanes. Due to the dulling of passengers' sense of taste, food appears less tasty at high altitudes. In order to make up for it, airlines frequently use stronger flavors in their meals, incorporating umami-rich products, spices, and herbs. In order to compensate for the reduced sense of taste, meals served on board are frequently more seasoned than they would be on the ground.

Airlines often provide two to three alternatives for regular meals. These typically consist of a vegetarian alternative, such as rice, pasta, or vegetable-based dishes, and a meat dish, such as chicken, beef, or fish. Additionally, several airlines provide a lighter choice, particularly for travelers who might prefer a less substantial lunch on long-haul flights. Airlines frequently modify their menus to accommodate local inclinations and customs. For example, Indian food may be served on flights to and from India, but Asian food may be served on flights to Asia.

Airlines are now serving lighter, more nutrient-dense meals as a result of the growing demand for healthier lunch options. Usually composed of nutritious grains, lean proteins, and fresh veggies, these meals are filling without being unduly heavy. Airlines frequently provide multiple meals on long-haul flights, such as a full meal followed by a lighter snack or breakfast before landing. In these situations, the second supper could be salads, sandwiches, or wraps that let guests eat without feeling overly full before getting off the ship.

Regular meals serve most passengers, however special meals that meet dietary requirements make up a large component of in-flight dining. These meals are categorized by airlines into three groups: religious, dietary, and medical. Passengers with medical issues such as diabetes or food allergies are catered for with medical meals. For instance, meals for diabetics are minimal in sugar and carbohydrates, and meals for gluten-free travelers are made for those who have a gluten sensitivity or celiac disease. When it comes to these meals, airlines need to exercise extra caution and make sure that cross-contamination is prevented, especially for passengers who have severe food allergies.

Meals on a diet accommodate individual choices, such low-sodium, vegan, or vegetarian diets. Vegan meals exclude all animal products, while vegetarian meals exclude meat but may contain dairy and eggs. Meals that are low in sodium and fat are designed for travelers who have to watch how much fat or salt they eat. They frequently include nutritious grains, lean proteins, and fresh vegetables.

Special meal planning includes religious meals in a big way. A kosher authority certifies that food is prepared in accordance with Jewish dietary regulations. To make sure they adhere to kosher requirements, each meal is packaged and sealed individually. Halal food is made with ingredients that have been certified halal and does not include pork or alcohol, in accordance with Islamic dietary regulations. In line with Hindu dietary customs, vegetarian or non-vegetarian options may be served at Hindu dinners, which normally do not contain beef.

Airlines utilize specific meal codes to identify and track these meals during the production, loading, and serving process in order to handle the complexity of special meal orders. By using these codes, travelers may be confident they'll get the food they requested. VGML for vegetarian meals, GFML for gluten-free meals, DBML for diabetic meals, KSML for kosher meals, and MOML for halal meals are a few examples of frequent special meal codes. By using these codes, the likelihood of errors is decreased and catering crews and cabin personnel can swiftly determine the right food.

Members of the cabin crew meticulously check the unique food codes throughout meal service to make sure the proper passenger receives the right meal. In order to prevent cross-contamination, these meals are frequently made in separate kitchens and are labeled prominently to avoid confusion. For instance, utensils required to handle special meals are not shared with ordinary food items, and gluten-free meals are stored apart from regular meals. Before serving the meal, the crew frequently makes sure the passengers are getting the correct food in addition to labeling it.

Cheese is a common feature of in-flight meals in luxury seats on airlines; it can be served as a standalone snack or as an addition to a multicourse meal. Cheese elevates in-flight food, particularly when combined with wine or dessert. However, because of the fluctuating temperatures and humidity in the cabin, serving cheese on an airplane calls for particular treatment.

Cold storage is necessary to keep soft cheeses like Brie or Camembert from getting too soft or runny. Hard cheeses, such as Gouda or Cheddar, are more tolerant and hold their texture better in flight. Despite these difficulties, the right handling and presentation of cheese when dining on board can improve the whole experience, particularly for first- and business-class customers.

Cheese is frequently offered as part of a cheese course in luxury cabins; this usually happens after the main meal or as a small snack. Passengers can enjoy a variety of textures and flavors since it is typically served with crackers, bread, fruit, or nuts. Airlines regularly give cheese and wine pairings, advising customers on which wines complement the cheeses they are serving. Airlines frequently sell cheeses that are representative of their home country or the destination of the journey; thus, the selection of cheeses is often affected by geographical factors. An Italian airline might provide Pecorino or Parmigiano-Reggiano, whereas a French airline might serve Roquefort or Comté.

To sum up, customized meals and menu design are important aspects of the whole in-flight eating experience. Travelers' needs and preferences must be carefully considered by airlines, which must provide a variety of regular meals and accommodate those with dietary or religious requirements. These meals are supplied precisely and securely thanks to the usage of unique meal codes. Cheese courses and wine pairings are additional luxuries enjoyed by premium cabin customers, which enhances the in-flight dining experience even further. Regardless of a passenger's dietary requirements or preferences, airlines may offer a fulfilling and delightful meal service with careful planning, execution, and attention to detail.

Cultural Influences and Beverage Service

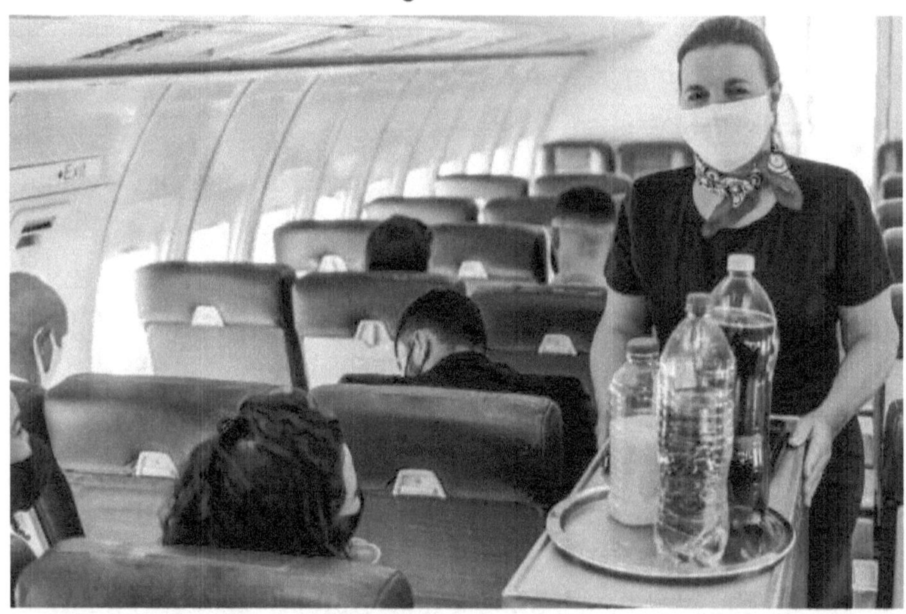

There is much more to in-flight meal service than just giving customers something to eat. Airlines have the chance to highlight the variety of cuisines from around the world, improve the entire travel experience, and engender comfort through food and drink. Airlines, especially on international flights, have devised menus that reflect the cuisines of different areas in order to cater to passengers from a variety of cultural backgrounds. In addition to meal selections influenced by Asian, Indian, and French culinary traditions, the food and beverage (F&B) service onboard consists of thoughtfully selected menus featuring international flavors. In addition, airlines provide a wide assortment of wines and liqueurs in luxury cabins to enhance the eating experience. In order to improve the in-flight eating experience, this section will examine how airlines create menus that cater to a variety of cultural backgrounds, the subtleties of F&B service across various cabin classes, and the significance of meal and beverage pairings.

Menu Items: Asian, French, and Indian Culinary Customs

Meal planning for passengers with different origins is a crucial aspect of airline operations. Menu selections on international flights frequently take into account the guests' diverse cultural preferences. Because of their diverse range of tastes and rich culinary traditions, in-flight menus usually feature dishes from the French, Indian, and Asian cuisines in particular.

French Food

Given its reputation for sophistication and attention to detail, French food is a favorite in first class and business class especially in premium cabins. When it comes to French food, airlines usually offer traditional dishes that prioritize flavor, presentation, and high-quality ingredients. Onboard, typical French appetizers could include foie gras, pâté, or a classy yet straightforward salad dressed with vinaigrette. Main course favorites that keep flavor and texture well after being reheated include coq au vin (chicken cooked in wine) and beef bourguignon (beef stewed in red wine). Rich sauces, a staple of French cuisine, are frequently employed to elevate these dishes because, at high altitudes where passengers' taste receptors are blunted by the low cabin pressure, they help conserve moisture and give depth of flavor.

Indulgent desserts such as crème brûlée, tarte Tatin (an upside-down caramelized apple tart), or chocolate mousse are typical of French cuisine. Freshly baked croissants or pastries may also be served at breakfast on French airlines, guaranteeing that travelers will have a classic French eating experience even while in the air. The addition of a cheese course, which serves a variety of French cheeses like Brie, Camembert, or Roquefort with bread or crackers, adds even more realism to the dinner.

Indian Food

Indian cuisine is a favorite on many international flights because of its strong flavors and fragrant spices. On their in-flight menus, airlines that serve routes to and from India or areas with a sizable Indian population frequently provide Indian cuisine. Indian cuisine is known for offering a wide range of vegetarian and non-vegetarian alternatives, with the former being particularly well-liked given the country's high vegetarian population. A few typical foods would be lamb curry, chicken tikka masala, or a vegetarian paneer dish. These would be served with naan bread, basmati rice, and side dishes like raita or chutney, which are yogurt-based condiments. Indian food is perfect for serving during flights because of its strong spices and complex taste profiles, which work well when heated up.

Indian desserts are typically made with components like milk, sugar, and cardamom and are rich and sweet. Popular options include rasgulla, which are cheese-based syrup-soaked sweets, gulab jamun, which are deep-fried milk-based dumplings, and kheer, which is a rice pudding scented with cardamom and saffron. Because these desserts maintain their flavor and texture even after being refrigerated and served onboard, they are especially well-suited for in-flight dining.

Asian-inspired Food

Airlines have the chance to design dynamic and varied meals that appeal to a wide range of palates because to the great diversity of Asian cuisine. Japanese food is a favorite in premium cabins because of its focus on pure flavors and fresh, premium ingredients. Sushi, sashimi, and teriyaki entrees, along with steamed rice, pickled veggies, and miso soup, may be served on airlines. Japanese bento boxes, which offer small servings of a variety of meals, are another well-liked in-flight option that gives customers a nutritious and aesthetically pleasing meal.

Menus served in-flight are frequently composed of Chinese food, which is renowned for its strong flavors and diversity of textures. To give customers a taste of authentic Chinese cuisine, airlines may provide dim sum, sweet and sour chicken, or stir-fried noodles. Seasonal vegetables and jasmine rice are frequently served with these dishes to provide a full meal that strikes a balance between flavor, texture, and nutrition.

Thai and Vietnamese cuisines, among others from Southeast Asia, are renowned for their vivid tastes and inventive use of herbs and spices like lemongrass, cilantro, and pepper. Thai green curry, pad Thai, and Vietnamese pho—a flavorful noodle soup—may be served on airplanes, along with fresh salads and dipping sauces to round off the meal. Asia's varied culinary customs enable airlines to provide a wide range of mouthwatering and fascinating meal alternatives, guaranteeing that customers have a pleasurable time when dining.

F&B Service: Providing Excellence in All Cabin Classes

First class, business, and economy all offer quite different standards of food and drink service. All cabin classes adhere to the same efficiency and care standards, but the premium cabins offer significantly more personalization, presentation, and attention to detail.

Efficiency and regularity are the main priorities of economy class. Meals are usually served in pre-packaged trays with a bread roll, dessert, side salad, and main entrée. These meals are made to be given to a large number of people in a short amount of time and to reheat rapidly. Airlines continue to make an effort to provide a balance of flavors and nutrition, even though the options may be more limited in economy class. In economy, travelers often have a selection of two or three main dishes, like pasta or chicken, with vegetarian options frequently offered as well.

On the other hand, first-class and business travelers enjoy a more upscale and individualized dinner service. Meals in these cabins are frequently provided as multi-course meals that guests customize from an à la carte menu. Appetizers, main dishes, cheese courses, and desserts are all served during the service and are all displayed on excellent china with real silverware. A range of wines and liqueurs, freshly baked bread, and individual attention from the cabin crew are all included in the lunch service in premium cabins.

The flexibility and personalization provided to passengers is one of the main distinctions in premium cabin service. Instead of adhering to a rigid schedule, passengers in business and first class are frequently free to select when they would like to eat, and the staff is taught to deliver a high standard of service that emulates dining in a classy restaurant. In order to guarantee that the cuisine in their premium cabins is not only excellent but also creative and up to date with current culinary trends, airlines frequently work with celebrity chefs to create the menus.

Liqueur Service: Improving the Dining Experience While Flying

Especially in premium seats, liqueur and wine service is a major factor in improving the in-flight dining experience. Throughout the flight, customers can choose to have alcoholic beverages such wine, champagne, and spirits either as an independent experience or as part of the meal service. Airlines choose their drinks deliberately to give customers a sense of luxury and pleasure while also complementing the meals they serve.

A prominent component of fine cabin dining is wine pairing. A variety of red, white, and sparkling wines that are hand-picked to go well with the meal are frequently available aboard airlines. As a welcome beverage, passengers may be served a glass of champagne or given the option to select a wine to go with their dinner. For instance, meat goes well with a rich red wine like Cabernet Sauvignon, whereas fish or chicken meals go better with a crisp white wine like Sauvignon Blanc. Wine recommendations can be made by the cabin crew, and some airlines even hire sommeliers to choose the wines that are served on board.

Usually offered after the main course, liqueur service might also include cheese courses or dessert. Popular liqueurs with distinct flavor profiles that go well with desserts' sweetness or cheeses' richness include Baileys Irish Cream, Amaretto, Grand Marnier, and Cognac. Amaretto, a liqueur with an almond flavor, goes well with desserts that contain nuts, whereas cognac is typically paired with strong cheeses like Roquefort or dark chocolate. The way liqueurs are presented and paired elevates the meal experience even more, especially for first class guests who receive more individualized attention.

Alcoholic drinks are normally sold in economy class, though on long-haul flights, some airlines provide free wine or beer during dinner service. Airlines nevertheless make an effort to provide a variety of drinks that meet passengers' interests, even though the selection in economy is less extensive than in premium cabins.

Matching Food and Drinks: A Fine Art

A careful balance of flavors is needed when matching meals to drinks, especially wine, as this improves the entire eating experience. Premium in-flight dining airlines frequently concentrate on establishing balanced food and wine pairings, taking into account elements like the dish's overall flavor profile, its richness, and its seasoning.

For instance, a robust red wine like Cabernet Sauvignon or Bordeaux would go well with a hearty cuisine like beef bourguignon since they accentuate the richness of the meat and the complexity of the sauce. On the other hand, a crisp white wine like Chardonnay or Sauvignon Blanc would go well with a lighter cuisine like grilled fish or chicken since it brings out the freshness of the dish without overpowering it.

Another key component of in-flight cuisine that is enhanced by thoughtful beverage matching is cheese. Stronger cheeses, such aged Cheddar or blue cheese, go better with sweet wines or port, while soft cheeses, like Brie or Camembert, are typically partnered with fruity, light white wines. Passengers will have a more pleasurable dining experience thanks to these combinations, which assist to temper the strong flavors of the cheese.

In summary, the meticulous design of food and beverage service along with the cultural variety of in-flight meals contribute significantly to the overall improvement of the traveler experience. Airlines, whether they fly in business or first class, are dedicated to provide wholesome, fulfilling meals and drinks that showcase different cultures' culinary customs. Airlines enhance the in-flight dining experience by matching meals with carefully chosen wines and liqueurs, providing passengers with a taste of luxury even at altitudes of 35,000 feet. By incorporating cultural elements and prioritizing high-quality service, airlines can craft an unforgettable and delightful dining experience that elevates each passenger's travel experience.

Chapter-12

Dangerous Good Regulations

Overview of Dangerous Goods Regulations

Transporting dangerous goods by air is a very complicated, highly regulated activity. Dangerous goods, also known as hazardous materials, present significant risk to health, safety, property, and the environment, particularly when transported by air. They represent an incredibly large range of substances, including but not limited to flammable liquids, toxic chemicals, radioactive materials, explosives, and gases-all dangerous under certain conditions. These risks, availed in a highly controlled and safety-oriented environment, have to follow strict guidelines by the aviation industry. International regulations on dangerous goods transportation play a vital role in ensuring the safety of all people handling, transporting, and storing hazardous materials.

The International Civil Aviation Organization, or ICAO, is the main international body with responsibility for setting the regulations that govern the safe transport of dangerous goods by air. These regulations are developed with the intention of standardizing procedures among airlines, airports, cargo handlers, and shippers, which in turn enables a consistent level of safety to be maintained globally. Regulating dangerous goods transportation really could not be more imperative. In an enclosed aircraft, with limited access and emergency response from the outside, even minor accidents with hazardous materials can have disastrous results. Strict adherence to regulations averts accidents, damage potential, and exposure to dangerous substances for passengers and crew. For this reason, every care needs to be taken that these regulations are followed to maintain the general safety in the aviation industry and to prevent any cause of deterioration of public health or the environment.

An important player in the enforcement of these regulations is a dangerous goods safety adviser. His responsibility is to know that all parties in the chain of transport of hazardous materials pay respect to relevant standards in safety and legal requirements. A DGSA's role has a vital influence on the establishment of a safety culture in organizations working with dangerous goods.

These range from monitoring the organization's compliance with national and international regulations regarding dangerous goods movements to training and guiding those employees who are directly involved in the transport of dangerous goods. The responsibilities of a DGSA will further extend to the investigation of incidents or accidents during the handling or movement of hazardous materials. The DGSA has to ensure that records concerning dangerous goods-related activities are accurately maintained, including documentation of training, incidents, and any corrective actions taken to address safety concerns.

In case of any accident or safety breach that concerns dangerous goods, the DGSA should carry out an in-depth investigation on the cause and follow up whether proper safety protocols were adhered to. At the conclusion of the investigation, based on the findings, recommendations of corrective measures would be presented by the DGSA to prevent recurrence of similar incidents. This has been a very key role in ensuring that necessary steps are taken by organizations to mitigate risks and follow the set standards for safety.

Training is one of the important duties of the DGSA. Staff involved in the classification, packaging, marking, labeling, handling, or transportation of dangerous goods should be suitably trained in the associated hazards of such materials and the procedures to follow for their safe handling. The DGSA must ensure that all personnel are sufficiently trained in the classification, packaging, marking, handling, and documentation of dangerous goods. This usually requires constant training to keep the personnel updated with the alterations that happen either through changes in regulations or otherwise best practices.

The significance of the DGSA's work underlines the gravity of possible failures' consequences to the regulations on dangerous goods. Non-compliance may cause an organization to suffer serious penalties: major fines, legal actions, and major damaged reputation. More crucially, accidents that are attributed to failure to follow safety procedures and policies may result in accidents affecting lives, properties, and the environment.

Non-compliance with dangerous goods regulations is not only against the law but also morally not acceptable. Every possible precaution should be considered to make passengers, crew members, ground handlers, and the environment safe. For this reason, the aviation industry needs to promote strict standards of safety and professional stewardship by professionals like the DGSA to reduce any remaining hazards associated with air transportation of hazardous materials.

Classification, Packaging and Marking of Dangerous Goods

Dangerous goods transported by air need to have proper classification, packaging, and marking so that the safety of the goods during transport is ensured. This proper classification would allow for the identification of specific hazards that different types of materials, through standardized packaging and labeling, give necessary precautions for their handling, stowage, and emergencies. In this way, together these components will be able to form the very basis of safe transportation of hazardous materials.

Classification of dangerous goods is the first and most important stage in the regulatory procedure. In developing a categorization system, ICAO classified hazardous materials into nine classes-each representing a different type of hazard: explosives, flammable liquids, gases, toxic substances, radioactive materials, corrosives, and other dangerous materials which create hazards during transport. Each hazard class is further divided into divisions based on the severity of risk presented by the material. This in turn provides for a universal understanding of material-specific dangers for everyone involved in the transportation chain from the shipper to the flight crew whereby proper precautions can be taken.

Packaging Once a material has been classified, it must then be properly packaged so it will be safe to be transported by air. The process for packaging dangerous goods is highly regulated as the requirements were developed to be strict to prevent any leaks, spills, or any kind of accident at any time during transportation. According to ICAO regulations, it is said that packaging should be able to withstand all conditions of air transport: changed pressure, temperature fluctuations, and the vibrations happening during flight.

The different packaging materials should be adequately sturdy to avoid any damage or bursting, and these shall be compatible with the hazardous materials they are carrying. Corrosive materials, for instance, shall be stored in containers made of materials that do not easily corrode. Liquids shall be packed in non-leaking containers, and gases shall be stored in pressure-resistant cylinders. Packaging for dangerous goods is subjected to extensive testing for its reliability in design and construction.

Salient features of hazardous goods packaging are the inner and outer packages, providing multiple layers of protection. The inner package may be glass or plastic containers containing hazardous materials, while outer packages are meant for extra protection and containment. This helps in reducing the risk of leakages or spills, even if the inner packaging has been damaged during transit. Absorbent materials can also be used inside the packaging to absorb the leakage in the event of an accident or damage to the package.

Dangerous goods are assigned into one of three packing groups based on the level of hazards they pose. Packing Group I is for materials that present the highest hazard levels and deserve the most stringent requirements for packaging. Correspondingly, materials falling under Packing Group II create a medium danger and less restrictive packaging, whereas in Packing Group III, there is less hazard and thus only basic precautions are necessary. This gives a good indication that packing groups allow the appropriate level of packaging concerning the type of dangerous good.

Proper marking and labeling are also crucial to safe transportation. Every package of dangerous goods shall be properly labeled to show the type of hazard it is. Labeling shall be in a manner consistent with the classification, utilizing easily recognized hazard symbols illustrating the danger inherent in the contents that handlers are exposed to, ground crews, and flight personnel.

The containers besides being marked with hazard labels, there should be an identification of proper shipping name of the material contained, its identification number, and handling instructions. The information is necessary to ensure that dangerous good packages are handled with caution during transportation. For example, packages of flammable liquids should be properly labeled with the symbol for a flammable liquid and must be marked to indicate that they should be kept away from sources of heat or ignition.

Another important feature of dangerous goods transport is the placarding, especially for larger shipments. Placards are large, easily visible signs placed on transport vehicles, cargo containers, or other units carrying the dangerous goods. These placards provide a quick visual reference to everyone that may come into contact with a shipment, including emergency responders in the event of an accident.

Proper classification, packaging, and marking form the bedrock of dangerous goods transport safety by air. Without strict adherence to these protocols, the risks associated with hazardous material transportation would increase exponentially. These are measures to ensure that from shippers to aeronauts and even in the event of accidents and emergencies, the handling and transportation of dangerous goods can be carried out in safety.

Handling, Transportation, and Safety Provisions

The safe handling and transportation of dangerous goods in aviation can only be made possible by strictly adhering to the laid down safety protocols aimed at reducing risks associated with hazardous materials. It is at this juncture that goods should be properly monitored right from the ground operation processes to flight operation processes so that handling is done in accordance with international laid down regulations. The critical aspects of handling and stowage, transport equipment and documentation, and the role of vehicle crew and training would be discussed in brief in this section.

Handling and stowage of dangerous goods involve a good amount of planning and precision in execution to avoid accidents which might arise out of their mismanagement. Before the dangerous goods are actually loaded onto the aircraft, the ground staff have to ensure that the materials are packaged, labeled, and documented correctly. Ground handling staff provide a very important link in the safe transportation of dangerous goods since they are used to move, store, and prepare dangerous goods for transportation. Every action within this process should be in line with ICAO recommendations, which state that dangerous goods should be kept separate from all other cargo and packed in such a way as to minimize the risk of any accidental release or coming into contact with incompatible materials.

Dangerous goods should be loaded into specific areas in the aircraft cargo hold, designed for hazardous materials, to keep them further away from the passengers and other sensitive equipment. The stowage should be adequately secure in order to avoid movements during flight that may result in damage or leakages. Finally, dangerous goods with special handling requirements, such as items requiring temperature sensitivity and fragile items, must be transported in conformity with applicable guidelines. The plans for stowage should be prepared with considerations in light of the dangerous goods class and specific hazards they pose, taking into account possible scenarios that could arise in event of an emergency during flight.

Documenting is also a very crucial element in the transport of dangerous goods because it ensures that information will be available to all parties concerned in the shipment. Each dangerous goods shipment shall be backed by a declaration, commonly referred to as a Shipper's Declaration for Dangerous Goods. The Declaration comprises a number of key elements of information: proper classification and identification of hazardous materials, quantity, packing group assigned, relevant handling instructions, and so on. This documentation should be accurate and complete. A single discrepancy in the paperwork can give way to severe deviation from safety.

In addition to the dangerous goods declaration, other relevant documents, such as the air waybill, need to show that dangerous goods are being carried by the inclusion of certain statements. This provides notice to all parties involved with the supply chain, from the ground handlers through to the eventual aircrew, about the potential hazard. The procedure for handling the goods and the actions in case of an emergency shall be given to the vehicle crew in writing. This is very important because it ensures that the situation will be contained and controlled as soon as possible should there be any incidents.

The transport equipment used in the movement of hazardous goods either on the ground or through air transport shall meet the specification standards for safety. Cargo loading systems, including pallets, containers, and aircraft cargo compartments, are to be designed and built to prevent any unintentional release or spill of dangerous goods. This equipment should be periodically inspected and maintained in order to sustain it in a good state. Besides, special equipment is needed with respect to vehicles providing ground transportation of dangerous goods, like airport trucks or trailers, while following specific requirements identified in the handling of hazardous materials with safety.

Members who belong to the vehicle crew and are involved in the conveyance of hazardous cargo should be properly trained on the risks associated with handling hazardous materials. Training programs should thus be comprehensive and take into consideration the most recent information concerning modifications made in the regulations or newly emerging risks. Such training covers a broad area, starting from hazard identification down to following safety procedures and the use of protective equipment. There is also the need for responses to emergencies by crew members, where there could be spills or leaks. Crew members have to be conversant with emergency procedures; these include dealing with fire extinguishers, personal protective equipment, and spill containment tools.

Other very important provisions are those of security in the transportation of dangerous goods. Because many hazardous materials, such as explosives or toxic substances, can be diverted for criminal purposes, security measures have to be implemented that deny access to dangerous goods by unauthorized persons. Vehicles transporting such items should always be kept under guard to preclude tampering with the cargo, and any dangerous goods should be accessible to only authorized personnel. Dangerous goods theft or sabotage can be avoided by the regulation of regular security inspections and shipment surveillance.

The safety of the transport of dangerous goods cannot be assured except with thorough coordination among the parties concerned in the shipment. Ground handling staff, vehicle crews, aircrew, and regulatory authorities have to monitor and manage collectively the associated hazards of hazardous materials. Established safety procedures, well-structured training, and effective communication will enable the aviation industry to safely carry dangerous goods without posing any threat to the safety of the passengers, crew, and even to the environment.

Compliance, Accidents, and Consequences

Compliance with international and national regulations provides the backbone for the safe transport of dangerous goods. Failure to comply poses not only the safety of aircraft, crew, and passengers at risk, but also carries heavy possible legal and financial ramifications against the organization involved. This section gives a brief overview of the importance of compliance with looking into the causes and consequences of accidents involving dangerous goods. Also discussed are general packing requirements necessitated by safety.

The regulatory obligation for compliance encompasses all levels in the chain of transportation: shippers, carriers, and receivers alike. Every person and organization in the handling of dangerous goods bears responsibility to ensure all the safety protocols are respected. International Civil Aviation Organization and International Air Transport Association among other bodies have strict regulations controlling classification, packaging, labeling, and transportation of dangerous goods. This is through regular inspection and audits by competent authorities that ensure organizations meet the relevant standards.

Compliance necessarily involves an authorization process. Some dangerous goods have special permits or authorizations as prerequisites to air transport. These are issued by competent authorities and are often given subject to particular conditions, such as being transported in limited quantities or in packages specially engineered for the particular commodity concerned. Dangerous goods may be transported in limited or excepted quantities, for which special provisions reduce the regulatory burden for small quantities of hazardous material. Even in these cases, though, strict standards of safety are followed.

Accidents involving dangerous goods can have devastating consequences, not only for the aircraft and its passengers but also for the environment and the communities affected by the incident. These accidents are usually related to the failure of compliance with the safety regulations. For example, improper packing results in leakage leading to fires, explosions, or toxic exposure. In some situations, misclassification of dangerous goods further leads to accidents where hazardous materials are not classified and hence are not subjected to proper safety measures.

The after-effects of road accidents that involve hazardous goods are great. Other than the immediate risk to human life and property, the accidents can cause immense damage to the environment. For example, toxic chemicals and radioactive materials, upon leakage, can contaminate supplies of water, soil, and air, thus continuing to affect human health and ecological balance in the long run. The financial consequences, too, in such disasters are huge, comprising cleanup costs, legal liability, compensation claims, and loss of prestige.

Investigations into dangerous good accidents often reveal lapses in the observance of safety regulations. These include poor training of personnel, lack of proper documentation, poor stowage, and deviation from established handling procedures. An organization found to have breached dangerous goods regulations may face severe sanctions, such as heavy fines, suspension of operation, or criminal charges for cases involving negligence.

General requirements for packaging, as stated by the dangerous goods transport, will be able to prevent accidents and ensure hazardous materials can be forwarded and stored safely. The different packages must be robust enough to withstand all the conditions encountered in the air transport, such as the variations of the pressure and temperature, and the shocks which may happen at the time of loading and unloading. They also need to be leak-tight to avoid hazardous materials from escaping and spreading contamination or injury.

Packaging of Dangerous Goods: The personnel responsible for packaging dangerous goods have to be trained in the particular requirements of a class or specific category of hazardous material.

The containers used for packing dangerous goods must be compatible with the materials packed therein to avoid chemical reaction that may cause leakage or explosion. Examples are that corrosive materials must be packed in containers made from materials resistant to corrosion, and the container for flammable liquids should be of such a type so that exposure to heat will not cause it to rupture.

Good packaging ensures safety for dangerous goods during transportation. Packaging that is in bad condition, unsealed, or poorly labeled highly increases the occurrence of accidents while in transportation. It is therefore a responsibility of the shipper to ensure that all dangerous goods are appropriately packed according to applicable regulations before they are handed over to the carrier for transportation.

Dangerous goods regulations may, therefore, ensure the facilitation of safety in aviation. Conformity with the international guidelines and correct classification and packaging of hazardous materials, and most importantly, that all personnel is well-trained reduces risks in the transportation of dangerous goods. A failure to adhere to such regulations results in severe consequences that include accidents that kill and cause unprecedented damages to the environment as well as costly ones. If applied stringently, the facilitation of dangerous goods transport by the aviation industry can be done safely through strict enforcement of safety standards and continuous monitoring of compliance to mitigate the potential risks they pose.

Chapter-13

Load & Trim

Understanding the Need for Weight Monitoring and Balancing

Weight and balance are basic ideas that are absolutely important in aviation to guarantee the safety, performance, and efficiency of an aircraft during flight. Monitoring weight and balance helps one avoid potentially hazardous conditions that can cause mishaps or compromise of aircraft performance. Continuous weight management is crucial for an aircraft since its weight distribution directly affects its stability, maneuverability, and general ease of control.

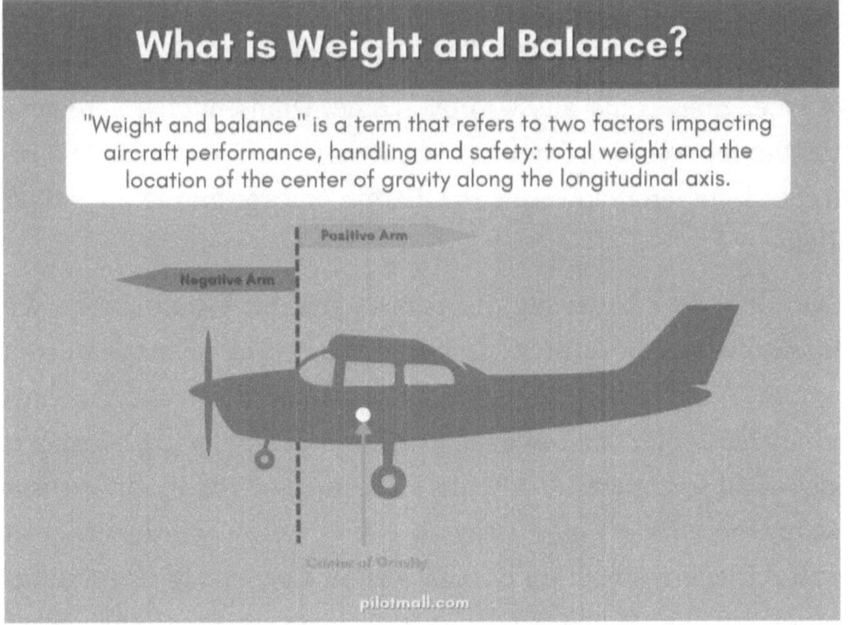

Monitoring weight is mostly motivated by the fact that an incorrectly balanced or overweight aircraft may cause major safety concerns.

An aircraft above its Maximum Takeoff Weight (MTOW) may find it difficult to climb altitude, call for longer runways for takeoff, or perhaps suffer mechanical engine and structural component strain. During takeoff and landing, the most hazardous stages of flight, this is especially important. Moreover, the weight distribution effects the center of gravity (CG) of the aircraft, which determines its controllability and stability. Particularly during pitch changes, the aircraft could become difficult to control if the CG is overly forward or aft. Maintaining the proper balance thus not only ensures safety but also helps to maximize performance and fuel economy.

In this setting, knowing fundamental flight theory is equally crucial. Flight dynamics is mostly based on the ideas of lift, drag, thrust, weight. While drag opposes thrust, the wings provide lift—which balances weight—as the airplane flies through the air. An aircraft's lift must be equal to its weight if it is to remain in the air; its thrust must offset drag. Should the weight distribution be off-balance or too heavy, the aircraft could find it difficult to provide the required lift or could suffer drag more than its engines could allow to overcome. Unintentional aerodynamic consequences resulting from this imbalance could also include a rise in stall speed, therefore lowering the margin of error during pivotal points of flight.

Not only does balancing the aircraft guarantee that it stays within its maximum weight restrictions, but it also helps to manage where that weight is found within the plane. Pilots and aircraft engineers have to precisely determine the center of gravity to guarantee the aircraft stays steady in all flying stages. Should the center of gravity be excessively forward, the aircraft's nose may be overly heavy, which would make takeoff difficult to pitch up or rotate with. Conversely, if the center of gravity is too far aft, the tail is too heavy and can cause the aircraft to become uncontrollable—especially during landing. Reaching an ideal balance means allocating the weight—including passengers, goods, fuel—such that the airplane stays stable and under control under all circumstances.

Effective comprehension and management of weight and balance depend on a knowledge of their language. In aviation operations, terms such Maximum Takeoff Weight (MTOW), Maximum Landing Weight (MLW), Basic Empty Weight (BEW), Zero Fuel Weight (ZFW), and Center of Gravity (CG) are routinely used to characterise an aircraft's weight characteristics. The maximum allowed weight for takeoff, or MTOW, guarantees that the aircraft may generate the required lift to safely depart the ground. Overcoming MTOW can have major repercussions including structural damage to the aircraft or inability to reach lift-off. Conversely, MLW shows the highest weight at which an aircraft is certified to land without running the danger of damaging its structural elements or landing gear. Whereas ZFW contains everything but the gasoline, BEW is the weight of the airplane with all its fixed operating equipment but without cargo, passengers, or fuel. As was before mentioned, CG is the point at which the aircraft's overall weight is thought to be concentrated and has to stay within specific restrictions for safe flying.

Not only do pilots but ground crew, flight dispatchers, and maintenance staff members engaged in aircraft preparation for flight depend on an understanding of these words. Correct weight monitoring and balancing guarantees that the airplane runs effectively, saves fuel, and—above all—operates within safe limits. An aircraft might rapidly become unstable or unable of executing necessary maneuvers without constant monitoring, therefore causing possibly disastrous results.

Maintaining Aircraft Weight Records and Components

The safe and effective running of every aircraft depends on accurate and current weight records. Maintaining these records is legally required, and they provide a basis for all those engaged in the operation of the aircraft—from engineers to pilots and dispatchers. These records follow the aircraft's weight at several phases of life, including its starting manufacturing weight, any variations brought about by repairs or modifications, and its operational weight at any one moment. Maintaining thorough weight records guarantees the aircraft stays within its operational range and helps to avoid overloading or imbalance.

Weight records have several elements, including the Basic Empty Weight (BEW) of the aircraft—that is, its weight with all fixed operating equipment installed but omitting any payload or fuel. Calculating the aircraft's overall weight prior to every flight starts with this BEW. Apart from the weight of crew, food, and other supplies required for the flight but excluding passengers, cargo, and fuel, the operating weight adds to the weight of these elements. Addition of payload and fuel modifies the weight to ascertain the actual takeoff weight of the aircraft.

The payload—that is, the total weight of people, baggage, and goods—is among the most crucial parts of the weight record of the airplane. Payloads are tightly restricted by airlines to guarantee the aircraft stays within its operational range. Should the payload surpass these restrictions, changes have to be made either in terms of fuel transported or offloading goods or passengers. Since it influences the flight's profitability for the airline as well as its safety, this balancing act is crucial. Overloaded aircraft could not be able to rise effectively to cruising altitude or might not have enough fuel to get to their destination safely.

Fuel weight is another important consideration that varies dynamically across a trip. Usually the heaviest single component added to the aircraft after the basic operational weight, fuel can make a significant portion of the takeoff weight. Not only does fuel weight define the overall weight of the airplane, but it also helps to keep balance. Usually found in the wings and fuselage, fuel is kept in several tanks scattered around the aircraft. The location of these fuel tanks might affect the aircraft's center of gravity, hence careful management of the fuel load is crucial to prevent moving the CG outside of reasonable bounds during flight. Fuel can be moved between tanks during flight in bigger aircraft to preserve balance and increase economy; this is particularly crucial during long-haul flights as fuel usage greatly lowers the total weight over time.

Monitoring aircraft performance depends on accurate fuel records since the weight of the fuel directly affects the range and fuel economy of the aircraft. Effective fuel weight management guarantees that, even as fuel is spent and the aircraft gets lighter, the aircraft stays within its operational limits all during the flight. The takeoff performance of the airplane depends also much on the weight of the fuels. To reach lift-off, a fully loaded aircraft with maximum fuel may need longer runways and greater speeds; a lighter aircraft with less fuel can take off more quickly and effectively.

In aircraft, also crucial are the several measuring systems and conversions applied in weight and balance computation. Usually depending on the location and the operator, aircraft weight is expressed in pounds or kg. Accurate conversions between these units will help to prevent miscalculations that can compromise the performance of the aircraft. A little mistake in converting fuel weight from pounds to kg, for instance, could cause appreciable differences in the aircraft's overall weight, therefore affecting possibly dangerous operating conditions. Ground staff, dispatchers, and pilots all have to be conversant with these measuring methods and make sure every weight-related computation is carried out precisely.

Apart from weight assessment, computations have to be done to ascertain the center of gravity of the aircraft. The CG must stay within a designated range for safe operation and is the point at which the overall weight of the aircraft is regarded to be concentrated. The CG's position influences the fuel economy, mobility, and stability of the aircraft. Should the CG be overly forward, the aircraft might be nose-heavy, which would complicate takeoff pitch-up. On the other hand, if the CG is too far aft, the tail could be overly heavy, causing instability and trouble controlling the aircraft—particularly during landing. Ensuring that the aircraft stays balanced during the flight and performs as best it can under all circumstances depend on accurate CG estimates.

Procedures for load and trim on airplanes are used to preserve the proper balance and guarantee that the aircraft stays within its allowed CG range. To reach the intended balance, these operations meticulously distribute passenger, cargo, and gasoline weight. Ensuring that the aircraft is correctly loaded and adjusted before takeoff falls on ground handling staff and flight dispatchers. This procedure include figuring out passenger seats, cargo placement in the hold, and fuel allocation among tanks. Any modifications to the load of the aircraft throughout the flight, including fuel consumption or cargo redistribution, have to be considered if we are to keep balance and safety.

To ensure the safe running of any aircraft, then, precise weight records and knowledge of aircraft weight components are very vital. Airlines and operators may guarantee that their aircraft stay within safe operating limits and that they run effectively across their trips by making sure that all weight-related data is precisely documented and watched over. Control of fuel weights, payloads, and other aircraft weight components guarantees not only passenger and crew safety but also flight economical feasibility.

Weight Measurement and Center of Gravity Calculations

Essential components of aviation operations include precisely weighing an aircraft and determining its center of gravity (CG). By means of their prevention of overload, maintenance of balance, and assurance of aircraft operation within its optimal performance boundaries, these chores guarantee the safety and efficiency of flights. With exact conversions typically needed to standardize measurements, several techniques and procedures are used to weigh the airplane including its components: fuel, passengers, cargo, and operational equipment.

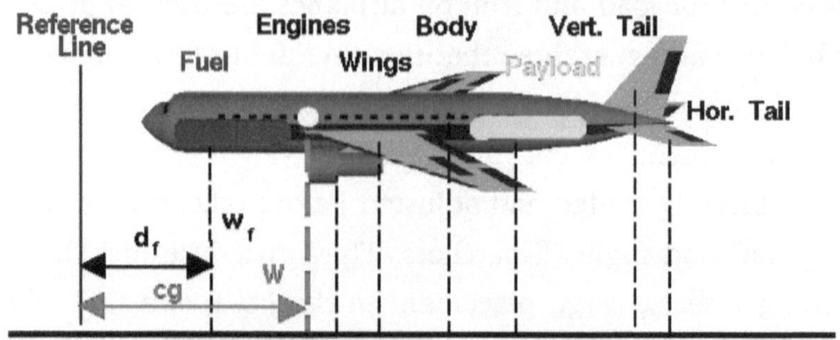

Each component has some weight w_i located some distance d_i from reference line.

Distance cg times the weight W equals the sum of the component distance times weight.

$$cg\ W = d_f w_f + d_e w_e + d_w w_w + d_p w_p + \ldots$$

$$cg\ W = \sum_i^n (wd)_i$$

The weight of an airplane is measured based on the area, but mostly in pounds (lbs) and kilograms (kg). Sometimes, especially when dealing with international teams or airplanes built in other nations, aviation experts must translate across several departments. For example, whereas many other countries measure weight in kg, the United States normally uses pounds. Accurate conversion between these units is crucial since even a minor miscalculation can produce major aircraft performance and safety impact by affecting its general weight. Since fuel weight is a major component of the aircraft's total load, converting fuel quantities is especially vital; even a small mistake may result in an incorrect fuel load, therefore possibly endangering the flight.

Calculating the center of gravity (CG) comes next once the aircraft's whole weight including its contents is known. Maintaining stability and control during flight depends on the CG, the point at which the overall weight of the aircraft is seen to be concentrated. The CG is computed by finding the weight balance along the longitudinal axis of the aircraft, thereby guaranteeing neither too forward nor too far aft.

For the aircraft to be safely run, the center of gravity has to lie within a particular range. Should the CG be excessively forward, the aircraft would nose-heavy, which would make it challenging for the pilot to elevate the nose during takeoff or sustain a consistent ascent. On the other hand, if the CG is too far aft, the tail may become too heavy, which would make the aircraft unstable particularly during landing or when changing altitude quickly. Using the weight data of the aircraft and the distribution of cargo, passengers, and fuel helps to avoid such hazardous circumstances by means of exact calculations.

Manufacturers of aircraft offer comprehensive instructions on the allowed CG range for every type, sometimes referred to as the "CG envelope." The design and structural integrity of the aircraft define this range; so, pilots and ground crew have to make sure the CG of the aircraft falls within this envelope before every flight. Should the CG prove to be outside the approved range, changes have to be made—perhaps by rearranging passenger seating, shifting cargo, or adjusting fuel distribution and amounts.

Usually, the CG computation procedure consists in multiplying the weight of every item or passenger by its distance from a reference point, sometimes called as the "datum." This gives each item a moment; the overall weight of the airplane divides these moments to determine the precise CG location. Although some circumstances, especially in smaller aircraft or less technologically advanced environments, still call for manual methods, modern aircraft and cargo systems often use automated tools to assist with these calculations. The proper placement of the CG helps optimize flight efficiency by minimizing drag and improving fuel consumption, so ensuring smoother and more stable flight dynamics.

Additionally shifting throughout flight is the CG, particularly in relation to fuel consumption. The airplane loses weight as it burns fuel, so the CG might shift. On long-haul flights, in which a lot of fuel is utilized, this is particularly crucial. Fuel is often kept in several tanks all around the aircraft to accommodate these variations; it can be moved between these tanks to maintain the aircraft's balance. To guarantee that the aircraft stays steady all through the flight, pilots and ground crews closely check fuel usage and the related changes in weight and balance.

At last, load and trim techniques come into action in control of aircraft weight distribution. These operations entail computing and modifying the load of goods, gasoline, and passengers to preserve the intended CG and guarantee that the aircraft's weight stays within reasonable bounds. In addition to increasing safety, a well balanced load increases the aircraft's performance, fuel economy, and general flying handling. Small control surfaces on the aircraft's wings and tail allow trim changes to fine-tune the balance and preserve steady flying.

Aircraft Weighing, Trim Equipment, and Special Conditions

Maintaining the safety and operational efficiency of aviation depends on two crucial chores: weighing an aircraft and applying suitable trim equipment. Aircraft weighing is the process of determining the real weight of the aircraft and its several components—including not only the aircraft but also its fuel, cargo, and passengers—by means of certain tools and techniques. Maintaining correct weight records for the aircraft depends on regular weighing, especially following changes or repairs that can affect its fundamental weight.

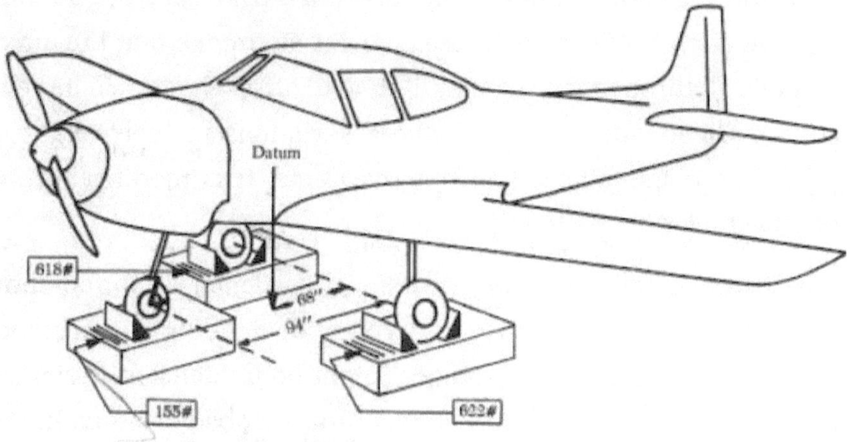

FIGURE 3-9. Weighing an aircraft using platform scales.

Usually, aircraft weighing is accomplished with calibrated scales or load cells under the landing gear. By carefully measuring the weight applied to every spot, these scales provide a complete weight computation for the aircraft. Particularly in cases of structural or system changes to the aircraft, this technique is essential to verifying that the recorded weight of the aircraft matches its actual weight. These weight measurements must be accurate since any differences could create improper load planning and maybe dangerous flying situations.

Aircraft weighing equipment has to satisfy high criteria of dependability and precision. This is a common use for load cells since they can offer extremely accurate measurements under the demanding environments faced in flight. Sometimes hydraulic systems are utilized in concert with weighing platforms to track the weight applied to every landing gear. These values are then aggregated to provide the aircraft's overall weight, which is noted and matched with the recorded weight data. Any notable variations between the recorded and measured weights have to be looked at and fixed to provide safe running conditions.

Maintaining the aircraft's equilibrium during flight depends much on trim equipment as well. By precisely positioning control surfaces—such as the elevators, rudder, and ailerons—trim controls let pilots change the aircraft's balance. These changes guarantee that the aircraft stays stable all through the flight and serve to offset changes in its center of gravity. On long-haul flights, where variations in fuel weight can cause the aircraft's balance to move over time, trim modifications are especially crucial.

Apart from regular running situations, particular attention should be given to weight and balance under very demanding circumstances. An aircraft's weight and performance might be influenced by elements including high altitude, scorching temperature, or bad weather. In high-altitude airports, for example, where the air is thinner, the aircraft may need more power to provide the same amount of lift, therefore maybe needing changes to the load or balance. In hot weather, similarly, the air density is lower, which might influence the takeoff performance of the aircraft and call for changes to the load or fuel.

The safe running of the airplane depends much on the weight and balance calculations under highly demanding conditions. Inappropriate balance or weight distribution might be more pronounced when combined with environmental elements and the inherent hazards connected with flying under demanding conditions. In such situations pilots might have to rely on automated equipment to control the aircraft's balance across the flight or change the trim more often. These disorders also usually call for longer runways for takeoff and landing as well as fuel load adjustments to reflect the higher power required to keep flight.

Managing the weight and balance of the aircraft depends also on last-minute adjustments (LMC) in weight or load. LMC is the modification of the aircraft's load—that is, cargo or passenger addition or removal—after the first weight and balance computations have been finished. Particularly if they influence the center of gravity, these modifications may greatly affect the performance of the aircraft. Any LMC needs to be meticulously recorded and included into the final load and trim calculations to guarantee the aircraft stays within its safe operating range.

Maintaining flying safety depends on effective handling of LMC. Little weight changes might affect the center of gravity of the aircraft, therefore causing instability or poorer performance. Pilots and ground workers must thus cooperate to control any LMC and guarantee that all weight-related computations are revised prior to the aircraft departure. Ignorance of these last-minute adjustments could cause dangerous conditions during takeoff, landing, or in-flight maneuvers.

To keep safe and effective aviation operations, the act of weighing an aircraft, controlling its trim, and accounting for unusual situations or last-minute adjustments is ultimately basic. Ensuring that the airplane runs best under all circumstances depends on accurate weight measurement, cautious balance control, and quick trim adjustments. Following these values can assist aviation experts guarantee the safe movement of goods and people, maximize performance, and aid to prevent mishaps.

Conclusion:

In the conclusion, the paper gives an in-depth analysis into different planks of the aviation industry concerning key aspects such as commercial operations, regulatory frameworks, safety standards, and logistics and operational issues. All these sections discuss how high standards are maintained in areas such as load and trim management, dangerous goods, and air charter services while creating a complexity of the topic and in areas of critical importance such as ensuring that aviation functions efficiently and, above all, safely.

Here the aviation industry demonstrates innovation and dynamism in facing new challenges, assuming new features, adjusting to technological change, and meeting an increasing demand for a globalized world. Sustainable activities and technology, including automation and digitalization, drive leaders in determining the future of aviation. The paper introduces how acceptance of these innovational possibilities can create improvements in efficiency and experience for customers at operational levels with the stringiest safety measures.

In fact, the interaction on the role of regulatory bodies emphasizes the requirement of a strong legal and safety framework. It is in line with international standards and safety standards, which would safeguard all activities across the aviation ecosystem from deviations due to any new player entering the situation. This framework not only means that passengers and cargo are safe but also that the world is going to have faith in the reliability of aviation.

The avionics industry is generally committed to progress as pointed out by the focus on operational excellence through proper training, safety guidelines, and continuous improvement. Professionals in the field need to evolve along with the changing technologies and expectations of customers, showing just how forward-thinking the industry really is.

The aviation industry therefore awaits a future of great challenge and great opportunity. All these are manifest in climate change and sustainability, ever-increasing expectation from customers, and the drive towards efficiency - factors that continue to accelerate innovation and change in this sector. And so, it is pro-actively facing these issues through increased cooperation across all sectors in aviation and active learning and adaptation processes.

It is this text's final fulfillment of great needs, being the first comprehensive resource on the detailed mechanisms underlying the industry of aviation. Instead of merely informing, however, it inspires professionals, students, and stakeholders to confidently and surely assume the future of aviation. Strategic planning, innovation, and an uncompromising commitment to safety and service will make the aviating industry soar to new heights in the years to come.